D0161799

DATE DUE

FEB 0 4 2002

Invisible
POWER

*The Elizabethan
Secret Services*
——*1570–1603*——

Invisible POWER

The Elizabethan Secret Services

—— *1570–1603* ——

ALAN HAYNES

ST. MARTIN'S PRESS · NEW YORK

First published in the United States of America in 1992

ISBN 0–312–08606–7

Library of Congress Cataloging-in-Publication Data

Haynes, Alan.
    Invisible Power : The Elizabethan secret services, 1570–1603/
Alan Haynes.
    Includes bibliographical references and index.
    ISBN 0–312–08606–7
    1. Great Britain–History–Elizabeth, 1558–1603. 2. Great
Britain–Foreign relations–1558–1603. 3. Secret service–England–
History–16th century. 4. Espionage, British–History–16th
century. I. Title.
DA356.H39   1992
263.2′83′094209031–dc20   92–8406
                                                                CIP

Typeset in 10/12 Times.
Typesetting and origination by
Alan Sutton Publishing Limited.
Printed in Great Britain by
The Bath Press, Bath, Avon.

Contents

Preface

This book gives exclusive attention to the Elizabethan secret services, organized to provide the spy masters of Elizabeth's Privy Council with evidence of enemy activity at home and abroad. It looks at their work and that of the intelligence clusters over a period of some thirty years – the successes and failures of two generations. To do this satisfactorily it is necessary to pluck out, isolate and probe complex material. There must always be anxieties about the sources, especially the State Papers, which are not easy to follow and interpret. Also, many have been destroyed that would have been cited if they had been allowed to survive, and the manipulation then of those that remain to us now has to be acknowledged. Even so, the long neglect of such a striking topic is still astonishing, and it can only in part be explained by the higher regard of many academic historians for 'clean' data. As John Bossy has recently written, 'spies are taken to be unreliable providers of information on matters in which few historians are interested anyway'. Probably they have also been coy about spying four hundred years ago because of the suspect popularity of spy fiction in the twentieth century; in the eyes of many critics a degraded genre defying serious attention. Indeed, much of it deserves this scorn, but not so the history of Elizabethan espionage. Of course, rarified ideas of historical scholarship and polite truth do not sit easily with mendacity, betrayal, apostasy, double-dealing, false witness, torture and executions.

Michel Foucault described the scaffold as a theatre of punishment, with the ruler present (as it were) in the person of the law. They did not have to be there in person (and if they were they took care to remain unseen) to demonstrate the ability 'to penetrate and control the natural body of the subject at the micro level of its parts'.[1] Even a woman could do this, as a surrogate king. Then villainy was engaged in a secret combat to be overwhelmed, and having subdued the base intentions of traitors by torture and executions, the final evidence of their impotence was the business of castration in public – ritualized sexual derision. In an act of darkness the victims of this revenge had fathered treachery. At the trial of the defendants involved in the Babington plot (1586), the attorney-general, Sir Christopher Hatton, declared that the inspirers of the crimes listed were 'devilish priests and seminarists' who *seduced* those 'whose youthful ambition and high spirit carried them headlong into all wickedness'. This plot had been aborted by the rapt attention given to it by the greatest of the Elizabethan spy masters – Sir Francis Walsingham. To emphasize at last the powerlessness of these young, virile men, some of them already fathers, their hitherto private parts were humiliatingly exposed and immediately severed before a large crowd.

In the middle of the sixteenth century the English had the sudden death of rulers at home and abroad perpetually in mind. In 1558, when Elizabeth, the last Tudor of direct lineage, ascended the throne, there were many of her countrymen (we may guess) who groaned inwardly, even despairingly, that the clumsy pantomime of Henry VIII's marital cavortings had settled so little about the succession question, with controversy ever flourishing. If the new queen remained unmarried, the bewildering search for a secure Protestant successor was sure to torment the politically empowered class. Their vicissitudes drove them to embrace an emerging option – the use of spies to protect a vulnerable woman from the worst her enemies could do. Sickness they could not control, and a chill or fever was enough to have them anticipating disaster. If she had succumbed to smallpox in 1562 the crown would likely have gone to the Catholic Mary, Queen of Scots, whose title derived from the marriage of Henry VIII's eldest sister Margaret to James IV of Scotland. Henry had himself sought to torpedo this possibility through his effort involving his last will (allowed by the English Parliament), which had it that if his son and daughters died childless the crown should pass to the Protestant Suffolk line of his youngest sister. Lawyers struggled with the constitutional meaning of all this, while others in government found a different mode for ensuring the future. The key appointment was that of Sir William Cecil (Gray's Inn) as the secretary of state, joined in the new privy council by Sir Nicholas Bacon (also Gray's Inn), his brother-in-law.

It was the collective agitation among the lawyers that led to their device which, for the purposes of the kingdom and the throne, assigned Elizabeth two bodies. These were the corporeal form subject to time, and also the timeless body politic. For many years she decked out the former with calculated extravagance and, towards the end of her long life, she displayed a particular reluctance to accept its physical limitations. Simultaneously the 'unerring and immortal' body politic was anchored in the nation. With her steely collaboration the lawyers annealed state and ruler. She embodied the nation as the Ditchley portrait registers, with her astride a huge map of England. So any threat, random or plotted, to the body of Elizabeth became a threat to the nation at a time when the country 'was ready to understand power in nationalist terms'. This component of government grew in strength throughout her reign and nourished manifest shifts in the national culture, especially the Protestant political culture, which required some uneasy borrowing and further development of ideas and mechanisms that had originated or been taken up by the city states and rulers of Renaissance Italy.

The case for espionage being the most significant is set out in this book. For those who studied law there was the progressive realization that in the circumstances spying could become an invaluable item in the government armoury – certainly Elizabeth herself came to think so. Yet the older generation, including some who had schooled her, like Roger Ascham, her tutor in Greek, resisted the source and bleated about it a decade into the reign. Nothing Italian merited attention; hence the delay in using spies until the rebellion of the northern earls revealed some shocking truths. By then Cecil, an acute political pragmatist, had decided to employ a man with first-hand experience of living and studying in Italy, where Spanish domination prompted his lively detestation. The son of a successful lawyer, Francis Walsingham had himself been to Gray's Inn before the Marian diaspora took him to Switzerland and then the University of Padua in the territory of Venice. At the same time, Robert Dudley, Earl of Leicester, the glamorous courtier who busily wooed Elizabeth in a spirited personal lunge to secure the succession (a notion that appalled many while it entertained the queen), was intrigued by Italian politics and culture without ever having been there. He was also admitted to a grateful Inner Temple, so all the first and second generation spy masters had a background in law.

These hugely ambitious men were the leaders of the political class, and so had to grapple with the constant shifts and perturbations of the unfamiliar. To do this they turned increasingly to the use of spies at home and abroad. Even then it was a daunting matter to prise out the truth, since paid agents and their myriad contacts might lie and lie. To jettison the dross and uncover more of the truth the spy masters allowed torture and defended its use (or threat of it), whatever more scrupulous men said about it being un-English. Indeed, the infamous rack actually made an appearance in Chapman's tragic drama, *Bussy D'Ambois* (1604), as did even more bizarre forms of torture in other Jacobean tragedies set in Renaissance Italy. This was a highly suggestive form of transference, although by then Elizabeth was dead. While now we may recoil from the real and sometimes ugly activities investigated in this book, there were peculiar circumstances that made this dismal feature of the reign an inevitability, especially since she 'would brook absolutely no challenge to the power inherent in her blood'. The many moments of discovery of a threat to her gave the spy masters and their immediate aides a cold-blooded momentum which helped to correct some of the brittle optimism of official propaganda also pushed out at their command.

Acknowledgements

Much of the first draft of this book was written in the delightful Brittany cottage of Kate and Martyn Chandler. Subsequent drafts were read in whole or in part by Dr Simon Adams (Strathclyde University); Dr Constance B. Kuriyama (Texas Technical University and President of the Marlowe Society of America); and Geoffrey Hodgson (Newcastle Polytechnic). Professor Kenneth Bartlett of Toronto University wrote to give encouragement just when it was needed. Charles Nicholl also took the subject seriously, enthused about it, and nudged me into some radical and unexpected rethinking. I am very grateful to all of them, and David O'Leary, for challenging weaknesses in the book. Of course, as is customary, I absolve them from any blame for the errors and blemishes that may remain. These I attribute to my sources.

I would like to thank the following for their kind permission to reproduce photographs: Ashmolean Museum, British Library (engravings from Richard Verstegen's *Theatrum Crudelitatum Haereticorum* (1587)), Courtauld Institute of Art, London University, Worshipful Company of Mercers, London, Mansell Collection, National Maritime Museum, National Portrait Gallery, The Marquess of Salisbury and Weiss Gallery, London.

My family have made a benign environment for most of the work, and the book is dedicated to them with love and gratitude. Finally, I owe thanks for financial assistance in preparing the manuscript for publication to the Hélène Heroys Foundation (Switzerland).

ALAN HAYNES
1992

Introduction

Treason begets spies and spies treason as Sir John Harington, a godson of Elizabeth I, noted in a puzzled reflection on cause and effect. There were almost as many compelling reasons for being a spy as there were spies themselves – belligerent conviction, self-interest, family necessity, vanity, desperation and perhaps a low threshold of boredom. Those named in this book, rescued from obscurity, were commanded by the great men of the Elizabethan Privy Council through their own secretaries. As reading aloud of any text became less common for the lettered class and the word on the page became silent (akin to secret), so spying became an accepted mode of penetrating this silence. Elizabethan espionage was the work of individuals collaborating, not whole departments. It was controlled by individual officers of state, but ultimately had a collective, that is national, purpose. It therefore shaped Elizabethan society, and grew parasitically on the body of the political nation, flourishing as it is like to do when a certain godlessness takes hold, earthly authority massing to fill the space evacuated. Clandestine debate led to secret intentions and then dangerous actions. To head these off, unfettered assistance was needed by the privy councillors who were vigilant, while still sceptical about a female ruler. They were right to be so given the notorious failings of Mary Tudor, Catherine de Medici, and Mary, Queen of Scots, mendacious and flirtatious. The latter was cherished and reviled almost equally, and became an active focal point for treason.

Others with a claim to the English throne were treated by Elizabeth with a cranky vindictiveness that must have made them regret their ancestry. Lady Catherine Grey, who enraged her by a secret marriage to Edward Seymour, Earl of Hertford, fetched up in prison, along with her husband who was still arguing the legitimacy of their prison offspring in the early 1590s. The Stanleys had a succession claim through the marriage in 1555 of Henry, Lord Strange, to Margaret Clifford, the granddaughter of Henry VIII's youngest sister. It could be bettered but not without dispute; Margaret's behaviour irked Elizabeth and royal irritation 'must have been intensified by rumours gathered by spies'. The government viewed the Stanleys as trouble, and informants of Sir William Cecil (later Lord Burghley), implicated family members in a plot to liberate Mary in 1570. By July 1571 Sir Edward Stanley was in the Tower with his brother and other prominent men beguiled by the royal refugee-prisoner; the earl of Southampton, Lord Lumley and Thomas, the brother of Lord Cobham.[1]

Those who planned to dethrone Elizabeth often found the unlikeliest mode, making it hard now to distinguish the real from the bogus. Whatever the follies and flurries in the background, in the foreground of political life and exchanges the queen 'was consistent in the displeasure shown to her possible successors'. What was worse according to the Catholic writer and activist Richard Verstegen, 'She had that instinctive malice which makes one prick out for hatred the very persons who have done one a good turn.' A biased view, but not without a grain of truth. She was sensitive to criticism, and confidence did stiffen later into arrogance, age heightening the bursts of ill-temper, and there were spasms of self-deceit that unleashed cruelty. She 'dressed to kill' in the costly, symbolically embroidered jewelled court dresses. In the 'Rainbow' portrait (Hatfield House) her cloak is scattered with eyes and ears – as if her extravagant claims made to a French ambassador to know everything that happened in her kingdom were possible through secret surveillance. The dominatrix of the English Renaissance, she pummelled, prodded, pinched and slapped those who aggravated her. When the private woman and public monarch fretted severely against each other, those close to her in council or kinship might suffer more than was appropriate.

Hunting spies for reasons of state, and animals for sport became the grand Elizabethan and Jacobean obsessions. Slaughtering deer which were then dismembered, mimicked the execution and dismemberment of traitors, done with relish for strategic public displays of limbs in London – a bloody routine no less shocking

Elizabeth I, *c.* 1570. The long, highly-charged reign of the last Tudor was vitally served by two generations of spy masters

when repeated for many years. Indeed, in the defiant atmosphere of raw suspicion, even the accusation of treason itself became as ritualized as hunting, so 'feeding the politics of calculated paranoia'.[2] No wonder when, in a period of livid religious antagonisms that swamped a weaker eirenism, power found expression in a torrent of tears, sweat and blood. The savagery of Richard Topcliffe, licensed to torture on behalf of the Elizabethan Privy Council, elicited a rictus of agony in the victim and, if he was a Jesuit missionary, very likely a taunting, beatific smile of elevated condescension. In the *Constitutions*, an intricately detailed account of how the Society of Jesus was to be governed, St Ignatius (or Inigo) of Loyola (d. 1556) had declared that a Jesuit 'ought to allow himself to be carried and directed by Divine Providence . . . as if he were a lifeless body'. After the attentions of such as Topcliffe this was often very nearly what he was; English Elizabethan Jesuits were haunted by fears of torture and then if captured went on to bear it with great courage. In this sado-masochistic ritual of martyrdom the government provided the whips, chains, rack and gibbet in a grimly obliging manner. Resistance to the Counter-Reformation was at its height after 1570, and it is a measure of its shadowy strength that in the aftermath of the Gunpowder Plot (1605) Robert Cecil, a second generation spy master, made such laborious efforts to find a Jesuit connection behind 'the devil of the vault' (Guy Fawkes).

Revulsion in England against Rome and its agents was at its height as the spy masters in the Privy Council took control of policy implementation, and convinced Elizabeth, who enjoyed exercising visible power, that no other way was safe. It was not a runaway despotism, but opponents with grievances of whatever kind quickly became enemies and they were then characteristically labelled 'devils'. So it was that the hapless Duke of Norfolk was at length denounced by his own clerk as 'a devil and no Christian man', when it was obviously untrue. The more curious and lurid the plots, the more a bitterly puzzled and vengeful government sought ways to undermine them, and as both the violence and invective increased, and the national psyche became more bruised and then embattled, so the position of ordinary Catholics was exposed to threats and punishment.[3] The most unruly, desperate men found a harsh comfort in plotting even when previous plots had failed, and after 1580 there was 'the almost annual parade of demonized conspirators to the scaffold'. The form became that of a sado-masochistic ritual as exampled by the precise form of the execution of the Babington conspirators in 1586 (see p. 80).

There was then a darting distress abroad in Elizabethan England. The greatest dramatist gave it mordant voice in the line 'the time is out of joint' – literally and dismayingly true when post-mortem dismemberment scattered the enemies of the state. As the reign reached maturity an official discourse of treason was widely used as propaganda by the government. Above all, it was Cecil's successor as principal secretary, Sir Francis Walsingham, never liked by Elizabeth, who did not waver in his conviction that a country without a standing army required strong government, and that without it England would slip into a calamitous civil war (such as almost happened in 1569), and find itself then invaded – a notion often contemplated abroad and once prepared for on a grand scale. 'Some kind of despotism was essential.' It was more useful then to have spies strategically placed than an army, because they could not band together to threaten the regime and everyone could be kept in a state of permanent anxiety. An abrupt event in nature like the earthquake in southern England in April 1580 reinforced this, with the divines and Puritan pamphleteers grimly discoursing on the terrors of the earth.[4] Walsingham's own gloomiest pronouncement was, 'There is less danger in fearing too much than too little.' For a Puritan like him the official abolition in England of Catholic paraphernalia in worship did not seem to diminish the hidden power of Satanic forces – rather the reverse. The export of despised Catholic church furniture became a nice little earner for Girault de la Chassaigne, butler to the French ambassador Castelnau.

The political nation, a few thousand who in some measure had power, paid for their advantages in nervous debility. There was the oppressive sense of enemies observing every move (with chess increasingly favoured at court). 'Fear eats the soul' and the priests funnelled secretly into England often claimed in compensation that they could exorcize evil spirits. A text dense with allusions to and appearances by malignant spirits – *The Tempest* – also has conspiracy as an essential component with Caliban defeated by the invisible Ariel as Prospero's intelligencer (a term first used in the 1590s).[5] It was Francis Bacon, brother of an intelligencer, who viewed all governments as 'obscure and invisible'. The guardian of Elizabethan state secrets was the principal secretary, within whose title appropriately was buried the word secret. The observable growth of a bureaucracy in the Renaissance state required skilled secretaries, and those who served a great man were involved in a tenebrous world of ruthless and competitive effort. Civil service rules of objectivity had not been established, so a sudden shift of favour, a political misjudgement, even an ill-timed bout of sickness, could expose the secretary to hostile forces. It was the way of the world and particularly dangerous if, in terror of his own fate, a stricken employer sought to shift blame on to his secretary.

Such was the cruel fate of the scholarly, loyal Henry Cuffe in the aftermath of the 1601 revolt devised at Essex House.[6] The Earl of Essex had cultivated (in both senses) friends in a manner perceived to threaten Elizabeth, and he had done it with that blurting freedom of speech that Tudor conduct books warned emphatically against. Essex forgot the importance of wariness in public and private utterance, unable to censor his thoughts before friends who, in a twinkling, might metamorphose into enemies. He ignored the superiority of a politically adept mind over a comely physique and natural courage so that Sir Robert Cecil could seize a precious advantage. He brushed aside clear advice from Francis Bacon on how he should conduct himself. The result was a mournful dramatic coda to the reign in a localized metropolitan tangle squeezed into a few houses and streets of the capital. The Essex rebellion fizzed with peculiar private animosities and Sir Gelly Meyrick, his household steward, wrote: 'We have envy and malice besides, to have it plotted and practised by those that my Lord [Essex] useth so near him.' The earl's calamity led Shakespeare to invent a friend for Hamlet, in the play most freighted by those terrifying events, who is the opposite of the agitators who clustered about Essex. Horatio represents that admirable person – the loyal, steadfast, tactful and virtually silent friend. In contrast, Hamlet/Essex under pressure soared into babble, with the earl under arrest in the Tower cravenly seeking the ear of anyone in power who would listen to his denunciations. The ruin of Henry Cuffe was assured.[7]

Portrait of Elizabeth I enthroned with Burghley and Walsingham at either side. From *The Compleat Ambassador* by Dudley Digges (1655)

The so-frequent mention of plots against Elizabeth in diplomatic and secret correspondence, often presented to her through the attentive, fretting, protective triumvirate of Burghley, Walsingham and Robert Dudley, the Earl of Leicester, all of whom directed their own private secret services that were yoked to serve the intentions of the regime, seems to have given the queen an authentic *frisson*, and with the passing years a sense of invincibility not always transmitted to her councillors who criticized her privately, but remained highly solicitous. Their sincere unease can be found too in the writings of the Protestant ideologues who in turn served them, with the official discourse in treason following the example of humanists such as Richard Morison during the years of Thomas Cromwell's commanding power. Government controls over printing (a developing resource) conferred a huge advantage, and anonymous pamphleteers wrote under the aegis of Christopher Barker, the royal printer. Yet, despite the best efforts of spies, collaborators and pursuivants, the exclusion of forbidden material was far from watertight. The right to search printing houses was renewed in 1576, but it has been estimated that at least 20,000 recusant works were imported into England and sold secretly before 1580. Girault and the French embassy cook, Réné Leduc, were among those involved in the clandestine importation of Catholic books. One of their depots on the Thames was the Half Moon Inn in Southwark. They paid out hefty sums to the landlord and to searchers in ports like Rye.[8] Even a historian like the estimable John Stow was raided by Bishop Grindal's commissioners, and moderates like the queen's mercer, Sir Thomas Gresham, believed in a hidden Catholic militant agenda for the assassination of Elizabeth followed by national turmoil. Cecil, Walsingham and Leicester had some differences, but on this they shared a view and the spy services took shape.

Cecil would have had an easier public role if the Elizabethan settlement of religion had permanently subdued Catholicism in England. But there remained a large confessional constituency that clung to it, longing to live unmolested, unmoved by the resistance of militant or papal Catholics to Elizabeth's rule. It was only a matter of time before what was directed from the south of England was challenged by the stubborn north. The region was emphatically Catholic, including not only farm labourers and small traders, but larger landowners and the aristocracy as well. Sir Ralph Sadler, the leading authority on Scottish affairs, after his appointment as Chancellor of the Duchy of Lancaster in 1568, declared that in the whole area of the north there were not 'ten gentlemen that do favour and allow Her Majesty's proceedings in the cause of religion'. Deserted by the church, one Elizabethan bishop complained that 'God's glorious Gospel could not take place' in the parishes where only refugee priests from Scotland and those lingering after being deprived of their livings for being Catholic remained. The secular conspiratorial leaders in the north were the Percys of Northumberland and Nevilles of Westmorland with a huge following among the people – allies of the Duke of Norfolk. They had contacts with the new and fervently papist Spanish ambassador, Don Guerau de Spes, who remained under surveillance even after the government restraints placed on him in January 1569 had been relaxed. As for the French ambassador, La Mothe Fénelon, he was trying to calm English fears, even as he saw hostility spreading like an ungovernable stain through all ranks in society.

A trade embargo was imposed on the English in Normandy, and English merchants' goods in Rouen were seized. Financially it was of little consequence, but before French assurances could reach London, the Privy Council was nervously assessing the possibility of the French aligning themselves with Philip II in an anti-English and anti-Protestant block.

Elizabeth and Cecil made a late decision over an opportunity that was certain to enrage Philip II and the Duke of Alva, his governor of the Spanish Netherlands. In November 1568 a fleet of Spanish treasure ships took refuge in English ports with a vastly tempting shipment of gold stowed on board, intended for the pockets of Alva's army. The consignment still belonged to Genoese bankers, so the decision to retain it, if not actual theft, was still a risk, and it resulted in a rupture with England's key export market, because Alva, invested with royal authority in northern Europe, was goaded into closing Antwerp to the Merchant Adventurers and, with the arrest of English traders, important secondary markets in Spain evaporated as well. It was a grave decision, endorsed by Philip, who acknowledged it would cause a great loss of revenue and damage to his subjects. It also did further harm to Anglo-Spanish relations at a time when Alva still believed that 'a friendly England provided the essential strategic and political link between Spain and the Netherlands' and was a crucial component in the trade that allowed a buoyant Antwerp to grow. Alva himself knew that de Spes was a threat to the security of this vision, but his injunctions were swept aside by the ardent ambassador whose clandestine meddling did spectacular damage, even though for a time Elizabeth would not allow him into her presence.[9]

It was the capitalist Italian merchants and bankers who tried to build bridges, approaching Cecil who had at that time strong connections with the Merchant Adventurers. The men of his own mind included Governor John Marsh, Thomas Aldersey and other Protestant stalwarts who were optimistic that Emden or more likely Hamburg could be developed as an alternative to Antwerp. The Florentine Cavalcanti brothers, with Roberto Ridolphi, made an approach to Cecil, and Alva

The rebellion of the Earls of Northumberland and Westmorland, *c.* 1569

himself was encouraged sufficiently to send a Genoese resident of Antwerp, Tommaso Fiesco, to London. His conference was to be with the well-placed Benedetto Spinola, a close associate of the Earl of Leicester, and very possibly the Italian who alerted London to the gold riding at anchor in its ports. Large sweeteners were proposed for Cecil and Leicester, and although both may cheerfully have accepted the bribes it need not be assumed that their decisions were swayed dramatically by a sum approaching £3,000. These triple negotiations, weaving together trade and politics, went on through the summer of 1569, with Fiesco arriving in June; there was a slackening of tension with the limited aim of the merchants being a 'simple restitution of the wares seized on either side of the sea'. At this time Spanish mariners held under restraint in England were released, and Alva devised a reciprocal gesture when English sailors were taken on the coast of Zeeland. The disturber of these efforts was de Spes who, in July, was using his freedom to intrigue with Mary's agents, and since he was under surveillance the motive of his watchers was obviously that he should ruin himself and his contacts. The difficulty of the royal interloper was that she could not be assaulted head on, while she was sufficiently vigorous in her Catholicism and adept in manoeuvring that her hopes of dislodging Elizabeth were by no means all pipe dreams. With Gallic and papal support for the Scottish cuckoo, Elizabeth might yet be crowded off the throne if Philip II could be inveigled into the tussle. The main obstacle to his participation was the possible advantage to France and the Guises, who could then attain that dominance in west European affairs which the addition of England to their sphere of influence might allow.

Therefore, it was the irksome presence of Mary that undermined the momentum of the informal exchanges that for a time seemed to presage a diplomatic resolve of the impasse. At the beginning of October 1569 the Duke of Norfolk was imprisoned in the Tower at the insistence of Cecil and his brother-in-law Nicholas Bacon, with the duke's friends making his case somewhat worse by smuggling letters in bottles, or rolled in black paper for a drop in dark corners. The 'bosom-creeping Italian' was also detained – Ridolphi was secretly acting for Rome. The Earls of Northumberland and Westmorland denied being disloyal, but were toppled by words and tears from their wives into action with Leonard Dacres, and Sheriff Norton with seven of his sons, although they were a time in agreeing their future courses. The release of Mary was their first undeclared objective; a clear avowal of this might have pushed Cecil into having her executed, so their public pronouncements were confined to religion and the removal of 'divers new set-up nobles' – meaning men like the detested Leicester whose hope of marrying Elizabeth had not been totally blasted. The secret involvement of de Spes, who reported the dominance of Cecil and Bacon in the Privy Council, led to the mistaken notion in London that Alva himself must be poised for some surprise intervention. Extreme disquiet was aroused by the arrival in England of the duke's second-in-command Chiappino Vitelli, Marquis of Cetona, who towards the end of November was privately warned by Leicester, who liked the envoy, that it was thought that he (Vitelli) was forwarding funds to the rebels.[10] On 14 November they invaded a welcoming Durham headed by the old device of the Pilgrimage of Grace – the cross and five wounds. After the emotional peak of hearing the mass said again in the cathedral, they headed south without real opposition to a small, fast-moving force that aimed to free Mary, then in captivity at Tutbury.

For some time Elizabeth had suspected the Earl of Sussex, Thomas Radcliffe, of protecting the sullen northern earls – he was after all an old political ally of Norfolk and no friend of Cecil, although he did profess to be Protestant. In the north she had the modest garrisons of the marches, dubiously loyal, and the force commanded by Sussex who was president of the council in the north. But his own brother, Egremont Radcliffe, had joined the aristocratic rebellion and, if he could have been certain of their triumph, the hesitant earl would probably have joined them himself. As it was, he decided to temporize, advising Elizabeth to come to terms with the rebels rather than 'hazard battle against desperate men with soldiers that fight against their conscience'. As the crisis, 'more of a popular rebellion than has been supposed', advanced across England, Cecil was ill, obviously with a stress-related complaint, but he made the crucial decision that Mary should be removed to Coventry with a strong escort that was forced to ride hard. With a sudden snap the rebellion faltered and the earls simply returned north to save their efforts, and to wait for Spanish help. No wonder, then, that there was almost equal anxiety in London, where unusually winter recruiting went on, about Vitelli, who was delaying his return to Europe so as to secure the consent of Alva. The new dizzying rumour went round that his actual purpose was to be on hand to lead an invasion force that would attack the south in the spring. In fact, Alva still wanted to negotiate and the only action taken by him was commercial – he had the Antwerp warehouses of English merchants forced open and emptied of perishable fabrics which were sold over the following year.

The queen's enemies might be willing to delay but her commanders were more mettlesome, although it was winter. Resistance to such an effort was impossible without firearms, and Northumberland and Westmorland fled into Scotland in mid-December. Alone Leonard Dacres fought and, after a defeat in February 1570 on the River Galt by Hunsdon and Scrope, he rode for his life to join the exiles. After such a brutal jolt to the system, when disaster was only just avoided, the government's response was correspondingly severe. Cecil had spent Christmas arranging punishments and was unseasonably unsparing. The leaders were tracked by a spy, Robert Constable, who managed to link up with them over the border. Directed locally by Sadler, and also by Elizabeth and Cecil, the soon-to-be knighted spy tried to lure the fugitives back into England, endeavouring to persuade Westmorland that his life would not be forfeited if he did return. Even Constable complained that his task made him a Judas to one who was a relation. Cecil, therefore, offered him a mighty cash bounty as 'Her Majesty is very desirous to have these noisome vermin'. As for Sussex, with the wider task of rounding up suspects, he seized the opportunity to reaffirm his loyalty, joining the Privy Council in December and, in mid-March 1570, he was sent against the earls with a punitive raid into Scotland. It has been estimated that some six hundred executions eventually took place with ringleaders dying at Tyburn, and the gentry involved receiving regular trials so that convictions could lead to the confiscation of estates. A rebellion that had at first been strikingly bloodless ended in a judicial massacre. Cecil's comment was abrupt and ugly: 'Some few of them suffered.'[11]

The rising stung the government, even though its failure might have suggested that internal Catholic discontent could not now serve as the primary element of a revolution. Many of the ancestral Catholics would probably reject papal denunciations of Elizabeth, even if converts did not, and the fact that the hostile forces were papal, Scottish, Spanish, was helpful, since nationalism could act as a deflecting shield. The concern of the government did not easily dissolve, however, because of this modest advantage, and the discomfiture can be followed in the tone and content of documents of the period. Indeed, the cruelly misjudged action of the saintly but hot-tempered Pope Pius V, provided further evidence (albeit late revealed in England) of Mary's disastrously provoking presence. Late in February 1570 came the paternal admonition, *Regnans in excelsis*, a bull of excommunication and deposition, woefully mistimed by a man who for a long time had personally admired Elizabeth.[12] Yet now, influenced by men such as Dr Nicholas Sanders, he told distant English Catholics that rebellion was actually a duty and obeying Elizabeth was a sin. The pontiff took on the mantle of aggressor and, in Elizabeth's mind as well as Cecil's, the bull identified the religion of perhaps half her subjects with covert treachery. They were particularly incensed that the northern earls escaped immediate retribution, with Westmorland escaping from Scotland during upheavals there and, after an excursion to Spain, fetching up in the Spanish Netherlands under Alva's protection. The taking of Northumberland only came about because he was surrendered by the Scots, and his execution in 1572 followed a stir involving Lords Dacre and Seaton, who hoped for the support of the Earl of Derby. He had done nothing to aid government or rebels in 1569 and, when he died three years later, their notion that he might lead a rising in Lancashire and Cheshire naturally folded.

Although not published in Spain or France, where the end of civil disturbances along sectarian lines freed Charles IX to support the widely touted idea that Mary should be restored to her throne in Scotland, the sudden appearance of the bull in the summer of 1570 nailed to the door of the Bishop of London's palace in St Paul's churchyard, was a sensation. Copies of it were hidden by Ridolphi in his employers' banking premises. It caught everyone off-guard 'and created new pressures for Elizabeth to strike a workable agreement with Mary', at a time when Cecil was bidden to make the best terms he could for her restoration to her unwilling subjects. Norfolk's followers, newly liberated, joined with Leicester in urging this scheme. Cecil and the pungently outspoken Bacon resisted it strongly, but the former could feel the ground slipping from under him in an undulating wobble that sickened him. Had he risked royal disfavour to such a point that Elizabeth would ditch him as she veered bemused and angry from one opinion to another? To try to smooth matters Norfolk himself was released, evidently in the hope that if he continued to correspond with Mary both would saunter into ruin. Cecil's rickety position was then further aided when the London publisher of the bull, a Catholic barrister called William Felton, was arrested. The grudge against him was deepened by Cecil's fear that unless he succeeded exile beckoned.[13] Felton was tortured but would confess nothing beyond the known facts, even denying having associates. He modified this at his trial with a claim of wide-ranging support among the peers, gentry and commons. His execution was watched by a horrified de Spes and Ridolphi, who may have seen him hand a diamond ring to Sussex, directing that it be given to the queen, with pious hope for her soul.

To deflect a threatening conjunction of the three strata in society, and to maintain the drive against those who secretly agreed with the dismembered Felton, Cecil wanted an even more significant public victim of government wrath and he found a candidate in an English-born exile stained with Protestant blood from the previous reign: Dr John Story. In the huge compilation history and witness by John Foxe, *Acts and Monuments* (popularly known as Foxe's *Book of Martyrs*), Story was cited as the most brutally zealous of Marian prosecutors, as befitted a lawyer and lay Franciscan brother. The great text was reissued in 1570, and had an extraordinary (perhaps unique) power to influence Protestant opinion, being often chained up in churches for hushed perusal of its horrors.* No wonder the name of Story was excoriated, especially if, as has been suggested, he did influence Philip II into bringing the Inquisition to Antwerp. This may not be so, but then it does not have to be, since few in England would have discounted the possibility, and the Inquisition itself provoked a powerful revulsion in England in 1568 when it declared the entire population of the Netherlands to be heretics and condemned to death. Story was hated as a brutal, meddlesome traitor and he was now in great peril as Cecil scrambled to shore up his own position. He was provoked into the first planned act of covert action abroad – modest in scale, being directed against one man – but sensational in its resolution.

---

* Along with the Bible, Erasmus's *Paraphrases* and Jewel's *Defence of the Apology*.

Chapter One

Abduction and Execution

'It's the job of an intelligence service to resolve a nation's obsessions.' Against the background of the rebellion of the earls, the Anglo-Netherlands trade rupture, as well as the publication of the contentious papal bull, the first major spy operation abroad under Cecil's direction was such a success 'that it set the standard for excellence throughout Elizabeth's reign'.[1] Given the difficulties that left him vulnerable if the queen's confidence in him ebbed, it was imperative that it should succeed. In addition, as the benchmark for clandestine operations it prepared the way for the future successes of Walsingham when he entered the office of Principal Secretary of State. The capture and later execution of Dr John Story emphatically established in the minds of European politicians that Elizabethan England was not going to be supine before threats. For Cecil's countrymen it was a stunning coup, underlining the attractions of striking at the enemy wherever possible, even if they were under the protection of Philip II. It was a particularly brutal rebuff for the Duke of Alva for giving condemned traitors like the northern earls, not merely shelter in exile, but as it seemed, active encouragement.

John Story was born in London and took a first degree in civil law at Oxford in 1531. He obtained his doctorate in the same subject in 1538 when he was already a lecturer. His privileged position in the élite of education did not lead him to curb his tongue or temper his views, even when he was elected to Parliament in 1547. In the second session his contentious declaration that rule by a child was a national disaster was strident and offensive, and caused a collective outrage. He was sent to the Tower by the House of Commons and only released after an apology. Since the regime still clearly displeased him, he left England shortly after for exile in Louvain. There he kept company with monks and awaited his opportunity to return to England. This came with the death of Edward VI and the collapse of the flimsy Dudley resistance to the succession of Mary Tudor. Back in England and royal favour, he was rewarded with the renewal of his Oxford lectureship and diocesan appointments in London and Oxford. He played a zealot's part in the return of the kingdom to Catholicism, notably in the government's pursuit of Archbishop Cranmer, at whose trial Story was Queen's Proctor.[2]

Story's power ended with the death of Mary. Given his recent public career he could probably only have escaped censure for a short time, but with the aggressive stance of the unrepentant he seemed to court it. Again he spoke in Parliament, this time scorning the Act of Supremacy. Though the government was slow to respond,

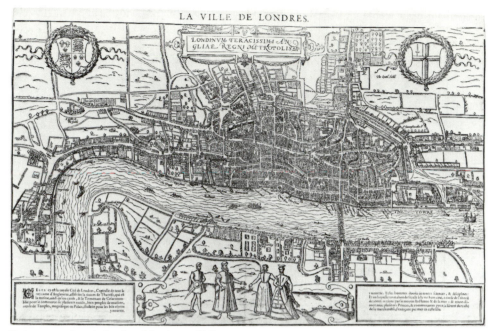

Contemporary French drawing of London, *c.* 1640

in May 1560 he was sent to the Fleet prison, until the pressure of legislation meant that he had to try to escape (again?) in 1563. The bill in question was aimed 'against those that extol the power of the Bishop of Rome, and refuse the oath of allegiance'. Since Story did that his predicament is apparent and he was exceptionally fortunate to be able to enlist assistance in an escape. He and another prisoner managed to get into the prison garden, scale a wall in darkness, and then take refuge with the Spanish ambassador. Having sloughed off the taint of prison he was then spirited to Flanders with the aid of the ambassador's chaplain. Though he took Spanish citizenship and received a royal pension, it was never enough to maintain his young family of four children, as well as nephews and nieces, and so he fell in with Alva's offer of sundry work. According to John Marsh, Story was 'a preferer of all English traitors' business' with easy access to the duke. His friends might think being a searcher for smuggled Protestant literature was demeaning, but Story accepted the work.

One of his closest contacts was John Prestall, whose dubious career as an intelligencer was likely prompted by Cecil. In exile, however, he maintained successfully the façade of being an enemy of Elizabeth and James VI. He and Story launched upon a plot for two royal murders and began to promote the possible prosecution of an invasion of England. By the spring of 1570 John Marsh was reporting that Cecil and Nicholas Bacon were also marked for assassination. Since he was reliable and well informed, Marsh had long been in Cecil's employ, and in 1569 and told him that the northern rebellion could expect assistance from Alva. Given the sour attitude that existed between England and the Spanish government of the Low Countries at this time, Cecil's notion of seizing Story for punishment probably went ahead with Elizabeth's approval. The strongly Protestant Marsh was perfectly placed to undertake the preparations for the snatch. As governor of the Merchant Adventurers, with Thomas Aldersey and Richard Saltonstall (later a lord mayor of London), he went to Brussels with government backing ostensibly to seek the mutual restitution of goods seized during the difficult trade embargo. Success in this matter was not important, for Elizabeth 'had every intention of keeping Alva at arm's length'. The negotiations instead became an excellent cover for Marsh's intelligence activities. In letters to Cecil he said little about trade, but he did report on the work of John Prestall, and he met other intelligencers – Lee, Taylor and Bradley (all called John). In Antwerp Lee lived at the sign of the Golden Stag and as a merchant knew the activities of the trading community. He also maintained contacts with a Jasper Himselroy who traded in English passports at the sign of the Gilded Head.[3]

In the kidnap of Story twelve men were employed by Cecil, with Marsh linking the spy master to the men in the field. Lee took the key role in Antwerp and proved his wits in improvising as late problems beset the scheme. John Bradley lived in Bergen op Zoom at the disused English House, where he was the porter on the premises, and he was taken on by Lee to hire a Dutch ship with master and crew. John Taylor in Antwerp dealt with funds, paying £60 to the actual kidnappers, Roger Ramsden, Martin Bragge and Simon Jewkes, traders in the Low Countries who anticipated a hike in their careers if they were successful. Another important figure was William Parker, like Story employed as a searcher and supposedly a Catholic exile. Lee may have bought him, or he could have been paid by the Privy Council to go into exile. It is possible that he was a brother of the archbishop who had many relatives in the wool trade. The plan devised by Lee, after discussion, was simple but well fleshed.[4] It hinged on Story being sufficiently zealous as a searcher that he would board an unknown ship to look for illicit items, especially books and pamphlets expounding the tenets of Protestantism. Knowing their man through Parker's assessment there was every reason to believe that he would indeed be lured, so Lee had to find an accommodating sea captain and crew. He settled on Robert Pygot who was already known to Cecil, but this choice was scuppered because the crew of Pygot's ship 'forsook the enterprise'. At least one of them was canny enough to suspect a plot, and on landing went to Parker to warn him in the belief that he was the likely victim.

If the plan was to go ahead this was where Lee had to improvise a solution, which he managed as Parker gently played down the dangers to himself. As far as the young kidnappers were concerned, Lee had to persuade them again that the inherent risks were worthwhile as their interest faltered. With trade taking a dive, however, and no immediate sign of an upswing, the appeals to patriotism were underpinned by hopes of reward from the most powerful man in the government. By the end of July 1570, the trio had become sufficiently motivated to take on the abduction. They travelled to Bergen, bought a ship that they considered again and resold, hired sailors and finally, through Bradley, found a Dutch sea captain for hire. They opted to rent his shop for a sum paid out of their own pockets, as they later recorded with regret as the prospect of reimbursement shrivelled. The whole effort now depended on the persuasive genius of William Parker and what he devised.

The operation itself was not as abrupt as some accounts have indicated. Parker told his colleague about three young Englishmen, all good Catholics as he also seemed to be, who knew of a ship carrying religious contraband. What reason he put up for passing on his information rather than acting on it is not known, but evidently he was glib enough for Story and so were the trio when he met them. He went to Antwerp to conduct a search and, moving from ship to ship in the huge and crowded harbour, spent days in company with them before the trap was sprung in Bergen. Lured to the English House, Story was then detained on board van Eyck's ship and 'clapped fast under hatches'. The vessel then sailed to Yarmouth carrying Parker and Story, nobody but Marsh knowing of the former's complicity and so effectively extending his career as an agent. Story yet maintained a robust attitude to his detention and, although in theory guarded by the trio, even managed a brief escape. Aided by a man called Gosling and an accomplice, his surge of good fortune only faltered because his kidnappers picked up the trail. He was recaptured after this brief flurry. No wonder instructions were sent requiring the slippery prisoner be kept incommunicado.

The bailiffs of Yarmouth then received their orders from the Privy Council. Story was to be sent under custody to the Bishop of London's residence, where he was to

Enemies (and even friends of the regime, like Ralegh) were often imprisoned in the Tower

be delivered to Thomas Watts, Archdeacon of Middlesex. He was experienced in dealing with elements like Story, but had no relish for the task this time. The prisoner was to be held safely to ensure he did not escape while the Lollards' Tower was prepared for him – new locks were thought necessary. Watts wriggled somewhat, declaring that only recently he had been dangerously sick of the ague and could still only venture out in fine weather.[5] However, by early September he had successfully discharged his duty and Story was placed in the Lollards' Tower which he knew intimately from his time spent examining Marian Protestants there. In December 1570 he was moved to the Tower of London, a fact which worried de Spes who thought it presaged torture on the rack installed there. Story remained in company with William Parker until the trial held in May 1571, and both seem to have lived a fairly comfortable existence because to differentiate between them might have aroused suspicions. The claim from the Lieutenant of the Tower for their charges, 1 February – 7 April, amounted to some £20 for diet, keeper, fuel and candles. Cecil's problem was now a judicial one – with what should Story be charged so that he might be executed without glaring discredit?

Whether in chains or not Dr Story had lost control of his own fate. Those who had brought him back to incarceration now found they were dependent too on the goodwill of Cecil and this brought sore disappointment. Ramsden, Bragge and Jewkes had set aside modest careers to undertake what had been set before them as their duty to their country and their sovereign. Having successfully completed the task, albeit with one major slip, soon rectified, they found their employer reluctant to reimburse them. They approached John Marsh, and he submitted their claim to Cecil and Leicester for some £300, but a week after a cool response from the top he proved much less supportive. Even so they did eventually retrieve something, though less than they had claimed, and no supplement for a job well done. Perhaps, as has been suggested, Cecil thought to use them again and this was his way of keeping them dependent. If so, it seems a very curious method and it looks as if they were shut out by Marsh himself wanting credit for the whole operation. Cecil, in one of his last letters to him on the matter, made the macabre joke that if the trio were not satisfied, they could have Story's remains (post-execution) to sell as relics. Simon Jewkes did return to the Netherlands by July 1573, no doubt rueful about the ways of great men. He does not seem to have been averse to a little intelligencing, for he wrote out material on political and military matters for William Herle, long an agent of Cecil's, and sent it to him in London.

In comparison with Bradley and Lee, the three kidnappers, if apparently ill used, did not suffer greatly. The former had simply hired van Eyck and his ship, but when this was made public he had to flee, leaving his wife and children behind. Alva's agents seized his property and his family was harassed by the Bishop of Antwerp; their situation worsened in 1574 when Bergen was occupied by Spanish troops. Marsh knew of this and did try to get help for Bradley, but their sometime employer seems to have ignored their plight. As for Lee – at first his part in the coup was overlooked, although the exiled Richard Norton, who had lost close relatives after the northern rebellion, did try to have him arrested for revealing all that had passed in Parker's house. Lee received a warning about this from an unlikely source – the Earl of Westmorland – and managed to hide the documents that would have incriminated him. Unlike his colleagues in the affair he did receive an annuity, but in the spring of 1573 he was arrested and his place in Antwerp was filled by another agent, Edward Woodshaw, whose task was to watch and report on Westmorland. Lee was probably executed.

Only Marsh and Parker flourished in the aftermath of the operation. Prestall was allowed to return to England, but only as a prisoner, and for years he was shunted in and out of prisons. Marsh continued to receive favours from Cecil, including a grant of concealed lands, but it was Parker who did best of all. Perhaps this was merited, for he had the most exhausting part and seems to have suffered some sort of breakdown on his return to England in company with the man he had betrayed. He recovered during the months he and Story were held, a lengthy period that requires an explanation. In the first place there was the hope that if Story was ignorant of just who had betrayed him, he might let fall some further useful information. Secondly, there was the possibility that Parker's career as a spy might be extended, so allowing him to penetrate more dissident groups. The notion was supported by the spy himself when he wrote to Cecil and mentioned his luck in sharing the family name of a noted Catholic exile since 1569, Henry Parker, Lord Morley. He had gone first to Flanders, where his health also broke down, and then removed to Spain where he died in 1577. There was also a third possibility – that Cecil was doing some forward planning to counter any conspiracy being worked up by the exiles, for the abduction of Story aroused strong passions among them.

William Parker was available as a trusted agent in the spring of 1571, when Cecil was applying himself to unravelling the complexities of the second Ridolphi plot.[6] In the first half of April that year as the third parliament of the reign assembled, Lord Cobham, Warden of the Cinque Ports, sent Cecil (now Lord Burghley) a mysterious packet. It contained letters, a copy of the infamous papal bull, as well as ciphered papers. Cobham linked these to a Flemish-Scot, Charles Bailly, who had arrived in Dover from Europe and was employed as an agent by the Bishop of Ross. Burghley gave the material his attention, but the letters concerning Mary, Queen of Scots, were relatively innocuous if they were being scrutinized for any hints of treason. The cipher items to Ross, Lord Lumley and Norfolk were immediately more suggestive and at least offered the hope of something incriminating. The obvious problem to be overcome was the absence of a key and, since it was thought Bailly might help to penetrate the mystery, he was held for a time in the Marshalsea. To get a very frightened young man to talk freely would require an agent with some expertise and Burghley's choice was William Herle.

Burghley's comment on the agent who had been in his employ for some time was that he was a man 'of very good quality'. This seems to refer to connections with several Catholic aristocratic families, and Herle was certainly well educated and a linguist.[7] His employment at this rather demeaning low level indicates the precarious finances of many men of his class, aggravated as they were in his case by the cost of supporting his sister and her children. Even so, being chained and left without a table, chair or clout for wiping himself did nothing for his pocket, and he claimed eventually that this period of extreme discomfort cost him £50. Secretly briefed by Burghley and not known as an agent by his gaolers, Herle made approaches to Bailly. His relief at finding someone to talk to (in French?) led him into indiscretions about the papers he had relinquished. On 11 April Herle reported that Bailly was 'the most secret minister of all ill-practices in Flanders'; an exaggerated notion, but still it led to removal to the Tower. Before this Herle was supposed to prise out details of Bailly's ciphers, but he failed, having inadvertently let slip something that alarmed the now silent courier.

Burghley clearly looked for a way of giving the prisoner a jolt to loosen his tongue. Bailly was therefore placed in the notorious Beauchamp Tower, and given the same room hitherto occupied by Story who had in the fashion of the day carved his name on the stone wall. On 1 May, Bailly was tortured and Herle actually caught a glimpse of him afterwards 'discoloured and pale as ashes'; 'more frightened than hurt' according to de Spes. Yet nothing weighty emerged with the groans – certainly not the cipher key. The compulsion to obtain it was heightened because Burghley had recently been contacted by the Bishop of Ross, one of the aides of Mary. The bishop said that he had learned of a packet of letters addressed to him being claimed by Dover authorities and their bearer arrested. He declared innocently that he was not yet certain of their contents, but that Burghley had his entire confidence in the matter. For a brief spell Herle himself had been able to waft messages from Bailly to the bishop, but this had stopped and Burghley decided to make a final play with Story.

The ruse was at once inventive and quite simple. Story had a wide-reaching

Dr John Story was the first recorded victim of execution on the triangular gallows

public reputation and Bailly, it was thought, was certain to respect, even revere him. If, late at night, a man who called himself Story was admitted to Bailly, he might succeed in drawing him out where torture had hitherto failed. As William Parker (for it was surely he) put it to Bailly when he went to his cell as Story, the meeting was allowed by 'the kindness of a gaoler'. Bailly accepted this with relief, as he did the pseudo-Story, having never seen either Parker or the man he was impersonating. Reverence for a Catholic hero made the messenger an easy target for Parker's fuliginous presentation. He counselled Bailly to decipher the captured letters and offer to become a government spy. With this opportunity present to him Bailly folded and surrendered the cipher key. His subsequent offer to spy was refused and still he could not understand why.

He would have been profoundly distressed if he had realized that by giving away the secret he had ended any use Story might have had for the government. On 26 May 1571, the sometime civil law expert, widely detested in London, was brought to trial. As has been noted, the problem had been with what he should be charged so that he might properly be executed. Burghley and Leicester, not always at loggerheads, seem to have conferred on the matter. Curiously, nothing Story had done in the past could now be construed as treasonable, though it was actually his service to Mary Tudor and his hot speeches as an MP that stoked their antipathy. So it was not until Easter 1571 that an indictment was concocted, based on the company Story had kept in the Spanish Netherlands. There he had mixed with other refugees, all under Alva's protection, and now the English government singled out Richard and Francis Norton, accused of treason following the rebellion of the earls. Story was, therefore, charged with consorting with traitors who plotted to kill Elizabeth. However, he still declined to make any plea on the grounds that he was now a Spanish citizen. Of course it was unavailing and he was condemned *nihil dicit* and very promptly executed at Tyburn with the towering cruelty of the day. It was the first recorded use of the triangular gallows.

Bailly's testimony presented a complicated picture. His mission to Antwerp had been at the behest of Roberto Ridolphi, the ubiquitous Florentine then based in London. He was active on behalf of various Italian trading and banking operations, including the Cavalcanti brothers whose public branch he ran in the 1560s. They were far from popular in English trading circles, but access to funds in money markets meant they could not be spurned, especially in the aftermath of Elizabeth's rupturing of trade with Antwerp in 1569. In October of that year even Ridolphi, whose clients included de Spes and the Bishop of Ross, had been arrested in London and held for a few weeks. He was twice closely examined by Walsingham and confessed his dealings with Ross. On Cecil's orders Walsingham went to the banker's lodgings to confiscate his papers, and there was a good deal of pleading that he would 'meddle no more with public affairs' before Ridolphi was released on bond. After that, Alva, who was striving for a *rapprochement* with London, was explicit in decrying the meddling of Ridolphi when instructing Guerau de Spes, the Spanish ambassador, and also when writing to Philip II, Burghley and his colleagues knew he was intriguing with Mary's representatives, and it was for this reason Ridolphi was freed. After a visit, probably embarrassing to both sides, Ridolphi quit Brussels for Rome and then Madrid. According to Bailly the intention was to land Spanish forces in eastern England to act in concert with a domestic uprising. The deciphered letters were spurious, distractions that allowed the delivery of the real letters to Ross. It was the bishop and de Spes who had cobbled together the substitutes to mislead Burghley. So how was he to get at Ross and the genuine letters sent him by Ridolphi using Bailly as courier?

It was made possible by William Herle. A scribbled warning to the bishop from Bailly was intercepted and Herle became the principal figure in a prison charade intended to establish his credentials. After examination, threats of the rack and so forth, Herle wrote to Ross begging assistance. The churchman was taken in, but only so far, and neglected to disclose the recipient of the original letters. Burghley saw with regret that his ruse had faltered and so decided to examine the bishop himself. On 13 May, three privy councillors, Sadler, Mildmay and Sussex, went to his house and elicited an admission. Mary had despatched letters by Ridolphi to Alva, the Pope and Philip II, asking for assistance in Scotland. The bishop then revealed the original letters had been destroyed by him, and when asked about the cipher merely identified '30' and '40' as the Spanish ambassador and Mary. He declined to say more and diplomatic propriety denied his questioners the use of torture. Burghley could, however, try to test the statement against what he knew from Bailly – that a Spanish force was intended for England rather than Scotland, and it was no surprise when de Spes and Mary denied the cipher. The bishop was then detained in custody by the Bishop of Ely and Mary's guards were required to tighten their grip. Shrewsbury was told to lock out Mary's servants after dark until daylight.

The trail seemed to have petered out, but as so often happened a new sequence erupted.[8] Burghley was told that John Hawkins was engaged in solo negotiations with Philip II that aimed to bring Englishmen taken into captivity at San Juan de Ulloa, back to England. Burghley had the London residence of de Spes under surveillance and began to ponder the meaning of all the comings and goings. When summoned before Burghley, Hawkins declared candidly that he had sought out de Spes and sent his friend George Fitzwilliam to Madrid as a means of freeing the captives. In his name Fitzwilliam was to offer to desert to Spain with some seventeen vessels and crews, although as Hawkins hastily pointed out it was all a 'practice'. When Fitzwilliam returned in May he reported a modest success, but with Philip II requiring a letter of recommendation from Mary, the minister sighted an opening to be exploited. Fitzwilliam was allowed to visit Mary to deliver letters and presents from the Count and Countess of Feria – the sometime Jane Dormer of Mary Tudor's court and of interest herself to Burghley. The Queen of Scots then declared her tender interest in all prisoners and Fitzwilliam got his letter which Hawkins sent to Burghley. Seeing no compelling reason to restrain Fitzwilliam, he was sanctioned to go back to Spain and the prisoners were released with a small tip to smooth any ruffled feathers. Hawkins, ever greedy, benefited from a huge dole made through Philip II's London agents, in the expectation that he would desert with his ships to Spain and be ready in the autumn to assist Alva in an invasion. Early in September Hawkins wrote to Burghley from Plymouth: 'Their practices be very mischievous, and they be never idle, but God, I hope, will confound them and turn their devices upon their own necks'. Fitzwilliam hurried home to warn Burghley of Norfolk's treachery in consenting to an invasion scheme.

Even before this arrived Burghley had another avenue to investigate. He had been sent a bag of money and ciphered letters, intercepted when forwarded from the Duke of Norfolk to his land agent in Shropshire, a man called Banister. The ultimate destination of such a package was Scotland and the Marian party. To establish a connection two of Norfolk's secretaries were, like Banister, arrested and racked.[9] Yet the duke did not do the obvious thing which was to destroy every incriminating paper – and Higford's confession led to seizure, despite the conflicting testimonies of the duke and Barker. To clarify this the Bishop of Ross was brought from his confinement with the Bishop of Ely, and bluntly told what treatment he would receive now if he remained silent. Burghley was bluffing, but his minatory stance induced Ross to speak in a way that was disastrous for the duke and Mary. He confirmed now what the brutalized Bailly had given away: that Ridolphi had left England with their approval, travelling after talks with Alva to Rome and Madrid to try to coordinate a landing in eastern England and a rising of Catholics; Mary would marry the Duke of Norfolk and replace the dethroned Elizabeth. With all this revealed Alva unhesitatingly refused to do anything, having already promised far more than was possible.

Setting aside his usual deference to ancient lineage, Burghley carefully prepared the Crown case against the duke. De Spes was summoned at last towards the end of 1571 before the Privy Council and expelled for conduct incompatible with his status. Even before he complied in 1572, the Spaniard insolently involved himself in a fantastical plot to murder Burghley – a notion apparently set up and foiled by Herle. As for Norfolk, the work for the verdict of guilty at his trial had been done; by then Burghley's political control was stronger than ever, though the spy master had to wait until June 1572 for the axe to fall.

Chapter Two

Home and Abroad

English foreign policy was given its particular configuration by geography, dynastic considerations, religion and above all trade. Sometimes privy councillors and diplomats expressed individual or collective views that would modify royal perceptions, such as the lengthy disposition of Elizabeth to be cordial towards her sometime brother-in-law Philip II, whose vast inheritance induced awe. Occasionally the views expressed were too extreme, as with Philip Sidney, whose intimate family links to Leicester and Walsingham availed him little once Elizabeth had been assailed by his raw opinions. 'Sidney learned early of his monarch's extreme standoffishness, and grew to dread the isolationism which he felt endangered England and the Protestant cause in general.' Insistent prejudices could have far-reaching effects on either side of the religious divide, as the placing of de Spes in London revealed. It was a pity that Philip II was so slow to grasp the distorting habits of mind of his lamentable choice 'whose influence was used to heighten rather than lessen international tension'. A few months before the envoy was expelled, Alva was forthrightly disparaging him in a letter to Philip, saying that de Spes had such a hatred of the sovereign and her countrymen that his judgement was impaired. Even years later Alva told an English diplomat in Madrid that if de Spes had not died in 1572 on his way home, he should have been imprisoned or even executed for his errant behaviour.[1] To balance against this there is the view that Alva himself was 'narrow-minded and politically short-sighted'.

The many printed volumes of English State Papers (often abbreviated from originals and supplemented by manuscript collections in private hands like the Salisbury papers at Hatfield House), have tended to obscure by pagination the fact that the Elizabethan policy-makers had to make weighty decisions on the flimsiest of briefing material. Their ignorance of the political realities of other countries was often startling. No one in London knew, for example, that Alva and de Spes were hopelessly split on policy. The famous stately dithering of Elizabeth was less an act of intelligent choice than an admission (albeit muffled) of ignorance. The need for accurate information was continuous and intensely felt, yet save for Paris there were no permanent English embassies abroad and the scope for pan-European misunderstanding hugely increased. As a result special embassies for the presentation of condolences, or the ever-useful Garter insignia, were always swollen since thirty or more pairs of ears and eyes were superior to ten.

Foreign envoys to Britain copied this mode. In 1569, for example, Alva sent as his envoy his second-in-command, the very personable Chiappino Vitelli, Marquis of Cetona, hoping to repair the damage caused by the grotesque miscalculations of de Spes. The sometime Florentine soldier of fortune arrived in Dover with a suite of forty-four, and most were required to remain in the port. Despite an initially frosty response from his hosts, Vitelli found a kindred spirit in Leicester who understood Italian and had a wide-ranging interest in Italian culture, so they talked principally about art. This link to the greatest patron of the arts at Elizabeth's court gave Vitelli access to her and he managed to charm her, although his true mission failed. It was a minor coup even so, since European envoys did not always have his deft ways in presentation and conversation. But then blunders by diplomats were not solely a foreign speciality. Philip Sidney was sent to Prague in 1577 to offer condolences to Rudolf II on the death of Maximilian, but used it to present a plea on behalf of Protestantism in the Empire. He also had a secret meeting with the Jesuit exile Campion for undisclosed reasons, just as when in Venice he sought out the self-exiled Catholic nobleman, Lord Windsor.

Less callow and less stern in his public prejudices was the semi-official resident correspondent in Germany, Christopher Mont.[2] In addition the government relied heavily on merchants and trade representatives like Christopher Hoddesdon, fluent in Dutch and a pioneer of the Moscow trade, who had lived for a time in Russia. Such men were rarely impartial, but they were often first with news that might have a bearing on business and profits. Finally, there was the motley caravan of unofficial eavesdroppers and intelligencers who scurried about hunting for anything that might enhance their income. Those with a career in mind, like Herle, usually found spying no more than an anxiety-inducing temporary option. The men who remained in it were rarities; spies at other times might be soldiers, academics, students, writers and musicians. The madrigalist Thomas Morley survived being discovered by the anti-Jesuit double agent Charles Paget in 1591. What the spy masters ruthlessly exploited was the impassioned but often thwarted desire of their employees to thrive.

Hitherto, the findings of Conyers Read on Elizabethan espionage have been unchallenged; the large subject ignored. Even in 1979 a wide-ranging history of Tudor government asserted yet again that Elizabethan privy councillors did not create anything like a 'sophisticated' spy system.[3] But the choice of this particular word is misleading and so is the conclusion then reached. It is unhelpful because today 'sophisticated' is freighted with a loose general meaning of lavish expertise, elaborate equipment and techniques. Sixteenth-century spies relied on simple methods of collecting material and rudimentary ones for transmission, like writing in onion juice. But there were successes and much evidence still that spying was a necessary item in the making of policy, underpinning the often sluggish deliberations of bewildered ministers and monarchs. As has been noted recently, it is possible to criticize the conduct of Elizabethan foreign policy, but not on the grounds of rashness and carelessness. 'Laborious weighing of alternatives, prolonged debate and frequent prevarication were the norm.' The spy masters eventually found access to limited public funds, but necessity (and anxiety) drove them to use their own wealth as well. Two generations of politicians did not do this out of idle curiosity; for over forty years there was an unshakeable conviction that espionage was vital.

Personnel with special skills and superior intellect were sought and employed. One of the most outstanding was a Cambridge MA (1577), then sent by the secretary to Paris to decipher any material that came his way. With remarkable grasp of cryptanalysis and foreign languages (at least French, Italian, Spanish, Latin and German), Thomas Phelippes did not disappoint his employer. Having adjusted the family name of Philipps to his liking, he often used pseudonyms, such names as John Morice (which meant writers to him had to pretend to be Catholic), and Peter Halins, merchant. His colleague was the seal-maker Arthur Gregory and the legend of their efforts has doubtless been puffed up by popular writers, but in spurning this vulgar approach historians have gone too far in discounting something of substance. The difficulty that has to be addressed is that as usual the evidence can be distorted and chaotically imperfect. The secretariat of each spy master was variously employed to do a great deal of preliminary reading and sifting. This could weed out the inconsequential which required no more response than a line of acknowledgement, praise or rebuke, and that not always very prompt. Sometimes important decisions could depend on the judgement of a trusted agent like Phelippes whose early experience in diplomatic affairs was gained under ambassadors Paulet and Cobham. This gave him an entrée into the world of invisible power with continual employment by Walsingham to follow. Phelippes may have been tutored in the clandestine arts by the writing master Peter Bales who in the 1570s and 1580s was at court, but without a secure post. A master of microscopic penmanship, he was also a deviser of ciphers employed by Hatton and Walsingham.

The fluctuations of news-gathering and intelligence for the conciliar triumvirate of Burghley, Leicester and Walsingham are somewhat easier to follow in the modest statistics than the murky efforts of their employees. In his last year as principal secretary, Burghley had items from 50 correspondents, and by 1585 his successor's list had swollen to 111. Yet Burghley went on receiving a substantial clutch of despatches and Leicester only surpassed him in 1582. After 1577 Walsingham's total only once dipped below the century mark, and in 1582–3 went over five hundred. The location of these letter writers (and it must be clear that not all had the subversive intentions of spies) was generally predictable, with the nations closest to England having most. Their efforts were intended to fill the startling gaps left by a severely contracting diplomatic service, something occasioned by confessional boundaries, political indifference and royal parsimony.

After Elizabeth's accession the Venetian ambassador and the papal nuncio were withdrawn, so in turn it was easier not to send envoys to reside in Venice or Rome. The English embassy in the Spanish Netherlands closed when Philip II went to Spain in 1559 and negotiations were then conducted through the Merchant Adventurers, while the controversial expulsion (or recall in the face-saving English formula) of John Man from Spain in 1568, left only the Paris embassy as the hub of English diplomatic and clandestine activity. De Spes, who came to London to replace Guzman de Silva, was not wholly lacking in ability, but it transpired that his political efforts were violently slewed in favour of promoting Catholicism at any cost. Explaining the expulsion of Mr Man (who had no doctorate despite the oft-repeated title), was the first event to tax his limited emollient powers. His private obsessions undoubtedly seeped into the public arena, and when he indulged in dangerous agitation it was hard for the Privy Council to resist real provocation; yet withal the Spanish embassy remained open for a further sixteen years, and only closed as Anglo-Spanish relations deteriorated rapidly and open war loomed. Even the absence of a resident ambassador there did not mean all diplomatic contacts had lapsed. Elizabeth sent seven ambassadors extraordinary to Spain and many *ad hoc* missions, some remaining a year or more. Sir Henry Cobham, for example, went in 1575 to reclaim, among other privileges, religious toleration for the English in Spain; a doomed mission even if he did indeed speak Spanish.

In 1572 Burghley had material from eight French cities, six towns in the German states and empire, five in the Low Countries, five in Italy, four in Scotland, two in Spain and one in Africa (Alexandria). The total dipped when he became Lord Treasurer, while by 1585 Walsingham's total had grown strikingly to some fifty foreign sources. Just before he died he was receiving pan-European material and this strength in depth (reports from twelve places in France, ten in Germany, as well as the Low Countries and more) is so strong it can at that point be dignified as a network. Even in April 1583 he had three men reporting simultaneously from Paris, nine from Antwerp, two from Middelburg and Strasburg. A little earlier, in January 1578, Paulet reported on a meeting with an anti-Spanish emigré Italian in Queen Catherine de Medici's household. Massino Delbene alluded to an agent called inscrutably J.B., who would reveal much of worth, and by the time of his next letter J.B. had tiptoed out of the shadows to bargain briskly for a sum to be paid by Elizabeth on her own estimate of his value. This approach may have been purposeful or foolish, but he promised in return information about the late Duke of Norfolk's affairs and 'certain practices' of the sometime French ambassador in London, La Mothe Fénelon. Above all, for a pension he would be Paulet's spy at the French court claiming he had great credit with Cardinal de Guise. Paulet's letter goes on: 'I know not how important his service may be in these old matters, but I take it to be most certain that in the occurrents of this present time he is able to do great and singular service, having good credit with the French and Spanish of better sort.'

The man was therefore hired, and Paulet was able to forward intelligence and stolen letters procured by 'my new acquaintance'. Walsingham's principal notion seems to have been that J.B. should trap Thomas Morgan, a key representative for Mary in Paris and virtually her secretary of state in exile. On 13 March the secretary's messenger arrived there with the 100 crowns Elizabeth had sent and a promise of future reward. Unfortunately, the spy affected to be livid that so modest a price should be sent when he claimed to risk his life. 'I cannot express unto you', Paulet wrote, 'how J.B. stormed and raged as well in words as in countenance.' Then he threatened to withdraw totally because he had proferred his services for eight years and received nothing. Paulet argued and then wooed him, so that eventually the spy relented, although later he did contrive a dignified hint that a higher bid from another source might shake his resolve. Finally Paulet was able to report with some glee that the spy was going to serve Elizabeth 'and doth promise to send me something in writing very secretly'. On 24 April Paulet wrote to Walsingham enclosing letters for Elizabeth which he wanted his senior colleague to look over before he submitted them. There was also the question of an enhanced payment to J.B., whom he thought was poised to reveal very important intelligence: 300 crowns and a promise of a pension of the same seemed a judicious amount. 'He hath refused the hundred crowns . . . and yet he hath borrowed of me sithence that time 130 crowns at one time, and 80 crowns at an other time, and I think it well bestowed, if I should pay it ten time of my own purse . . . It is easy to see that he dealeth plainly and frankly. I write openly unto you . . . as I trust my letters shall come safely unto you.'[4]

The ambassador had a cluster of assistants to help him with secret service matters. However, the transition from one ambassador to another was not always easy. In 1583 Sir Edward Stafford complained to Walsingham that Sir Henry Cobham had made the excuse of protecting his sources and declined to show him anything 'which might instruct me what course to take . . .'. Secrecy then was obviously as obsessive a concern as it is today among unimaginative bureaucrats. Looking at the arrangements of a secretariat to receive such material, Burghley's modest set-up was noted approvingly by two of his younger contemporaries. Nicholas Faunt and Robert Beale both wrote extended essays on the office of principal secretary, and Beale's attention was given added piquancy since he was one of Walsingham's brothers-in-law. Both essayists worked as private secretaries for Walsingham, but withheld praise for his occupancy of the great office of state because they preferred the example of his predecessor Burghley. Faunt thought the use of numerous assistants led to confusion and a distressing lack of secrecy. His line may have been partly governed by self-interest, for he held the view that two personal secretaries were sufficient, with a division in their labours so that only one dealt with intelligence matters. Faunt never did become Walsingham's chief aide.

Burghley certainly shared some secret service matters with his secretariat; despatches of known spies were sometimes endorsed by a secretary. But, being a cautious man, it was done with signal discretion and Burghley preserved as much as possible for his private, single scrutiny. Henry Maynard was chiefly responsible for foreign elements in the Lord Treasurer's affairs after 1582, so one of the hands-on despatches was probably his and it is likely he had access to his employer's ciphers. Even so, letters to Burghley were often deciphered by him alone, and his passion for order in his papers was unflagging. Such was his reputation that many of his correspondents apologized for noting material they expected he knew already, but they were driven to include it because omission might be suspect. Writing to Burghley in code or not could make the brow moist and prickle the palms of hands.

The secret service of a courtier-politician like the Earl of Leicester is even more difficult to trace. Much of what would have constituted a major archive has been destroyed. Still, his secretariat provides some hints to the breadth and texture of the work done for one of the most strangely underrated of Elizabeth's circle of close advisers. One of his most gifted employees for a time was Edmund Campion (b. 1540), a noted scholar whose conversion to Catholicism led to his becoming an exile and a Jesuit after 1573. In later years Leicester employed Jean Hotman and Gabriel Harvey before Arthur Atey snatched the coveted position in 1579. Once

Sir William Cecil (later Lord Burghley),
1520–98, may be called the founding father
of Elizabethan espionage

also an academic like Harvey, Atey had been with John Man to Spain in 1566. For
the earl he took control of secret intelligence correspondence and the activities that
led to it. Atey was very likely responsible for decoding cipher material, and he had
as well his own correspondents in Europe who sent him information which he sifted
for Leicester. Other men at various times employed by him were John Wolley,
Edmund Spenser and Edward Dyer, who might have become secretary of state in
1590 on Walsingham's death if the earl himself had been alive.

The political slant of Leicester's career, his contacts at home and abroad, though
ill recorded, suggest with remaining data that he would have wanted a wide-ranging
clutch of informers and intelligencers. To hold his own against Burghley he needed
them, and so one of those who moved for a time into Leicester's orbit was the
resourceful William Herle. By the spring of 1581 he was residing in Lambeth,
brushing up his study of foreign affairs, especially in relation to France and Spain,
and by November feeling able to claim that he had 'means to decipher the Spanish
ambassador's actions' to the earl. Herle had somehow discovered the diplomat's
clandestine mode of sending material abroad. The means was apparently a rare
female courier, 'the letters hanging from the woman's waist, next her skin,
downwards'. Mary, Queen of Scots' efforts to correspond with her allies called for
even more varied techniques: alum used for writing on paper or cloth; books in

which the material being transmitted was to be found on specified pages; letters hidden in the heels of slippers or the linings of trunks. They failed – Walsingham knew them all.

The official posting arrangements of the government also had drawbacks. This was despite the efforts of Thomas Randolph from 1568, occasionally a special ambassador to France, and then Sir John Stanhope, much favoured by Elizabeth so he held the office of Master of the Posts for life and was followed by his son. There was an increasing expectation that the organization they headed would smother unofficial services, leading to a proclamation in 1591. At the same time there existed the Merchant Strangers' post, an operation for foreign merchants which had historically given the users considerable freedom in the matter of correspondence, as well as in trade. They seem to have selected their own postmaster, and the death of Christian Suffling in 1568 led to a dispute about his successor.[5] Raphael van den Putte was the nominee of one group, and the Catholic Godfrey Marshall of the Italians. Given the importance the government attached to posts it is not surprising that the Privy Council selected van den Putte, whose appointment was confirmed by Randolph.

Freer communication was anathema to the Elizabethan hierarchy. It was intended that posts should carry official letters exclusively, and the ordinary post was a man on a permanent post route (or specific variation), who regularly carried mail from one point to another. It was a routine for which he was paid a fixed daily fee, and he had to do the work in person, not execute it through a deputy. Increasingly, private letters did seep into the official post, a fact acknowledged by the official injunction that those riding with the packet 'and having by-letters, or private packets' would be dismissed for opening public or private mail. Special posts outside England were paid according to distance and their expenses. When Stephen Lesieur, who later worked for the Merchant Adventurers and then Sir Robert Cecil, travelled from Elizabeth to the Duke of Parma and the Duke of Cleves in February to October 1582, he submitted an itemized account:

> London to Dover post horses: 33 s.
> Tournai to Mons   "   : 26 s.
> Antwerp to Bruges   "   : 10 s.
> A messenger from Cleves to Antwerp: 25 s.
> Messengers between Lesieur and Daniel Rogers: 18 s.
> Dover to Windsor post horses: 33 s.

Horses were the key to a moderately efficient system and Master of the Horse, Leicester, took an informed interest in breeding them. But this was principally for the court and the post horses were often of low quality and 'evilly used' so Walsingham, for example, kept a stable of over sixty mounts. Moreover, there was always a shortage caused by the abuse of placards or 'passeports', which were the permits for the use of the post horses. In 1566 the Privy Council tried to end this by tightening controls on their use, and when the keeper of the post horses in London was required to have six horses in his stable, he was told to hire them only to 'such as bring sufficient commissions'. Ailing horses or animals absent, for whatever reason, led to a faltering service and there were constant complaints about slackness and unwarranted delays. The result was that the injunctions on letters for speed became ever more urgent in tone and extended. A letter of 1597 was marked 'haste, haste for Her Majesty's service', while in the same year, with a characteristically dramatic flourish, Essex wrote on a letter to Sir Robert Cecil: 'For Her Majesty's especial affairs. Hast, Hast, Hast, Hast, Post Hast, Hast for Life . . .'.

By the 1580s there were five principal post routes in England and three on the continent to Paris, the Low Countries and Italy. Other countries had their own postal systems and an English diplomat in Spain might well have had to consign his correspondence to the employees of Philip II. The major handicaps at home and abroad to an efficient service were low pay, indolence, contamination of the service with extraneous items, equine failings and poor roads. Given all this and a heavy correspondence, Burghley, Leicester and Walsingham had to maintain large households of servants not simply for ostentation, but to have messengers they thought they could trust available immediately. Abroad, the staff of the Paris embassy and personal servants of the ambassador, were all employed. James Painter, the Paris post, often carried material in his head, so the interesting question arises as to whether he used a memory system, especially since he seems to have dabbled in espionage. Another messenger for Walsingham on the Paris route was the painter John de Critz who wrote a series of letters to his employer in 1583, and who carried letters to Stafford from 1585–8.

As it was, safe transmission of both routine and secret material was always a worry and taxed ingenuity. To increase the likelihood of safe delivery from somewhere as distant as Constantinople, multiple copies might be sent by different routes, and for secret items an invisible ink preparation of milk and lemon juice might be used. This meant that a blank sheet of paper in a packet was suspect and on one occasion when wily old Sir Ralph Sadler, then the guardian of Mary, found some virgin enclosures, he tried fire and water to see if anything emerged, but nothing did. The use of cipher was another option despite its many attendant problems, even at a time when English was comparatively little known and no distinction is made here between code and cipher. As Duke August of Braunschweig-Lüneburg, author of the *Cryptomenytices* wrote 'the hidden meaning of the document or epistle should be, either quite unintelligible or intelligible only after great labour . . .'. Burghley had a long acquaintance with the theory and practice of cryptography. In 1552 Girolamo Cardano (Cardanus) was in London staying with Sir John Cheke, whose sister Mary was William Cecil's first wife. Cardano, a Milanese doctor and mathematician, was the deviser of the cardan grille. This was a piece of sturdy material pierced with rectangular holes at irregular intervals. The same height as the script, they varied in width allowing access to whole words, syllables or letters. Each was randomly numbered and by placing the grille on a piece of paper the message was spelled out in the number order – at this point still a clutch of letters. These were further disguised by incorporation in an apparently innocuous message. A decoder with an identical grille placed it on top of this text to read the message in the correct order. Widely used for many years, it was the covering message that usually alerted the attentive reader, by its clumsiness.

It is known that Cardano met John Dee at Cheke's home, and it is inconceivable that the polymath Englishman did not question Cardano about ciphers. Indeed, it may have been these exchanges that alerted Dee to the cryptographic works of Abbot Johannes Trithemius of Sponheim (d. 1516). In his *De Rerum Varietate* (1557), Cardano attacked both the method and personality of Trithemius, who was for long believed to be an exponent of demonic magic, despite the denials he had made in his lifetime. For those with a particular interest in ciphers the unpublished 'Steganographia' (covered writing) and *Polygraphia*, published in 1518, were key texts. The latter's several volumes contained hundreds of alphabets in which words and phrases could be substituted for the individual letters of an item. The most famous was the Ave Maria cipher with its 384 columns of Latin words from which equivalents could be selected so that the plaintext message could be disguised as a piece of devotional writing.[6] In the early 1560s John Dee wrote excitedly from Antwerp where he was staying with his printer Willem Silvius, to William Cecil, that he had found an extremely rare manuscript of the 'Steganographia' which, in its extended title, refers to the art of writing secret messages and communicating them long distances by occult means. The maverick scholar was agog with excitement and spent ten days preparing a copy. A lingering flavour of the fierce controversy over this text can be found in the recent disagreement of scholars who have studied it and its circumstances. One view is that 'the book offers no more than a system of double codification by cipher'. The alternative view is that, although the first two books deal with ciphering, they were a device to obscure the third book with its presentation of demonic magic.

Ciphers did become an indispensable tool of international diplomacy and war. The relative decline of Latin for despatches and the growth of ciphers coincided with the view of the educationist Richard Mulcaster that even tradesmen should learn some Latin. Intelligencers and soldiers used them, as did resident observers and senior merchants, who often had a second career in information-gathering. Elizabethan ciphers had two principle forms: transposition, where characters were shuffled but retained their actual meaning; and substitution, which omitted the change of sequence while replacing characters with other letters or symbols – often numbers served this purpose. In fact, all kinds of whimsical terms could be pressed into service and Burghley had a particular leaning to the signs of the zodiac. In a code for Thomas Bodley sent to the Low Countries in 1590 and written out by the Lord Treasurer himself, the Duke of Parma was Aries; Prince Maurice of Nassau, Gemini; the Estates General, Cancer; the Council of State, Leo; then Sir Francis Vere, amphora and so on. The following year, when Sir Henry Unton at last arrived in Paris to replace the wayward Sir Edward Stafford, the same sort of device appeared in a code drawn up for him. This time Elizabeth was Aries; Philip II, Scorpio; Normandy, Virgo and so on. Days of the week could be used to denote people and things – the French ambassador became Sunday; soldiers, Tuesday and victuals, Saturday. In an early cipher of William Cecil's, Catherine de Medici, who had some sexually alluring female spies in her employ, became *tout*; King Charles IX, *rien*; the Prince de Condé, *petit*; and Gaspard de Coligny, *seul*.

The cipher mode most frequently used in Elizabethan material was number substitution for a name or word. In April 1583 Robert Bowes was using it for communications with Walsingham: France is 54; Scotland, 70; James VI, 91; the

Letter in cipher from Elizabeth I apparently to the Earl of Moray, Regent of Scotland, 1569 (translation opposite)

Right trusty and right webeloved cosin we grete you wl. By your leters lately written to our secretary 14 amongst other thinges we perceve how princly you ofer the service of your self and all that you command to the help of suppression of a certen commotion in the north of our realme styrrid by tuo unloyall subjectes the Erles of Northumberland and Westmerland, for the which your kyndnes we do hartely thank you. Having had also intelligenc given us of your like offer made to our Marshall of 14* and of this disorderid attempt we dout not but you well understand the originall cause to be for the R.‡ Wherfore we think good that yourself with such as be your frendes shuld be in good redines, lest the fautors of this quarrell there in Scotland specially towards our frontyers might conspiring with our rebells bring some daunger to you, specially whan our rebels be forced to flee into that realme, as likely they will, considering what forces we have in redines to march agaynst them in the south. And in this matter we think good that you be advertised from the Erle of Sussex and the Lord of Hunsdon and Sir Rafe Sadler to be at York, of the proceding of the rebelles, and as they advise you to come to the Borders, and other wase require you to procede, so we ernestly pray you to do.

Your lovinge frende

Elizabeth R.

* Probably Berwick.
‡ Mary, Queen of Scots.

Earl of Lennox, 870; Elizabeth, 32 and Mary, 23. By 1585 Walsingham and the special ambassador to Scotland, Edward Wotton, an Italianate Englishman who had spent some years in Naples as the secretary's agent, had revised this so that Elizabeth was now 3; France, 32; Mary, 11. All this could be made a little more perplexing even to the trained eye by multiples replacing letters. Thus, William Davison had a cipher in which A could be replaced by 24, 91–9 and 100; B by 23, 89–91; C by 22, 86–9, continuing to Z which was replaced by 1 and 12. The larger the number of possible substitutes the better to baffle, but neither John Somers nor Thomas Phelippes working for Walsingham were easy to throw off. Indeed, for the correspondence of Mary in her English captivity, they were aided, not hindered, by the invariable use of cipher. English government correspondents were more restrained and partial cipher probably gave less clues to anyone prying into intercepted letters. Another reason for restraint in use was that preparing ciphered material was time-consuming and many became thoroughly bored by the effort. Certainly, if an individual or place was given a specific symbol, this might be more resistant than ciphering each letter when frequency and repetition could provide a clue – 'e' being the most frequently used letter. One variation that could be introduced into letter substitution was the use of *nil significantia* – letters or characters which had no meaning for the decipherer. A tiny mark might be used on a character to show that it was to be treated for a null. Transposition ciphers could became complex and were less easy to break, but it was the case that whichever was the preferred method ciphers caused problems even to the users. In September 1576, for example, when Sir Amias Paulet went as ambassador to France he discovered that the symbols for key figures in the religious factions were missing. Clerical errors could add to the confusion, so in 1583 Bowes had to point out to Walsingham that a copyist had written 31, instead of 91, for James VI. Cipher keys might stray through accident or theft, or be forgotten before a journey. Since they required sustained attention, especially when unfamiliar, many users seem to have maintained an extravagant optimism that what they were using had not been broken. In fact, loyalty or lethargy could both be costly, yet a request for a new cipher was not always met promptly.

Chapter Three

An Enigma and Secrets

Zeal and bigotry are unlovely kin. In his analysis of Sir Francis Walsingham's motives as a spy master, the American businessman and historian Conyers Read declared that there was but little bigotry in Walsingham's persecution of the clandestine priests. 'Protestant as Walsingham was, he was first of all a statesman, and he habitually looked upon religious and political problems alike from a statesman's point of view.' Also, one might say, from the point of view of a lawyer, albeit one who had never completed his studies, and property owner. The return of Catholicism threatened economic consequences that would have been particularly felt by men like Walsingham, Cecil, Bacon and Robert Dudley.

Born shortly before his lawyer father William Walsingham died in 1534, Francis was raised by his mother Joyce, the daughter of Sir Anthony Denny, with whom

Sir Francis Walsingham, 1534(?)–90. The Principal Secretary (or the Secretary of State for Foreign Affairs) managed his spies and agents with ruthless authority and compelling dedication

the then Princess Elizabeth and her servants were lodged at Cheshunt (Herts) in 1545. Joyce Walsingham remarried in 1536, and her second husband was Sir John Carey, whose brother married Mary Boleyn. Mary Walsingham, his sister, married Sir Walter Mildmay, one of the leading Protestants at the accession of Elizabeth and also a brother-in-law of Peter Wentworth, the radical Puritan MP who went to prison rather than not speak out in the way he felt compelled. The interrelationship of the Walsinghams with such deeply Protestant families indicates clearly the family cast of mind. Francis Walsingham went to Cambridge and, rather later than some of his generation, matriculated from King's College, although no degree is recorded. There from 1548–50, he may then have gone abroad, although by 1552 he was at Gray's Inn, then in a surprisingly rural setting, for its fields were not yet laid out formally. With the accession of Mary Tudor, and his family having been concerned in the Wyatt troubles, he went to Europe, travelling at first with his three Denny cousins who enrolled at the University of Basle. He went on to Padua, a university with a pan-European reputation for tolerance and excellence. 'Consiliarius' of the tiny English 'nation' in the faculty of civil law in March 1556, he seems to have left in April and between then and November 1558 he was again in Basle. Only with the accession of Elizabeth did he return home and Cecil engineered his seat in the 1559 parliament, Bossiney being the gift of the Earl of Bedford, a strong Protestant.

Early in the 1560s Cecil employed a number of men to provide him with political information. Abroad, for example, there was Christopher Mont; at home Thomas Randolph, Master of the Posts (1567), who also did work in Scotland before marrying Anne Walsingham, one of eight female cousins of Francis. The question of exactly when he was first employed by Cecil is a little muddied by a remark of Francis Mylles in a letter of October 1586, when he claimed to have had twenty years of service with Francis Walsingham. But the latter did his first recorded work for Cecil in August 1568, so perhaps for two years he had done modest clandestine work following his second marriage. Walsingham's first wife was Anne Carleill (widow of a London wine merchant); his second was Ursula (née St Barbe), the widow of Sir Richard Worseley of Appuldurcombe, Isle of Wight, where they lived until he bought a house in Cripplegate. They moved from there when he bought 'The Papey', to the east of St Mary Axe, and over the road from his close friend Thomas Heneage (the ancient 'Hospice of Poor Priests'). When he handed over a list of suspicious arrivals in England during the previous three months, he also forwarded an alarming, if unspecific report from an Italian spy of a plan to kill Elizabeth. The timing of Walsingham's approach to the heart of government (despite Elizabeth's lack of warmth) is significant. It coincided with the appointment of de Spes as Spanish ambassador – a man Cecil falsely believed to be a tool of Alva. As early as June when John Man named de Spes, he remarked on the 'very secret interview' between the envoy and the Catholic exile, Sir Francis Englefield. De Spes arrived in a lowering climate of opinion and at the deepening of the 'Black Legend' of Spain. Norris, who remained in Paris as ambassador until August 1570, was assiduously feeding back rumours of plots to London, and he recommended an Italian as a reliable secret agent.

Tommaso Franchiotto was a Protestant soldier from Lucca and had long been paid a retainer by the French crown.[1] Throughout the rest of 1568 he and Walsingham were engaged in intelligence work, with the latter arranging with the lord mayor, Thomas Rowe, for weekly reports on all strangers who took lodgings in the city. Franchiotto, again in France, dredged up evidence of hostile plans aimed at toppling Elizabeth. These he reported to Walsingham, following up in October with the news that preparations were being made in France for the invasion of England. A year passed and it was Walsingham who was employed by Cecil to watch the suspect Florentine financier Roberto Ridolphi whose links to the northern rebel earls required investigation. Given his training in law and his fluent Italian, Walsingham was perfectly suited to supervise Ridolphi's interrogations (see p. 8).

In 1570 Walsingham was instrumental in the political ruin of the titular Archbishop of Cashel in Ireland, Maurice Fitzgibbon. For this minor coup he employed a Captain Thomas, an Irish intelligencer who had served under the French king in the civil wars. Walsingham's reward was promotion to the pivotal post of resident ambassador to France, going there in December with his family to replace Sir Henry Norris who had followed Thomas Smith, who later took over the duties of secretary of state. Geographically, France was in a key position as a conduit for news, with all the post routes passing through the country. No surprise then that news-gathering was formally included in Walsingham's instructions. As ambassador he had access to many sources and was in touch with leading Huguenots. Even so, he often had to wait for information, not being able to go out and challenge sources. As a consequence the alertness and skills of his staff became an important factor in success or failure, and a good many men did remain in service from one ambassador to the next. One such was Giacomo Manucci, a letter-bearer who lived in the parish of St Andrew Undershaft, informant and spy for a number of years. Also employed was the Florentine Tommaso di Vicenzo Sassetti. Both eventually moved to London and Sassetti became a bodyguard, with a £50 pension, to Leicester.[2] In 1581 Sassetti was back in Paris furnishing Walsingham with news.

On his return to England, Walsingham was briefly without a government post and was able to rest, but this did not mean he was unemployed. He continued his valued intelligence-gathering from former contacts now scattered across Europe. The information gleaned so went to Burghley and almost certainly to Leicester. Then, in December 1573, Walsingham's successful and methodical application won further recognition when he joined the Privy Council as joint principal secretary with Sir Thomas Smith who remained in office until 1576. From 1577 his colleague was Dr Thomas Wilson, a humanist scholar with longstanding Dudley links, who also had a hand in intelligence work, directing for example the mission in the following year to Constantinople of William Harborne, possibly not the first time that the latter had acted as an agent under the camouflage of trade. The office of secretary was one that grew startlingly in importance during Elizabeth's reign. Walsingham contributed mightily to this, especially in the field of foreign affairs. With this in mind he sought to spread the burden of business and, as has been noted, the expansion of his secretariat led to criticism from Robert Beale. In his treatise addressed to Sir Edward Wotton, he remarked 'Burthen not yourself with too many clerks or servants . . . Let your secret services be known to a few.'

Thomas Stukeley, 1525(?)–78, bending the knee before King Philip II of Spain

Like Burghley, Walsingham employed a chief secretary. From at least 1577 it was Lawrence Tomson who dealt with incoming correspondence from the Paris embassy, the semi-official correspondents in the Low Countries, and numerous special envoys sent abroad. It is important to remember that the absence of a resident ambassador in a country did not always stem from the severing of diplomatic relations. Tomson might occasionally touch on secret service activities and in the mid-1570s he undertook deciphering when his employer was especially busy. In fact, many agents wrote directly to Tomson requesting that he should pass on their submissions. Routinely there were three other secretaries directly involved in secret service activities and the deciphering of intercepted letters – theft of such being routine. For a time one of them was Beale who had worked with Walsingham in the Paris embassy and who in 1574 became a clerk of the Privy Council. He worked with the ciphers Walsingham used, knowing most, if not all, of them. He decoded incoming letters and occasionally fell to working on an intercepted item. However, it was John Somers who was primarily responsible for revealing the material in the coded letters sent to Mary, Queen of Scots, while he and Thomas Phelippes undertook the breaking of particularly tricky cipher letters from Europe.

The duty requirements for Walsingham's other secretaries varied. Francis Mylles was largely responsible for matters concerning the capture and examination of Jesuits and seminary priests (who arrived in far greater numbers), as well as for Irish matters. Such an arrangement was necessary, since by the mid-1570s all Ireland was in revolt, with the majority of the native population still loyal to Rome. Papal intervention in that permanently troubled country was manifested through certain individuals, including the quixotic and cloudy-minded Thomas Stukeley. The secretary purposefully tracked this riotous individual through agents. In January 1577 Walsingham heard through Henry Gilpin, a merchant in Naples, of

Stukeley's representations to the Pope. When Stukeley moved to Flanders one of his letters strayed into Dr Wilson's hands so that Walsingham was appraised of the direction of papal policy against England. In the same year, Christopher Hoddesdon, already well established in trading activities in eastern Europe, and then with royal authority doing the same for English trade with Germany and the Netherlands, was in Hamburg where he got news from Rome. It was that with the support of Moris Clynog and Owen Lewis of the English College there, Stukeley was preparing an expedition against Ireland. It was set to leave from Città Vecchia, a detail then confirmed by Sir Amias Paulet in a letter to Walsingham. Hoddesdon's Roman contact had no trouble following Stukeley about until the sailing. The hilariously ramshackle armada was actually one leaky galleon with four small cannon, manned by an extraordinarily motley crew. Included in the force were three Sienese noblemen and two Corsicans who were pursuing a vendetta against the Sienese and had joined simply to murder them.

The next news of Stukeley came from Paulet in June 1578, when he wrote that the political adventurer had been spotted in Lisbon by an Irish friar, Thomas Bowser, who had added the startling rider that Stukeley's destination was now North Africa. In a dramatic swerve he had decided to join the last Mediterranean crusade. Wilson confirmed it by sending a man to Portugal to watch the flighty quarry. Stukeley perished with the army of King Dom Sebastian at the Battle of al-Qaṣr al-Kabīr – a rout that had a real political significance in mainstream European politics. Stukeley was not in himself significant as a leader, although he had important Irish connections, but the effort successfully mounted to track him was a measure of the rapid development of intelligence work. If secret services existed only in skeleton form in 1572, five years later the work being done was beginning to show a modest efficiency, a sound basis for the growth in effort in the tumultuous 1580s, when Walsingham's employment of spies became systematized, turning his opponents' weapons against themselves.

While Stukeley was scampering about for his airy Irish 'invasion', the English government was coping with more trouble there stirred up by the instigator of the Desmond Rebellion in Ireland, James Fitzmaurice (Fitzgerald). In the late spring of 1575 this perpetual dissident was driven from his country to France where for the most part he remained, first in St Malo, then in Paris, his activities being monitored by successive English ambassadors there. Dr Valentine Dale employed Captain Thomas to pose as an English Catholic refugee to gain Fitzmaurice's confidence. The ruse worked and the renegade Irish mercenary revealed Fitzmaurice's plans for raising forces. But Thomas himself was well known in France and he was arrested by agents of Catherine de Medici; it was a struggle for Dale to secure his release. Fitzmaurice, as Walsingham was informed, had in the mean time travelled to Rome. There he won papal support and after that he was tracked to Spain and Portugal.

By 1581 Walsingham himself was in Paris for the protracted marriage negotiations between Elizabeth and the Duke of Anjou. While there he learnt of a project for the invasion of Scotland which had won the approval of the Pope who commended it to Philip II. The secretary had long had contacts with English Jesuits in the city, as well as other English catholic refugees, or the tale may have been nosed out by Thomas Rogers, who spent some time as a secret agent in Rome. It was there that the Scottish Jesuit, Father Creighton (or Crichton) had gone in the spring to discuss Scottish affairs with the head of his order and the Pope. All their interest focused on Esmé Stuart, sieur d'Aubigny and cousin of the young James VI; the Jesuits certainly saw the charismatic French courtier as an instrument to bring first Scotland and ultimately England back to the faith. In June 1581 the regent of Scotland, the Earl of Morton was beheaded on the command of the young king. Freed from his restraints James was quickly seduced by the powerful personality of d'Aubigny who paid lip-service to Scottish Calvinism, while secretly a Catholic and a friend of the Guise faction in France. Made Duke of Lennox, he was given charge of one of the principle gateways of Scotland, Dumbarton Castle. Early in September the Spanish ambassador in London, Don Bernardino de Mendoza, got in touch with a clutch of leading English crypto-Catholic noblemen who agreed to convey an unnamed priest into Scotland. He was to discover from Lennox whether James VI would convert. The notion was that when he did, and when he invaded England, there would be a Catholic rising in the north of England to declare him heir to Elizabeth and to release his mother from her imprisonment. If Elizabeth sturdily refused to allow the conversion of England, she would likely be deposed.

When the priest returned to England the six Catholic nobles were in prison and Mendoza decided himself to take the matter forward. Although the priest (probably William Watts) had not ventured too far with d'Aubigny, he had broached matters with Lord Seton who seemed to think that James could indeed be won over to Catholicism. Reporting this to Father Robert Persons, Mendoza must have relished the prospect for he sent news of it also to Pope Gregory XIII. Persons had to dash quickly to France to avoid capture, but before leaving England he sent two priests to reconnoitre Scotland – Father Watts and Father William Holt. Creighton was now on his way home and stopped on the orders of the father general to see Persons; he took him to see the Duke of Guise. Once in Scotland Creighton had secret talks with Lennox, together with Holt. Walsingham knew of this, having heard from Cobham in Paris that Guise was enthusing about a scheme to invade Scotland. In October his servants intercepted a letter from Mary to James Beaton, Archbishop of Glasgow and her ambassador in Paris, which revealed her knowledge of the matter.

In February 1582 Father Holt was back in London, and while hiding in Mendoza's residence he revealed that Lennox and some other Scottish lords were even willing to force James to embrace Catholicism if Mary agreed. They wanted 2,000 soldiers, preferably Italians, who could be transported from Friesland to land at Eyemouth. Mendoza wrote to his monarch of the pros and cons of intervention, acknowledging that most depended on how things fared in the Low Countries where Philip was endeavouring to suppress the Dutch Revolt. Mendoza's original emissary arrived in London at the end of March disguised as someone who pulled teeth, and since he had walked from Scotland was clearly a hardy individual. He carried two messages from Holt and Creighton, who wanted Mendoza to meet them as soon as possible in Rouen. They asked too that Mary should have Beaton prepare two sets of credentials for Seton's two sons, one addressed to the Pope, the

Departure of Mendoza, the Spanish ambassador, after he was implicated in the Guise plan for invading England

other to Philip II. Mary herself received a letter from Lennox and it appeared from it that Creighton had led him to expect a papal army of 15,000 men. Mary was intrigued, as she wrote to Mendoza the project was 'highly desirable' and she pondered the inclinations of the Pope and Philip.

Mendoza did not intend to leave his post and his message to Holt and Creighton made this clear. However, it arrived too late and by the end of April the latter was in France for a series of high-level conspiratorial meetings. The invasion was indisputably vital to the cause, but Guise thought 8,000 men enough, while Lennox now asked for 20,000 by the autumn and a matching immediate sum of crowns. Creighton moved to Rome to consult the Pope; Persons to Madrid; while Holt went back to Scotland to inform Lennox and work on James. If this project had been undertaken so then no doubt England would have been engulfed by a calamitous war and concurrent civil war. That it failed was partly due to Walsingham whose agents had intercepted the tooth-drawer on the border and found papers hidden behind his mirror. They were sent to the secretary by Sir John Forster, the ageing warden of the Middle Marches. It was also partly due to a coup in Scotland when the pro-English Earl of Gowrie seized the person of James VI in September, and George Douglas, one of Lennox's envoys to France, was taken and tortured for a confession that was sent on to London. Then a letter of Mary's was intercepted and the clerk of the signet, the son-in-law of Sir Ralph Sadler, John Somers (who had been acting principal secretary when Walsingham was ill in 1577), deciphered it. In May 1583 English spies in Scotland tracked down Holt to Leith where, in disguise, he was about to board a ship. Walsingham claimed that Elizabeth wanted him tortured, only James allowed him to escape. As the design fluttered apart its ruin was completed with the death of Lennox in June, but Creighton was only captured the following year while crossing the Channel. In the Tower he confessed everything. As the papal nuncio remarked ruefully 'we must now prepare some new design'; the enterprise had failed but the intention remained.[3]

If the Catholic-Jesuit provocation had achieved nothing for their cause, it had proved strikingly useful to Walsingham. One of the key items that emerged with the capture of George Douglas was his admission that Mary used the French ambassador in London to pass on her secret correspondence. Walsingham intended to put his own man in the embassy and achieved a very considerable advantage when Mauvissière's secretary, de Courcelles, proved to have an appetite for bribes.[4] It was through him and the invaluable spy Henry Fagot that the principle secretary became aware of the activities of Francis Throckmorton and for six months he was shadowed until his arrest in November, followed by interrogation and torture. When Throckmorton finally revealed the Guise plan for invading England he implicated Mary as well as the meddlesome Mendoza. On 19 January 1584, the Spanish ambassador, who was surrendering his eyesight out of duty to his king, was summoned before the Privy Council to be berated in Italian by Walsingham who ordered his hated enemy to leave England in fifteen days. Sylvanus Scory, who was a Catholic convert in service to Leicester, was bold enough to escort the departing ambassador down river. Mendoza seems to have left his affairs in the hands of the merchant Pedro de Zubiaur.[5] Mendoza, writing to Philip, claimed that he had railed at the Council and spoken of a necessary war. In fact, the idea of a Spanish invasion of England had already been outlined by the Marquis of Santa Cruz, but given his compelling difficulties in the Low Countries, Philip had scarcely considered the projection.

Mary had fled from Scotland and the evidence of her domestic miscalculations, in 1568. It was the year Walsingham began working for Cecil, and very soon the former had concluded that she had to be destroyed. Although a cultured man, Walsingham conceived of the Scottish queen an unwavering and unfeigned loathing, based on the threat she posed to the stability of his queen and country. The somewhat unequal tussle between the two began with a success for Walsingham when a youth named Steward was taken and confessed that he carried letters from Mary to her Scottish friends. He said he received her packets at Doncaster from a Scotsman named Alexander Hamilton, then the tutor to the children of the Earl of Shrewsbury. Hamilton denied everything, even as Steward maintained his story. Since the young man absolutely declined to return to England after questioning by the English diplomat in Scotland, Henry Killigrew, Walsingham as yet was stalled, although clearly servants of Shrewsbury were suspect. The work to trace secret correspondents went on and in January 1576 he received from Regent Morton a copy of instructions given by the Bishop of Ross to his servant Leslie. Elizabeth was told and, as a result of further investigations, a London bookseller, Henry Cockyn, was accused of being an intermediary between Shrewsbury's servants and those of the bishop. Cockyn was further believed to have had dealings with Thomas Morgan (once a servant of Shrewsbury) and the executed Duke of Norfolk. The book dealer was examined by a three-man commission after denying anything untoward; he did agree that he knew those named but claimed them as customers for his wares. Walsingham thought him venal and paid for by Mary, so he proposed to his two colleagues that Cockyn should be offered an abrupt choice: a pardon and a bribe for a confession; or torture if he declined. It was shrewdly judged and the bookseller now allowed that he had been an intermediary between

Hamilton and the servants of the bishop – also that he had carried messages from Mary to Norfolk. To set this off further he added that several of Shrewsbury's servants and one of the servants of the French ambassador carried clandestine correspondence for Mary.

Walsingham's tireless ferreting had won him an advantage. He had learned that he could not trust Shrewsbury's household under that easygoing master, and he had been put on his guard about the earl's reliability as a royal gaoler. Furthermore, he could begin to gauge the temper of the recusant nobility and even the opaque attitude of Elizabeth to Mary. With the discovery of the latter's connection with Mauvissière, surveillance extended in all respects. Concentration on the ambassador was maintained with the assistance of the poet-scholar and spy, William Fowler, a near kinsman of the intelligencer William Ashby. The former had studied in France and had even loaned money to Mary, but his imprisonment in England had undermined any dissident loyalties and very likely he agreed to spy as a means of obtaining his release. Through his connections Fowler was able to supply news from France and Scotland, and he became the obvious first choice as an intelligencer in the embassy. One item that surfaced through him was that Mauvissière was sending letters by a gentlewoman (alas unnamed and one of the few so involved) travelling to Scotland. A search of a ship at Gravesend revealed three letters from Mauvissière to Mainville, the French representative in Scotland, and these were passed to Walsingham. His explanation of this interference had the limpid quality of the best diplomatic 'economy with truth'. It was claimed that the letters had been seized in error since they were thought to be passing between Jesuits in England and Scotland, and Bowes (one of the English representatives there) wrote that Mainville was satisfied by this line because the seals on the letters remained intact. His confidence was probably misplaced for Phelippes may have already been using Arthur Gregory as seal-maker.

Robert Bowes was a hard-working ambassador between September 1577 and October 1583 – albeit, not continuously. His employers can have had no complaints about his diligence, for hundreds of his despatches and letters have survived. He began his public career serving under his own father in defence of the border between England and Scotland, and in 1569 assisted his brother George at Barnard Castle during the rebellion of the northern earls. In 1575 he became treasurer of Berwick and the Scottish appointment later naturally derived from his local knowledge; his experience in intelligence work was gained after taking over from William Drury. When not in Scotland, Bowes stayed in Berwick, never idle, building an active intelligence cluster and making use of as many sources as possible. Although, as he wrote to Walsingham in 1583, he was suspicious of strangers, he did not miss the opportunity to take on the Italian Rocco Bonetti (Mr Rocke). Some years before Bonetti had been employed by the Earl of Leicester, but he was also well acquainted with Mauvissière during his ten years in London. Indeed, in 1583 Bonetti was in Edinburgh to transmit letters from Mainville to Mauvissière. He let on about this work to the Fleming Eustace Rogghe (well known to Walsingham) and Rogghe told Bowes. The offer of a meeting between Bowes and Bonetti was made and, after suitable hand-warming payments, Bowes got to see everything the courier was carrying.[6]

Lord Henry Howard, 1539–1614. A learned crypto-Catholic courtier detested by Protestants, he was still periodically favoured by Elizabeth and so survived the reign to become Earl of Northampton

As early as 1580 the letters written by Bowes were dense with intelligence matters, and an interesting rivalry sprang up among his recipients. On taking up his post he had been instructed by Elizabeth to deal with Walsingham. Later, however, Burghley nudged his way in and clearly irked the secretary, who now felt that in intelligence matters he had primacy. He acknowledged that Bowes could not altogether cease writing to Burghley, but required that he should write 'privately to me'. Intelligence material for Walsingham and the queen were to be put into cipher lest 'in my absence from the Court, my private letter should be opened'. By the end of 1582, the envoy's correspondence with Burghley had diminished, and the Lord Treasurer was probably reduced to reading second-hand material from his colleague. Given this stir it is not surprising Bowes was not completely at ease in his assignment. Following the fall of Morton at the end of 1580, his problems were compounded as 'most men openly fly the English company'.

Walsingham had the spy called Henry Fagot in the French embassy in London by mid-April 1583. He was not identified for Fowler whose letters to Walsingham signed 'A' date from October 1582 to December 1583, but we know that he was the embassy guest Giordano Bruno, fiercely anti-papal and rejoicing in his secret support of Elizabeth. Fagot was joined later by John Florio, tutor to the ambassador's daughter Katherine-Marie and an interpreter for Mauvissière himself. Fagot induced Courcelles to betray his employer so that Walsingham obtained a copy of every letter that passed between Mary and the ambassador. Courcelles also gave the secretary a useful list of all who thronged the embassy or who used it to write to Mary. By his account the 'chief agents of the Queen of Scots are

Mr Throckmorton and Lord Henry Howard. They never come to the ambassador's house except by night.' The watch on Throckmorton was maintained until early in the morning of 2 November 1583, when he was seized at his home in Paul's Wharf. When his papers were searched a list of Catholic noblemen was found; a plan of certain harbours for the landing of foreign forces and some pamphlets attacking Elizabeth. 'Turning Courcelles was a priceless tactical achievement of Elizabethan policy.'

The Throckmortons were an ancient Worcestershire Catholic family; Sir John Throckmorton's career as a Justice of the Peace and administrator had shrivelled with accusations of maladministration and Jesuit sympathies. His son Francis had studied at Oxford and the Inner Temple before being sent abroad on a European 'grand tour' with his brother John. On his travels he had encountered prominent and active Catholic exiles, notably Thomas Morgan and Charles Paget with whom he discussed English Catholic cooperation with the Guise faction. Back in England in 1583 Throckmorton organized communications between Morgan and Mary, and her links to Mendoza. Questioned by a committee of the Privy Council he denied everything at first, but then under repeated questioning told contradictory fabrications. He was subjected to the rack, but refused to reveal more until the prospect of more pain galvanized his memory and his tongue. He told of the spot for the landing of Guise's army and its notional strength, as well as the names of all the Englishmen prominent in public life who had promised assistance. Then he told of the past history of the plot with the correspondence and connivance of the Jesuits, the Pope, Philip II, Mary and Mendoza. He told of the secret reconnaissance of Charles Paget in England visiting the Catholic enclave around Arundel in Sussex where he sounded out the local gentry. His aim was to contact men like William Shelley of Michelgrove who rapidly fetched up in the Tower. He told more than enough to sign his own death warrant, and as he waited for execution he struggled with the full burden of remorse for telling.

One of the consequences of the Throckmorton treason was to increase the alarm of Walsingham at the scope of Mary's correspondence. To increase vigilance she was put under a much stricter guard after Shrewsbury became involved in a matrimonial hubbub with his wife that even further diverted his attention. Sadler and Sir Henry Neville temporarily had the job until she was removed to Tutbury and the altogether sterner regime of Sir Amias Paulet. As the agitation subsided a little a feeling of gloom replaced it when another plot came to light. It was apparently the fumbling effort of Dr William Parry (ap Harry), a Welsh blusterer and spendthrift whose career ended miserably.

Parry came from a middle-ranking home in Northop, Flintshire, went to grammar school in Chester and later seems to have worked for a lawyer. The doctorate is something of a mystery and was either gained at the Sorbonne or else was an unearned honorific. In London he entered the service of William Herbert, Earl of Pembroke, until the latter's death in 1570. Despite marrying money, Parry squandered a fortune and ended up in debtor's prison.* His release was probably

---

* Parry married two widows and seduced his own stepdaughter, according to a propaganda tract.

Dr William Parry, failing in his attempt to assassinate the queen

due to Burghley, the result of an obscure family connection. What was required of the ex-prisoner was that he should spy on exiled English Catholics, though in the years 1577–9 he was back in England. Then he disappeared abroad again, before in 1580 striking out at one of his domestic creditors. The death sentence was reprieved by Elizabeth, who had other Parrys about her – Dr Henry Parry, a scholar who was her chaplain, and her long-serving confidante Blanche Parry, who was godmother to Dr John Dee's son Arthur. Parry left England again to return to routine spying, for all that he seems to have been converted that year. In 1583 he quit Paris where his links to Burghley were known, and went first to Venice, then on a second journey to Lyons and Milan. In January 1584, back in England, having shared certain Catholic interests, he regaled Elizabeth with a vivid tale of the Pope, Thomas Morgan and a plot to kill her. In March he received a letter from Ptolomeo Gilli, Cardinal of Como and papal secretary of state, which seemed to underpin his story. Having used the letter advantageously, in the later summer he was back in Paris on a twofold mission for Burghley. He was to gather intelligence as well as act as cicerone for the young hunchback Robert Cecil, who was to have an improving period abroad after lengthy paternal hesitations.

On returning to England the travellers both had seats in parliament – Parry at Queenborough, so obviously his crimes and debts had been forgiven. Yet, he could not stifle his outrage at new legislation against Catholics, declaring it was 'full of confiscations, blood, danger, despair and terror to the subjects of this realm', and he had also distributed seditious literature. The House of Commons was startled by the vehemence of his rhetoric and commanded him to the custody of the sergeant, though the next day he was freed on Elizabeth's orders. The maverick managed to mollify his shocked colleagues while still holding to the general drift of his outburst. The queen and Burghley held back and Parry was soon in disgrace again with a double-dealing remedy for his money problems. He put it to Edmund Neville, already under suspicion of treason, because he was a cousin of the exiled rebel

Westmorland, and claimant to the barony of Latimer, that they should assassinate Elizabeth in the Palace Gardens at Westminster. The gambit might have worked, but Neville was too nimble, telling someone at court who told Elizabeth. Both men fetched up in the Tower where Parry was examined by Walsingham and confessed that Morgan had devised the plot. When he was tried for plotting to murder Elizabeth it was after he had outgrown his usefulness as a spy. After an extorted confession, he was executed in Palace Yard on 2 March 1585, while Neville was released a decade later. This time Elizabeth eschewed making his execution even more savage, waiting until the Babington plot was shattered for a gruesome revenge. As for Morgan – she wrote formally to Henri III to demand her enemy's extradition, and he did fetch up in the Bastille.

Compared to so many other misjudged plots, the clumsy effort of Parry seems absurd or childish rather than any sort of real threat. But he deserves a little attention because the autumn of 1584 was 'a jittery time for the Protestant rulers of Elizabethan England'. At home and abroad the intentions and actions of the militant Catholics seemed a severe threat, putting a quarter of a century of work at risk. To reverse this trend and all its baleful possibilities, Elizabeth's senior advisers came up with the Bond of Association with her authority. It was a notable piece of political symbolism and propaganda, drafted just before the opening of the new parliament in November. The Bond stemmed from intelligence that said 'the life of our gracious sovereign lady Queen Elizabeth hath been most traitorously and devilishly sought'.[7] In addition, Walsingham was given every reason for a calculated attempt to undermine and even dispose of Mary. A martyr to boils, he knew the relief to be gained from lancing a source of deep distress. This was the climate 'in which Catholic activities were converted into conspiracy at a time when the nature of the Catholic mission to England was entirely debatable, creating a discourse of treason, regardless of whether a given "treasonous" plot was real, imagined or contrived by the government.'[8]

Chapter Four

'Men must dissemble'

For a decade after the accession of Elizabeth, Catholicism in England was in dismal retreat, a decaying component in the life of the nation. Some nine thousand parish priests were content to live with elastic consciences, to read the book of Common Prayer, and to preserve their livings. Their former bishops were dead, imprisoned, paroled or exiled, but Rome made no attempt to fill the vacant sees or even to provide for ecclesiastical organization and controls. Everything was left to private enterprise so that a nation pestered with religious divisions for thirty years was now able to catch its breath in a short period of rest and growth. Before 1581 the government allowed a very modest space for a private, hushed defiance of the law, notwithstanding the indignation of parliament with its savage additions to the coercive legislation against Catholics. Action had to be taken in just four distinct cases where religion became tangled with politics. In his list of Elizabethan martyrs compiled in the eighteenth century Bishop Challoner allowed for only three victims of the penal code before 1581.[1]

To resist this dramatic decline of Catholicism, a seminary, founded almost single-handedly by Dr William Allen, was established at Douai in 1568. It was very quickly a remarkable success for the sometime Oxford academic, being conveniently placed for students, and offering free board and education to all-comers. Young men with catholic tendencies, infatuated with the idea of martyrdom, 'lost and wandering lads', students in difficuties in their college in Oxford or Cambridge, found it irresistible. So did poor serving men, soldiers and future spies; all deserters were welcomed by Allen.[2] Walsingham's rise to power coincided with the founding of Douai and surveillance began as early as 1571. Four missionary priests were sent to England in 1574 and six years on as many as a hundred had arrived. By then, with the assistance of his friend Dr Owen Lewis, Allen had founded a second college in Rome, much to the satisfaction of Pope Gregory. Walsingham's intention was to recruit men who could be infiltrated into the colleges to wreck them; the names of Solomon Aldred, Gilbert Gifford, William Gifford, Edward Grateley and others must pepper any narrative of the principal secretary's secret service.

Serious attention to confessional infiltrators began in 1577, and soon it was reckoned there were some forty in the country. The first fatality was Fr Cuthbert Mayne, but his execution had more to do with greed than faith.[3] He had been given sanctuary by the wealthy Cornish landowner Francis Tregian, whose home was zestfully raided in June 1577 by the newly appointed sheriff of the county.* Richard Grenville was a man who in fits of rage chewed glass, and he nursed a deep animosity towards Tregian whom he had targeted as a suitable husband for his daughter, only to have the plan collapse. Some sheriffs, lords-lieutenants and bishops had their own domestic spies and pursuivants who wore an identifying badge called the 'scutchion'. Watching the ports and the post fell to Walsingham, as well as his assistants, who had travellers looked over by searchers (often reported as corrupt). But key men and much clandestine written and printed material got through for distribution, with seminarists risking entry using a variety of pseudonyms and disguises. They came as merchants, soldiers, gentlemen or even as sometime galley slaves.

When Fathers Robert Persons and Edmund Campion arrived separately in June 1580, with the whole country on alert, they were disguised as a jewel merchant and an army officer. The searchers had descriptions and two woodcut portraits, yet still failed to arrest them, although detailed information from the spy Charles Sledd did lead to the capture of Thomas Cottam. The only two Jesuits then in England devoted themselves to different but equally dangerous tasks. Persons undertook a defiant, politically slanted peregrination around the clandestine Catholic communities then seething with rumours of a great foreign invasion and news of papal troops landing in Ireland. Edmund Campion, devout, zealous and eloquent, travelled with equal alacrity to say mass, and to preach to eager listeners. One gentleman who offered hospitality to them was Sir William Catesby (father of Robert Catesby), and it led to his arrest in August 1581, for not only were Jesuits and missionary priests like Dr Humphrey Ely, who had come with them after teaching canon law at Douai, Rheims and Pont-à-Mousson, considered traitors, but so too were all who harboured them. Once, when pressed very hard, Persons, who had a charmed life, had no option but to take refuge with Mendoza.

In July 1581 the sweet-tempered and much-loved Campion was in Berkshire at Lyford Grange, home of the Yate(s) family. Mr Yate was then a prisoner in London while his family held on to succour priests and even clandestine nuns. Against his better judgement Campion was persuaded to return to the house for a Sunday mass that drew people from as far as Oxford. Unfortunately for the Jesuit a spy called George Eliot was loitering in the vicinity. A former Catholic servant of Lady Petre of Ingatestone, he had recently been made a yeoman of the chamber. With a pursuivant he turned up at the gate only to meet an old fellow servant, a cook, who let on that mass was about to be celebrated. Mrs Yate had sought to exclude all strangers, but Eliot was persuasive and redoubled his effort to get in when the celebrant was named. The pursuivant was dismissed, but not before Eliot had rattled off what was happening. He was sent to the local magistrate for a warrant and a company of a hundred men.

Eliot went in for the mass and sermon, and was briefly minded to arrest Campion on the spot in his vestments, whatever the risks. Instead, he left the house in a

---

* The historic rhyme for children, 'Goosey, goosey gander', records the sinister enthusiasm frequently shown by the searchers.

P·ROBERTUS PERSONIUS ANGLUS
Soc·Iesu Socius et Superior P·Campiani in
priã Missione Anglicana obiit 15 Ap 1610 Ætat suæ 64.
Ascendit ex adverso et opposuit murum pro domo Israel·Ezech·13

Father Robert Persons, 1546–1610, Jesuit activist

flurry and so aroused the suspicions of Mrs Yate. The look-out sent by her to a high window spotted that the house was surrounded and Campion with two resident priests dived into a hiding place squeezed into a space over the entrance. When Eliot and the searchers entered, all items of worship had been hidden and the search became a rather dispirited, lame affair lasting the afternoon. Local men did not relish their chore and the magistrate eventually withdrew them with an apology. Eliot was enraged, proclaiming that they were aiding a priest and demanding a further effort.

As they moved over the house again Mrs Yate feigned illness and rebuked the crestfallen magistrate for maltreating a sick woman. He agreed to let her retire to any single room in the house to be undisturbed further. Naturally she seized the chance to have her bed moved to the room adjoining the secret hiding place. She pretended too that Eliot required an aide – thereby hoping to hear of any plans he made. The search went on into the night and so she ordered quantities of ale to be served in the hope of inducing a falling off in the effort. The notion was rewarded and, when the stir had subsided, the priests were released into her bedroom where they were visited by the Catholics who had remained behind. Incredibly, they asked Campion for another sermon and this he consented to deliver in a whisper. At the end there was some confusion and noise as the group dispersed, and when one of the priests fell over in the gloom, the guard did eventually appear. By then, however, all had scattered by a secret exit.

The next day 'Judas' Eliot, as he came to be known, had the search continued, and after baffling delays only discovered Campion and the priests at prayer when the disguising wall was sounded and pierced in a final effort. The Jesuit, Ford and Collington, made no resistance and were carried off to London – Campion's arms bound and a note affixed to his hat reading 'Edmund Campion, Seditious Jesuit'. After imprisonment in the infamous 'Little Ease', the cell that desperately restricted movement to little more than a twitch, he was put on trial at Westminster Hall with Thomas Cottam and others in November 1581. Found guilty of treason Campion was executed the following month. It was a thrilling coup for Eliot, the apostate spy, though he might have preferred to capture the political Persons rather than the guileless Campion who died for him. Indeed, some of Eliot's glee was dissipated by the breathless opportunism of another agent, Anthony Munday, who had been apprenticed to the stationer John Allde for eight years in 1576. He had scrambled to find a patron in a high position as well and, on Lord Oxford's advice he had been to Rome in 1578–9, as a convert, but now he seized the opportunity to write a hack piece called 'A Discoverie of Edmund Campion and his Confederates'. Munday became a recusant-hunter because he panicked when Oxford was arrested and in the Tower from April to August. His terror was reinforced by the earlier exemplary executions of the Nortons, Felton and Story which he had seen.[4] Eliot's own version of the events was published later and said sourly of the rival text that it was as 'contrary to truth as an egg is contrary in likeness to an oyster'.

At Campion's trial evidence for the state had been presented by the spy Sledd, sometime servant to Dr Nicholas Morton, English penitentiary at St Peter's, Rome, in 1580. More discreet in his covert activities there than Munday, he was at pains to present detailed material to his employers. His dossier of information on those he had encountered, nearly three hundred priests, soldiers, merchants and students, gave motivation to the spies and spy masters. It was the students who presented the rector of the English College, Moris Clynog, with acute problems, for he had little chance to decide on the genuineness of an applicant before he admitted him. How could he know who was honourable and pious? Munday and his even younger companion Thomas Nowell were admitted on letters of recommendation. Were these genuine or fake? Nowell cheekily claimed to be the nephew of Dr Alexander Nowell, Dean of St Paul's; it gave him a status that enhanced his quality as a convert.

Clynog's difficulties were made worse by the clashes of nationality and temperament within the college.[5] There was no way of easily dissipating the hostility between English and Welsh students – very satisfying for Munday who stirred up the English element against Clynog himself, and as a punishment was made to sleep in a cupboard. Better that than 'Little Ease'. By 1582 Munday had become a regular agent for ferreting out popish plots, while running down priests. Richard Topcliffe, who was assigned to track down Campion's publications, described him to John Puckering as a man 'who wants no sort of wit'. By 1584 he was one of the messengers of the queen's chamber, obviously advanced by Leicester, and from then on was frequently employed as a pursuivant. Between 1588 and 1590 Munday was Archbishop Whitgift's chief hunter of the Martinists, snooping in booksellers and listening to conversations. He was still doing this in some measure in 1611–12 when he testified against two gentlemen, Hugh Holland (who is best remembered for his sonnet on Shakespeare in the First Folio) and Thomas Bell.

The young men who fled abroad to preserve a faith that might be passionately held but ill-defined, were by nature eager, adventurous and disputatious. Away from the restraints of their families, loving or otherwise, they could often be wildly undisciplined, even though short of money, ill-clothed and restless, with physical as well as spiritual hungers. When their studies were completed and they returned to England in disguise, sometimes penniless despite Cardinal Allen's best efforts, there were still problems since it was a natural tendency to cluster in London. In the city they trampled on each other's coat tails and were shadowed by spies until picked up, imprisoned, exiled again or executed after torture. The government claim that no man was ever tortured for his beliefs was cynical propaganda and does not stand scrutiny. The problem of Catholic organization stemmed, of course, from the lack of superiors in England. As secular priests (albeit taught by Jesuits) they were ordained for normal work in a diocese subject to a bishop's guidance. But England had no Catholic bishops, and authority fell to the continuously exiled Allen.

Nor did the Jesuits have a superior until the landing in England of Father Henry Garnet in 1586. At dawn on 14 July, Garnet, Robert Southwell and William Weston rode out of London to Hurleyford, a house two miles from Marlow in Buckinghamshire. There they conferred for a week, with Weston giving the other two details about Catholic houses 'and plans were laid for the systematic organizing of resistance county by county and house by house'. Unlike the seminarists there were never enough Jesuits for the tangles that ensnared their co-religionists. Moreover, Jesuits were inculcated with a dutiful obedience to their superiors (it was what brought Campion back to England from a moderately comfortable exile), and Persons, wherever he was, did not let them forget it, even if they had personal reservations about his conviction that the conversion of England needed the powerful support of Philip II. The seculars and their supporters were prepared to treat with Elizabeth and her government; the Jesuits and theirs were not. This division of philosophy and intent allowed Walsingham and his associates to penetrate deep into Catholic clusters abroad.

In Italy one of the secretary's first efforts concerned Edward Unton, a distant relative of the Earl of Leicester, and Solomon Aldred, who appears in the picture in 1583 when he went to Rome. Having re-embraced Catholicism he moved to Lyons and a job as a tailor, which he abandoned the following year. Remarkably (and not all his English contemporaries were friendly in their remarks), he received a pension from the Pope on the intercession of Dr Owen Lewis, Bishop of Cassano and leader of the Cymric faction at the English College, perhaps because he had been intercepting letters to the English ambassador in Paris. A visit to Milan led to Aldred's incarceration by the city's Inquisition. In prison he met Edward Unton whose brother Henry, prompted by Walsingham, went to Rome (from Lyons) to pay a large fine for his brother's release. All three men then went back to Lyons before returning to England. Unton thought Aldred unstable and dishonest – Walsingham agreed, so he was courted and apparently persuaded to become an English agent. Thereafter, his behaviour was spectacularly freewheeling and it is not always clear what Walsingham gained from employing him, apart from useful connections in Rome.[6]

More important lay individuals were active in France and must be given some attention before any detailed scrutiny of the Babington plot. The divisions among the exiles were particularly noticeable there because one group avowed rebellion. Such men as the Earl of Westmorland and his follower Leonard Dacres were, by their own actions, driven from the mainstream of English society, and faced a bleak future unless a Catholic monarch took the throne. Others, less extreme in their intentions, still had hopes of winning the approval of Elizabeth, with a pardon as her supreme gift. Their enmity towards their birthplace was modified by hope – the hope of returning to enjoy their properties. Two such were Charles Paget and Thomas Copley, whose lands remained intact while the Crown took the revenues. From exile Copley solicited the aid of Burghley and then Walsingham, even offering a *douceur* to the least corruptible of the queen's servants. Having refused to respond to a royal summons from England, he became a papal pensioner. Paget did come over in 1583, but it was a clandestine visit to see if certain Sussex gentry would fall in with the projected invasion of the Duke of Guise. After the Throckmorton plot he was joined late in the same year by his brother, Lord Paget, whose forfeited estates provided the revenues later for the expenses of Mary's household at Chartley. Joined by Charles Arundel, they formed a nucleus of plotters, all under the surveillance of ambassador Cobham and the embassy spies. When Stafford replaced Cobham he had a specific brief to watch the refugees from his residence on the Quai de la Tournelle and report on their movements. But in this he was more inclined to act on his own intiative, keeping in contact with Arundel, through whom he approached Guise and the Spanish ambassador, Don

Bernardino de Mendoza. It led to a thoroughly dubious bout of double-dealing. In the controversy transmitted from Rome like a virus, between the Jesuits and the seculars, Cardinal Allen eventually sided with the 'English' group of Persons, Arundel and Fitzherbert, along with others. On the 'Welsh' side were the Pagets, Thomas Morgan, Thomas Throckmorton, Dr William Gifford, Father Edward Grateley and Dr Clitheroe; Gilbert Gifford quarrelled with Arundel. The benefit of these divisions was of course to Walsingham, who had stealthy dealings with a number of the latter, bolstered by information from Thomas Rogers (alias Berden).

Rogers was one of the most considerable spies employed during the 1580s. He emerged first from obscurity as a servant of a well-placed and rich young Catholic English layman – George Gilbert. A convert of Persons, Gilbert shone as an educated man of action, one whose spiritual agitations led him into intense prayers and mortification of the flesh. The many admirers of his charm and good looks that clustered about him took a vow of chastity; some were or became actively homosexual like Lord Oxford and Lord Henry Howard, younger brother of the late Duke of Norfolk.[7] With Vaux, Throckmorton, Tichborne, Habington, Stoner and Thomas Pounde, they devoted themselves to smuggling priests, as well as shifting students abroad to study. Some fared better than others; Thomas Pounde badly, although he was not executed. A first cousin to the father of the Earl of Southampton, he was a devoted friend of Campion and a Jesuit lay brother who spent a large part of his life in prison. There he managed still to dress as became his rank and fortune, and on at least one occasion bribed his way out of the Marshalsea for a brief respite. In mingling with Protestants these young men were not required to argue their case flatly, but 'to pry into corners', putting likely converts in touch with priests after the administration of preliminary instruction in the faith. Another task was the printing of Catholic literature, so Persons established a secret press in Greenstreet, East Ham, before having it removed to Henley Park, the house owned by Francis Browne, brother of Viscount Montagu.

In 1583 Rogers wrote to Walsingham from Rome and it seems his loyalty to the emigrant cause was under scrutiny, and for a time he was imprisoned in Castel Sant' Angelo.[8] Cheerfully promising fidelity he was released and travelled to England. In January 1584, in a letter to Thomas Phelippes, he protested that he undertook missions to serve his country, not out of venality and 'you shall always find me resolute'. It was a claim Walsingham and his immediate associates heard frequently, but with Rogers it did carry conviction and his service with Gilbert had given him a particular advantage. This became evident when a priest called Ithell arrived in London in February 1585 and asked Rogers to act for Catholics exiled to Paris. He may have declined because he was busy – spying on Catholics in London, dining with a priest called Edmunds (alias Hunt) and setting down the names of those at dinner with him. In late March he came across a servant of Dr Allen called Richard lodging in the city and he asked Walsingham if he should have him arrested. The secretary stayed him a little and Rogers reported a fortnight later that he had talked to this Richard. He asked about papists coming to England and the servant let on about Allen's preparations for each priest.

Probably much of the routine work was undertaken by Persons who made a modest establishment in Rouen. In 1582 he had set up his third press there and took on a manager, a pious merchant called George Flinton. At Rouen boats for crossing to England were arranged, books were prepared for clandestine distribution, like the notorious attack on the Earl of Leicester called in brief 'Leicester's Commonwealth', which was also made available by Girault de la Chassaigne's import system, along with vestments too. Later, an agent of Robert Cecil, called William Wollastone, reported that an Irishman who had lived in Rouen for years acted as a broker, sending books for mass from Newhaven to Ireland. Richard the servant said priests coming from France often used boats going to pick up coal in Newcastle. The customer there was a Robert Highcliffe, a covert Catholic like his wife, and he allowed men and printed material into the country.

Through the summer of 1585 Rogers continued his work, and in July it was agreed he should be put into a prison to see what he could glean. There he met a priest called Barber (also known as Stansham) and he received from him letters of introduction to the Jesuit Thomas Fitzherbert. From Ithell he probably got the same sort of items for contacts with the Pagets and Arundel, so the emigrant community in Rouen and Paris was about to welcome a guileful interloper into their midst. His first report from the city was written on 11 August 1585, and naturally he noted the divisions in the community. Of more immediate weight was the fact that he gave names of refugees accounted reliable to Catholicism who had access to the English court, and he discovered a new, significant postal connection. The exiles had arranged with the new French ambassador in London, Chateauneuf, to convey letters to their English friends after the delivery of his packets. The culmination of a period of woes for them was that they marked out Rogers to be their agent in London. It was in this guise that he returned to England and because of the security Walsingham sought to maintain, one of London's leading priest-hunters, Richard Young, almost arrested Rogers.

For the next two years he was working in London. His pursuit of priests was more subtle than that of men like Richard Topcliffe, and for a price he could win freedom for selected men. This double-dealing won him great credit among the exiles, their sources having failed them on his true allegiance. When Walsingham, at his prompting, spared the life of Christopher Dryland, he acknowledged the same in a letter of November 1586 – 'they suppose that some friend at my request moved your Honour therein'.[9] Very likely he benefited financially since, if they thought he could use bribery effectively, money would have been forthcoming. Papal or Spanish, it hardly mattered, and it provided for a well-cushioned retirement when at last in 1587 exiles began to suspect him of treachery. Rogers decided it was time to leave the shadows and in 1588 he became briefly purveyor of poultry to the royal household, a department he had worked in before. Leicester was then Lord Steward and he was anxious to replace the 'fine purveyor' John Raymond and his underlings, since they were very unpopular in the trade. Henry Windredge and Rogers jointly took over from Raymond, but reinstatement came for him after Leicester's death and his family continued to hold the post well into the seventeenth century. One of Walsingham's most successful agents, Rogers certainly merited a reward for his canny and responsible behaviour. Indeed, it was a model of sagacity compared with the erratic course of a well-placed contemporary in the diplomatic service, Sir Edward Stafford, protégé of Burghley and avowed hater of Leicester, whose discarded bed-partner Lady Douglas Sheffield, he had married, for all that she had an infant, Robert Dudley.

At this time Walsingham's distributor of funds and letters in northern France was the Genoese merchant Horatio Palavicino. His business connections made him extremely useful, especially in foreign exchange dealings, and it was he who paid Rogers while the latter was in Paris, and dealt with his despatches. Another task for the Italian, who was later denizenated and knighted, was to observe Stafford, with whom he became friends, and he became uneasy when Stafford began to show signs of an acute addiction to gambling. As an ambassador Stafford seems to have believed that he should be allowed a free hand to undertake whatever intelligence schemes he thought necessary. One thrust that he tried hard with, though not very successfully, was placing spies in the homes of important figures in Paris, such as the Archbishop of Glasgow, the Duke of Guise and of course Mendoza. The effort failed, although some of Mendoza's servants seem to have accepted his money, while Stafford himself seems to have sold information to Mendoza, whom he loathed, to fund his rampant gambling. The question of what he sold and indeed whether it was worth buying has been debated by two historians of the Elizabethan period. The evidence seems to favour the view that, like all unstable men trapped into selling information, he had to reveal far more than he intended originally to receive his reward.

Palavicino's liking for the man and his manifest embarrassment at his ungovernable behaviour led him to voice his fears to the ambassador. Stafford may have flinched but he ignored the warning and the merchant, after ruminating on the matter, wrote most deliberately to Burghley to warn him of Stafford's unreasoning, possibly calamitous infatuation with cards.[10] He hoped that Burghley would rebuke the ambassador before Elizabeth got to hear of matters from a less friendly source, though on that score Stafford was well protected, since his mother was long an intimate of the queen. Palavicino was actively hiding Stafford's outrageous behaviour. Leicester also knew of the situation and took time to write to Walsingham somewhat queasily of doubts being raised about the Italian. Such a thought must have been particularly uncomfortable for the earl since his campaigning in the Low Countries in 1586–7 was made possible by Palavicino's financial muscle in London. The Puritan-inclined group on the Privy Council did regard Palavicino uncertainly because of his known links to Burghley and the peacemakers. Yet in mid-1586 Palavicino was in Germany as Elizabeth's agent in Frankfurt to negotiate the recruitment of a German Protestant army to invade France. With him as his secretary was Alberico Gentili, sometime protégé of Leicester. As for Stafford – had he not so continuously undermined his own position, he might have proved a first-rate envoy. He had been educated in the household of the Prince de Condé and, by the time of his appointment in October 1583, he had already been on five missions to France between 1578 and 1580 as the extended wooing of Elizabeth by the Duke of Anjou required.

With his towering passion for knowing everything, it is not surprising that Walsingham looked for a spy to check on Stafford. The man unusually ill chosen for this delicate task was Walter Williams, whom one writer has alleged was 'a villain of the blackest dye'. Perhaps – but probably not. Certainly he was a venal trickster who had once been a servant of Thomas Copley (a regular correspondent with Burghley), and had come to Walsingham's attention when exchanging letters with the exiled landowner. Arriving in England, Williams was then put to work in August 1582 in Rye prison, a town where the searcher was thought to be a Catholic sympathizer, although the generality of people there seem to have been anti-Catholic. Williams failed to find any evidence of a conspiracy at that time, but he did learn that a man named Large, one of the main post operatives, was a conveyor of papist letters. For his pains Williams was still in Rye gaol in December without uncovering anything important, while the priest held for questioning was more amused than dismayed. As for his investigation of Stafford, that too proved a failure because Stafford got him drunk. Williams was dropped as an agent and reduced to mere letter carrying.

Chapter Five

Mayhem and Money

In a number of ways Elizabethan England resembled a Latin American or African country today. The economy was scrappily underdeveloped although it had an unrealized potential. Equally rickety was the administrative infrastructure, with corruption at all levels, because it primed the pump for action. Other familiar and raw aspects of Elizabethan life included violence in the streets, the exploitation of women and children – the latter the outcome of 'demographic diarrhoea', to use Michel Tournier's provocative phrase. The consequence of this population problem (one patriarch of the gentry class fathered twenty-five children) was the swelling abundance of fiercely ambitious university graduates with scant opportunities for making any sort of living without recourse to well-placed patrons (a pattern repeated today on a dizzying scale in India). Since there was no standing army to take on the younger sons and obligingly kill them, many did this for themselves and private enterprise aggression in Ireland, Europe or the Caribbean was tolerated. For those who took part it offered a much craved opportunity for betterment – or beggary. The Earl of Leicester's great expedition to give military aid to the faction-riven Dutch rebels against Spanish overlordship late in 1585, had young English and Welsh men of standing flocking to serve him. His stepson Essex's even less promising attempt to subdue Ireland in 1599 was similarly supported. A prisoner taken could bring a useful ransom.

Without a regular army to fight in and with no obvious career networks based on merit to sustain their hopes, young men with an education could only welcome an approach from the spy masters. As it happens Burghley was chancellor of Cambridge University and Leicester was a reforming chancellor of Oxford. Candidates for service often studied at the Inns of Court without intending to be lawyers or barristers, and Leicester was also an important figure in the Inner Temple. A Cambridge MA such as William Ashby began his career in the foreign service as a letter carrier for the principal secretary. Between 1576 and 1588 he was often employed in Europe as a confidential messenger, travelling to and from English representatives in Brussels, Frankfurt, Augsburg and other towns. After a decade of this Ashby may have felt well-enough entrenched to branch out to do some work for Sir Christopher Hatton, who had a private interest in intelligence-gathering. In June 1588, during the Armada crisis, Ashby achieved the sort of promotion men of his ilk dreamt of and then some times rued. He was appointed ambassador to the court of James VI and, as he was to discover, it was a difficult assignment (so little time had elapsed since the execution of Mary, Queen of Scots), and required nerve-straining vigilance.

Altogether more shifty and coarse-grained than Ashby were two more university-educated men. Barnard (or Bernard) Maude is presumed to be the man of that same name listed as a scholar of Trinity College, Oxford, who received his BA degree in 1566. At much the same time Robert Poley (pronounced 'Pooly') was at Cambridge in the humblest of the ranks of students, the self-financing sizars, who did menial tasks in college. Despite their education, poverty trailed these men like the threat of a disease. Since Poley and Maude were to figure as government agents in the Babington plot, and Poley was to have a remarkably lengthy career, it is worth considering the social and financial imperatives that thrust them into intelligencing.[1]

After graduating and a period of service with Edwin Sandys, Archbishop of York, Maude at some point had attached himself to service with Sir Robert Stapleton of Wighill in Yorkshire. In May 1582 the latter arrived with Maude in his party at the Bull Inn, Doncaster, where they encountered Edwin Sandys, whether by accident or design is uncertain. Whatever – it was a misfortune for the cleric, since he and Stapleton, already acquainted, disliked each other, and when the latter's sketch of employment in London was briskly rejected, Stapleton planned a revenge and involved Maude in it. The shabby little plot involved the innkeeper, William Sisson, who told Stapleton that the churchman had made a lewd suggestion about Sisson's wife. Maude persuaded Sisson to pimp with his own wife so that when she was with Sandys the room could be stormed and the archbishop blackmailed by Stapleton. This grubby plan was undertaken and though a chastened Sandys balked at £800, he did agree to £600 and a lease. Only when further demands were thrust at him did he go sheepishly to Burghley with the mortifying story. On hearing of it Elizabeth ordered an investigation and trial of the culprits. Stapleton had well-placed friends like Hatton and Mildmay. Maude was much more exposed and had an unsavoury reputation. The upshot was that he not only had to pay Sandys back the money, but he also had to hand over £300 to Elizabeth. He went to prison for three years as well and just avoided having his ears slit by a timely confession tricked out with remorse. Trawling the prisons for potential agents Walsingham got him released after a time, and in March 1586 Maude was mingling with Catholic dissident conspirators at the Plough Inn, Temple Bar.

'Theatre – the art of upstarts, opportunists, would-be aristocrats.' So too espionage. Poley's career was shaped by his social circumstances and finances, and perhaps we should add a dash of transcendent resentment too. He seems to have developed an appetite for expensive comforts and by 1588, well into his furtive career for Walsingham, it was estimated that his rooms in the premises of a Mr and Mrs Yeoman were furnished by him at a cost of some £40. This compares startlingly with the brutal circumstances of his contemporary Robert Barnard who, in his official letters for the brief period he was employed, used the initials P.H. Like agents already cited, he was an educated man, employed throughout 1582. Yet, in a letter to his employer he wrote that he owed his landlord over £4 and the man unkindly threatened to imprison him for non-payment. 'I have not received anything from you in these three months past. I beseech you to give me order whereby I may, with less trouble to your Honour, receive monthly that which it may seem good to you to bestow upon me.'

One of the constraints on employing large numbers of spies was the cost of such an effort. The data on this is wretchedly scrappy, even contradictory, but it has often been adduced that because Elizabeth underfunded the arrangements for espionage, Walsingham in his zeal paid men out of his own pocket. Unlike some of his lesser contemporaries in trade or finance, he was never rich, although he had a comfortable family life in London and Barn Elms. The cost of this and the secret service may in part account for the strain that developed between him and Leicester in dealing with the cost of the funeral of Sir Philip Sidney, an event on a grand scale that was delayed for some months after his death in battle. To have a funeral that matched the public reputation of the lamented dead man, and to pay off his debts according to the many particulars of his will, was a challenging matter. Walsingham appealed to Leicester for assistance just at the moment the earl himself was facing bankruptcy under the burden of fighting in the United Provinces. The fact that he had manifestly not been very successful did not reduce his charges. Walsingham declared that after his son-in-law's death he had paid out some £6,000, and after Leicester's refusal of funds it has been assumed that Walsingham wrecked his own finances to pay the entire debt. This seems uncharacteristic, not to say odd, and later figures given by Robert Sidney's accountant, Thomas Nevitt, say nothing about such an effort. And despite proclaiming the hardships that had fallen on him Walsingham 'undoubtedly did remove several thousands of pounds worth of movables from Penshurst'.

Calculations of the annual sums spent on his secret service offer amounts varying between a few hundred and thousands of pounds. Read and then Lawrence Stone a generation later say that in 1582 it was £750; £2,000 in the crisis years of 1585–8 and £1,200 in 1589 to cover the whole range of activity! W.R. Scott was certain that successive Catholic plots added greatly to the cost of government at home, so that in 1588–9 as much as £30,000 was spent.[2] Read based his figures on Thomas Lake's copy of secret service accounts in the signet book. One of Walsingham's secretaries in 1590, Lake estimated that his employer received £250 in April 1585; £250 in October and £600 in February 1586. The figures are rather different in the signet book itself, with over £800 noted for 1585. If these sums all appear incredibly low then Frederick Dietz was more generous, although his figures on every aspect of the Elizabethan economy are now widely contested. He has £4,655 in 1583; £4,220 in 1584 and over £13,000 in 1585. A pity he had no explanation for the huge jump. In 1610, another spy master, Robert Cecil, Earl of Salisbury, prepared a memorandum with secret service details that show from the accounts of the Entry Books of Issue and Pells Declaration Books some remarkable figures:[3]

1583–4	£5,753	14 s.	$\frac{1}{2}$ d.
1584–5	£10,030	9 s.	4 d.
1585–6	£9,455	16 s.	11 d.
1586–7	£13,260	0 s.	0 d.

The clamour of unpaid spies was an unavoidable element in the lives of the spy masters. Thomas Rogers might take a substitute for cash, but others had to solicit much smaller sums than the £50 he got for procuring the release of two priests. The quaintly named Maliverny Catlyn once wrote that unless he and his family received something quickly they were going to have the most wretched Christmas ever; Walsingham had Phelippes send him £5. Pensions, which in theory at least required regular payment, were much rarer, although Gilbert Gifford for his part in sabotaging the Babington plot received £100 a year. At the beginning of the 1590s, Chateaumartin, consul of the English merchants in La Rochelle, directed a bill to Burghley for his services. Its detail is striking and may say as much about the man to whom it was being submitted, as it does about the Frenchman who prepared it. The delivery was made by Adam Brisset whose journey from London to Bayonne was costed in stages: London to Plymouth (via Exeter), 9 crowns; passage to La Rochelle, 10 crowns; 5 crowns for the section of the journey to Royan and then 12 crowns for horses from Bordeaux to Bayonne, so that the total with supplement-aries was 73 crowns.

Chateaumartin besides claimed 20 crowns for horses used at various times for journeys to St Jean de Luz; 66 crowns and 15 sous for Adam Brisset, including expenses to San Sebastian; 50 crowns for the courier for return journeys to Madrid; 216 crowns and 40 sous for the agent there in the period March to July; 122 crowns to the man in Biscay for the same period; 20 crowns to those he entertained; 12 crowns for minor messages and letters; 30 crowns for the man in Aragon; 100 crowns to M. Masparrant; 10 crowns for thirty days lodging for Brisset – in all just over 700 crowns. In December 1589 Chateaumartin had received £100 (that is 333 crowns and 20 sous) in cash and a letter of exchange for £500. He had also drawn 100 crowns from Francis James – a total of 933 crowns and 20 sous with 214 crowns left to administer. When Walsingham died, Elizabeth had to wait for the return of Palavicino for reports on the Frenchman's employment, so until then he was allowed to keep the balance. His claims for future intelligence work were pitched high, and Burghley often scaled down the allowances while still expecting value for money. Thus, £366 sought for an agent in Biscay became £200; £120 for someone to travel to Seville and Lisbon became £100.[4]

Bayonne was not only on the itinerary of spies and their ancillaries, it also attracted English traders. In 1599, for example, Henry Norton had a licence to transport corn there and since his patron, Sir William Bevyll, had dealings then with Sir Robert Cecil, who had recently revamped the Cecil spy network, it would not be surprising if Norton also did some intelligence work while abroad. He was the eldest son of the Inner Temple lawyer and poet Thomas Norton, who had died in 1584. Co-author with Thomas Sackville (Lord Buckhurst) of *Gorboduc*, the first blank verse tragedy in English, Thomas Norton was a radical puritan who fetched up in the Tower for indiscreet trumpetings about puritanism both in and out of parliament. He was one of the commissioners who examined Edmund Campion and his rigour in the dealings with the Jesuit may have had an additional private prompting. Norton's second wife, Alice, was the daughter of Archdeacon Edmund Cranmer and she fell prey to religious mania so that by 1582 she was held to be insane. It seems to have been a family terror, for in 1607 her nephew too was regarded as mad. For nearly two decades after Norton's demise Alice lived with her eldest daugher Ann, who had married George Coppin (or Coppen). By the turn of the century he had been an informant of Robert Cecil's in Burghley's household when the old man was seriously ailing, and so at the mercy of assistants and servants. With Cecil wanting to know what passed in his father's establishment so that he could protect him and his own interests, it is not surprising that at much the same time he infiltrated a young servant into the household of an increasingly suspect Earl of Essex.

Thomas Norton's name appears on the torture warrants that were prepared for the officers of the Tower and Bridewell. Some writers about Tudor England, especially those leaning to Catholicism, have occasionally betrayed an unseemly glee at the fact that torture was most pronounced in Elizabeth's reign. Common law did not allow for its use as a means of obtaining a confession, but this hallowed exclusion was set aside by the Privy Council. Their aim was to protect the state they administered for the queen, and mostly that meant preventative torture to identify and forestall plots and plotters.[5] The excessive severities of the treatments meted out by the prerogative courts (that is those that claimed to be superior to the common law), mostly citing punishment for treason, excited anger in England and indignation abroad. The protests became so loud that it was considered necessary to bring out a pamphlet to refute such views. It appeared in 1583 ascribed to

Methods of Catholic torture: example B shows the acute constriction of the body held in manacles

Burghley, although more likely it was the work of Norton. Against voices like that of Sir Thomas Smith who regarded torture with public disdain, Norton proposed that it be used with restraint so that no one was racked 'until it was rendered evidently probable, by former detections or confessions, that he was guilty; nor was the torture ever employed to bring out confessions at random, nor unless the party had at first refused to declare the truth at the Queen's commandment.'

The collated torture warrants for the period 1540–1640 only number some eighty, which might suggest that the opponents of such a procedure had some success.[6] Yet, since a number of names of known victims, such as the creative joiner who made priest-holes, Nicholas Owen, do not appear in the warrants, secret torture was done by Richard Topcliffe, who appeared on Burghley's payroll in 1581 employed as a pursuivant. The instruments of suffering were the rack, manacles (described by Richard Verstegen as 'An instrument of iron which presses and doubles up on man into a globe shape'), and the eponymous Skevington's irons, the invention of Sir Leonard Skevington, Lieutenant of the Tower in the reign of Henry VII, which held the neck, wrists and ankles in a linked restraint. The first of these grim items was used in the Tower, although Topcliffe is said to have boasted that it was nothing compared with his. The rack was introduced into England in the reign of Henry VI and consisted of a stout oak frame raised several feet off the ground. The prisoner was placed under it on his back, with ankles and wrists lashed

A prisoner is confined in a tiny cell above the door to view the operation of the rack below; he may be next

by ropes to two rollers at the end of the frame. By means of levers worked in opposite directions the body of the prisoner was pulled up level with the frame and thus left suspended by ankles and wrists. If his silence was maintained the levers were moved and the cords pulled on the joints until bones started from their sockets. When Charles Bailly was imprisoned Burghley required the Lieutenant of the Tower to oversee his examination: 'You will ask him for the alphabet of the cipher, and if he shall refuse to show the said alphabet, or to declare truly the contents of the said letters in cipher, you shall put him upon the rack; and by discretion with putting him in fear . . . you shall procure him to confess the truth with some pain of the said torture.'

The rack in the Tower was 'the accustomed torture' until 1588.[7] That was the year Richard Topcliffe was first noted on a warrant against Tristram (the name used in Spanish records but actually William) Winslade. He had been captured on board the galleon of Don Pedro de Valdés in the Armada fleet, his life having taken its peculiar direction as a result of his father's involvement as a leader of the Prayer Book Rebellion (1549). Winslade fetched up in the Tower, while other captives from the Armada went to Bridewell, which now also served as a religious prison. If the rack in the Tower was indeed somehow a milder instrument than that later employed by Topcliffe, who did not really flourish until Walsingham died in April 1590, it could explain how, after his release in February of that year, the unfortunate Windslade could actually become an itinerant harpist. The lamentable suspicion must remain that he was not a very good one.

From 1589–1603 torture was generally carried out at Bridewell, the sometime royal palace given to the city of London by Edward VI in 1553. Originally intended as a remedial institution for the destitute poor, by 1590 it had substantial debts and was threatened with closure. It may explain why Bridewell had no rack and relied instead on the gauntlets, the victim having a hand inserted and a lever tightened to compress it. With wrists so clamped he was then suspended on a beam with no foot support. This mode of inflicting agony may also have been used in the Tower. In 1592 the Jesuit poet Robert Southwell was there, having been betrayed by Anne Bellamy, the daughter of Richard Bellamy, the oldest of the brothers who suffered for aiding the Babington plotters. The calamities that befell the family continued when Anne was raped by Topcliffe, who was not above, it seems, making indecent remarks to a remarkably complacent Elizabeth. When Anne's pregnancy showed she was further humiliated by being married off to one of Topcliffe's servants. As for Southwell himself, through the Copleys he was a cousin of the Bacons and the Cecils. Sir Robert Cecil attended at least one examination after which he marvelled with cool wonder at Southwell's resistance. Though not racked the Jesuit suffered the gauntlets: 'We have a new torture which it is not possible for a man to bear. And yet I have seen Robert Southwell hanging by it . . . and no one able to drag one word out of his mouth.' Topcliffe's zeal cost him a spell in prison, but only because the government did not want Southwell to die under torture. In his 'Supplication', written before his capture and addressed to the queen who licensed Topcliffe's outrages, Southwell noted that men were whipped, starved, deprived of sleep, racked and very possibly had their genitals mutilated, although he was too polite to refer openly to this savagery and did not have to submit it. The manuscript seems to have been much prized and, when Topcliffe obtained a copy in 1594, he lent it to Francis Bacon, who grudgingly admired it.[8]

Topcliffe did not mellow with age. Even at sixty he was a grizzled agent of revenge Protestantism, although he may have been raised as a Catholic. It is hard to find anything, even anecdotal material, which alters the long-held view that he was an ideological sadist, albeit acting under orders.* But he was not an illiterate thug, for all the typical idiosyncracies of his orthography. Topcliffe came from a well-connected northern family. He had links with the Fitzherberts of Derbyshire and Staffordshire, and Thomas Fitzherbert's attempt in 1595 to bribe him to eliminate two relatives, when it was disclosed, led to another short period of imprisonment for maligning privy councillors. Nicholas Fitzherbert later became a secretary to Cardinal Allen and was his first biographer. Topcliffe's vendetta against them was powerfully nourished by the thought of the family's estates, and though they held on to Norbury and Swynnerton, he did get his hands on Padley, acquired from Thomas Fitzherbert.

The grandson of Lord Burgh, Topcliffe does not seem to have become rich through the sweat and blood of his victims. There is even a suggestion that his marriage faltered because of his alleged failure to pay his wife adequate maintenance. His greatest satisfactions seem to have been pathological, such as the execution of the Jesuit Edmund Jennings and six other Catholics in December 1591 at about the time Southwell was writing in a white heat of emotion, his 'Supplication'. However, it should be pointed out that not everyone arrested by him was tortured, even in the fuss surrounding the lost play *Isle of Dogs*. In August 1597 Topcliffe, Thomas Fowler, Richard Skevington, Roger Wilbraham and Dr Giles Fletcher, were commissioners appointed by the Privy Council to apprehend and interrogate several of the players of this mysteriously lewd and seditious drama. Those arrested by Topcliffe were the actors Gabriel Spencer, Robert Shaa (Shaw) and Ben Jonson, who had collaborated with Thomas Nashe in writing it. They were detained in the Marshalsea until released in October and there is no hint of torture although Topcliffe, Skevington and the recorder of London had the previous year been authorized to use the manacles when examining eighty 'Egipcians and wanderers'. The Council got details of the play first from Cecil, he from Topcliffe, who in turn had been alerted by an informer of his own.[9] Topcliffe's alacrity in dealing with such a matter may be explained by his desire to exploit the matter in order to polish up his reputation. In the aftermath of the Cádiz expedition (1596), Sir Anthony Ashley, who shared with Sir George Carew the charge of detailing the treasure and coin taken, had fetched up in prison for theft and Topcliffe's son Charles (Ashley's clerk) was involved in this shady business. Since he got off with only a rebuke, it is possible to infer that his father had come to his aid. Even so, in 1602, as proof of his long memory for transgressions, Cecil chided Topcliffe for not having his naughty son 'cleansed'.[10] Theft by others the rackmaster could not abide. Once he maltreated a suspect Scottish thief with such ferocity that the man's indignant employer told the lord mayor 'that cannibals would not use any as his servant was used'.

* He had been employed by Burghley and Leicester in the 1580s, but not as a torturer.

Chapter Six

Agents and Conspirators

Although the Babington plot was in the second order of Elizabethan crises, it edges ahead of other threats to the queen because of its complexity and personnel, and it is of special interest in any detailed consideration of the secret service formed by the methodical Walsingham. Above all, the plot had a political consequence of the first magnitude; it led inexorably to the long-anticipated execution of Mary, Queen of Scots. That was certainly a talisman as far as the secretary was concerned, but those at home and abroad who dipped into (and even skipped out of) the affair had other motives. While the initial motion of a plot came from one faction of disenchanted and edgy English Catholics, the shaping and momentum behind it tilted to the government's advantage. This seems to have begun very early, long before the formulation of the plot, because the Duke of Guise in 1582 made a disastrous error of judgement. Then he called together a conference to discuss invasion and the removal of Elizabeth, allowing the Jesuits a prime position. This enraged laymen like Charles Paget and Thomas Morgan, sometime cipher clerk to James Beaton, the Archbishop of Glasgow, for they held that such business was for laymen, not priests. Guise was not above offering a reward for the murder of Elizabeth and so Walsingham began to assemble a list of men who hankered for it. With the murder of William of Orange in 1584 vigilance became even more vital, and the tense response under the leadership of the Earl of Leicester was the Bond of Association, intended to bind the nation together at a time of gloom.

One of those seemingly baited by Guise was George Gifford, a gentleman pensioner who went to France only to be judged untrustworthy, if not authentically a double agent. His brother, the priest Dr William Gifford, was also in France supporting Paget and Morgan, along with their young cousin, Gilbert Gifford. Both Giffords were apostate secret agents when they met with another priest, Christopher Hodgson, and also John Savage. From 1581–3 the latter had been soldiering for the enemy in the Low Countries. A product of Barnard's Inn, he entered the English College in Rheims in May 1583 and remained there until mid-August 1585. According to John Charnock, a colleague in arms, 'he was an excellent soldier, a man skillful in languages and learned besides'. Yet he proved less purposeful than Gilbert Gifford (b. 1560), a second cousin of John Gerard and educated at Douai from 1577. In company with Edward Grateley he had entered the English College in Rome in 1579, where he had been quickly sought out and suborned by an English agent, Solomon Aldred, an inveterate troublemaker, one of a clutch of disaffected men who put themselves at Walsingham's disposal. Initially highly regarded in the college, Gifford became a cranky member of the troubled establishment, and after eleven months was expelled. Following a gap and an apology to Cardinal Allen, he was allowed into the institution at Rheims in 1582. When his temper betrayed him again he quit and returned to England. Within a short time No. 4, as Gifford was called in London, had crossed again to France, writing to Allen from Paris, and arriving in Rome a year later. In April 1585 he became a deacon at Rheims for cover and left in October.

Thomas Morgan's career was almost equally chequered. In 1584 he fetched up in the Bastille, as we have noted, for plotting against Elizabeth, but despite this hiatus he 'carefully maintained his contact with the Scottish queen'.[1] To do this he approached Christopher Blount, having once saved his life. Even so, this was extraordinarily risky, almost provocative because it was as if Morgan was now signalling to London his seething discontent. As it happened Blount was to have a somewhat lurid career, but at this time he was loyal to Elizabeth. He was one of the two surviving sons of Thomas Blount, who, until his death in 1568, had been a key figure in the Earl of Leicester's household, and Mary Blount (born Poley), from a Suffolk Catholic family. According to Anthony Wood, Christopher was privately tutored in Louvain by William Allen, but at this time he was following his father by serving Leicester.[2] Blount's contact with Morgan was surely with the earl's approval and Walsingham's knowledge. It is given heightened interest in that his mail carrier was Robert Poley, one of the most nimble agents ever taken into Walsingham's network. Morgan did not at first trust Poley; the man's demeanour was unsettling, and in recommending him to Mary he proposed that she should test Poley's loyalty. Morgan wanted a representative for the exiled Catholic seculars like himself, the Pagets, Thomas Throckmorton and so on, in England and he looked for a time to Dr William Gifford to undertake the work.

Solomon Aldred bobbed up again to arrange for William Gifford, later named by Savage as the initiator of the Babington plot, to meet the English ambassador, Sir Edward Stafford. All at the prompting of Morgan who must have learnt from Mendoza that because of his gambling Stafford was vulnerable. It seems that Morgan was prodding Gifford for two reasons: first, it might distract Walsingham when plans were afoot to renew Mary's correspondence with her supporters; secondly, if William Gifford could lead a schism in the Rheims seminary and return then to England with government protection, he could still act for the exiled seculars under the moderately benevolent eye of Walsingham, himself always eager to wreck the seminaries. Aldred's dealings with Father Edward Grateley were part of this. The latter had gone to Rome probably with the intention of sowing discord between Persons and Allen, the sometime chaplain of the Earl of Arundel being rather an adept in such matters. The essential link from Morgan and Gilbert Gifford's point of view, between the proposed disruption of the seminaries and the regicide plot, was the book of anti-Jesuit slanders, planned and eventually written by Gifford and Grateley. In December 1585 it was Gilbert Gifford who came to England, rather than his cousin who was ailing and frightened, and Stafford and Aldred ceased their dealings with him. As far as an irritated Walsingham was concerned, Dr Gifford was a potential source of embarrassment, so it is not especially surprising that the exile was eventually condemned to death as a prime instigator of the Babington plot. He informed Gilbert Gifford that his cousin deserved that 'we both write and speak bitterly against him'. William Gifford, despite his breach with the Jesuits and, most particularly it seems, Robert Persons, whose class notions he resented, was never unequivocally won over to the views of the government in London and can be placed among the 'National Catholics' who argued for toleration. Despite one or two dips of confidence Gilbert Gifford was similarly disposed, although when he landed at Rye in December 1585 he was carrying a letter of recommendation from Morgan to Mary. The intention was that he would negotiate with Walsingham on behalf of his cousin, and would also go about setting up a safe letter carrying system for the isolated Mary. 'Safe for whom?' is the looming question because by 1585 the loyalty of Morgan to Mary was severely strained. The cluster of plots hitherto had all failed; he had been imprisoned in the Bastille; he was poor when someone like Grateley had made a lot of money stealing from Arundel. Even if Morgan did not intend to betray Mary his choice of Gifford was dangerous. If he did intend to betray her it was probably not Walsingham's money that led him in that direction, rather the captive queen's own funds, which he, as her representative, controlled. Walsingham never publicly avowed that he wanted Mary executed; his undeviating attention was devoted to rendering her politically impotent and crushing the threat from the Jesuits. In this view he became the perfect ally for Morgan who buried his own retreat from the Marian cause because of the additional dangers to which it exposed him in Paris.[3] Charles Arundel left the city for Spain in the autumn of 1586, with both sides declaring him loyal, although Mendoza qualified this. When Arundel returned to Paris in 1587 he was dead within the year and Stafford wrote that Charles Paget had

Sir Amias Paulet, 1536(?)–88. Before his ambassadorial experience in France (1576–9), this avowed enemy of Catholicism had spent several years as governor of the openly Presbyterian community in Jersey

poisoned him. Morgan did not need to be a seer to know the risks attendant on any suspicion that he had reneged on the Marian cause.

Since 1585 and the appointment of Paulet this looked ever more etiolated. From Tutbury Mary's letters were directed to Mauvissière, the official channel for all her correspondence, and subject to scrutiny by Walsingham. Even this faltered as Walsingham became more and more interventionist, and the pretence of royal privacy was abandoned. Incoming correspondence was equally controlled through the hands of Stafford in Paris, and Morgan's search for alternative routes and messengers (like Poley) failed to break the English stranglehold. With the Gifford family home near to Tutbury, it was felt that the personable young Catholic gentleman ought to be able to find a way to smuggle letters to Mary without alerting her captors. But first Walsingham wanted the satisfactory report of Thomas Rogers on Gifford confirmed by day-to-day scrutiny in London, so he put the latter in company with Thomas Phelippes, then living in premises in Leadenhall market.[4] He could set about deciphering the letter Gifford was carrying from Morgan to Mary, and he could weigh the general acumen of the beardless young agent. Moving Mary from Tutbury as was planned had a psychological component to it; a new home ought to suggest new opportunities to be exploited. The problem was to find an alternative safe residence; Chillington, the Gifford home was rejected because it lacked ale-brewing facilities and Chartley nearly fell on the same score. The latter was owned by Essex, who had been brought up there with his brother and sisters, and he was reluctant to hand it over. Since his mother was from the Puritan Knollys family and his stepfather Leicester was an ally of Walsingham, this presents a small mystery. But the move to the moated house was made and Paulet was pleased to be able to receive Phelippes in the Christmas and New Year of 1585–6. The elderly Puritan gentleman then confirmed that Mary was effectively quarantined. From his own observations of the dynamics of the household, it may have been Phelippes who devised the barrel mode of delivering letters to satisfy the intense craving of the queen for outside contacts. But since he was mistrusted by Mary's household there is a good case for saying it was Gilbert Gifford who thought of the idea and put the notion to Chateauneuf. Familiarity can help nurture unmerited trust and since the brewer was a Catholic and partisan of Mary, he was welcome to the house. An offer by him to smuggle letters in and out was bound to be authentically tempting, so the resourceful Phelippes, with a devious idea to nurture, must have consulted Paulet about suborning the man. He acknowledged the brewer's private worship, but said he was an 'honest man' – by which Paulet meant someone ready to pocket a bribe where there was no risk attached and do what was required of him. And so it proved. When approached by Phelippes the brewer agreed for a price to deliver packets of letters in a cork tube which was slipped through the bung-hole of the barrel. Collecting the empty cask he was to look again for the tube which was to be passed to no one but the 'secret party': Gilbert Gifford.

Before setting out for Chartley, Gifford had several difficult transactions to carry out. The most important of these was to establish links with the diplomats at the French embassy. Apart from Morgan's letter of recommendation addressed to Mary, he had also brought with him similar items from Morgan, Paget and others addressed to the new ambassador Chateauneuf. He went to put these before Cordaillot, the secretary who dealt with most of the business connected with Mary. Gifford explained his courier mission in flawless French and for heightened colouring sketched out some of his own personal biography. He claimed, for example, that having been absent from England for over a decade even his father and sisters would not recognize him, and such an advantageous invisibility could not let him down. He would deliver letters to the embassy for forwarding abroad, and take anything sent via the embassy to her. Properly wary, the French reception he received was coolly cautious, and Cordaillot wanted some evidence that the man before him really was linked to the prisoner-queen.

Gifford then took himself off to the neighbourhood of Chartley, apparently having re-established contact with his father. In Staffordshire he settled into premises that were provided for the estate's steward.[5] That done he rode over to Burton to meet the still anonymous brewer and he handed over Morgan's letter to Mary, together with his covering note. The following Saturday the brewer made his delivery at Chartley and, having unloaded, announced he would collect the empty cask the next day as he went back to town. Given the requirements for secrecy in a household of hired watchers, this did not allow much time for discreet letter writing and ciphering. Even so, the arrangement was followed and at a judicious distance from the house the reply packet was retrieved. It was handed to Gifford who returned to London. There Phelippes set to work deciphering what proved to be very modest, low-key contents: an acknowledgement of Morgan's letter and two more items for all that Mary was still uncertain about Gifford. When the work was done, he could take the packet to the French embassy, all the seals counterfeited with exceptional accuracy by Arthur Gregory, whom Walsingham employed especially for this skill, and who later joined Robert Cecil's secret service.

Cordaillot remained an unwilling participant in the effort, but he relented enough to hand over a letter from his ambassador to Mary. It was in cipher, but cautiously contained nothing compromising or important and, since Gifford had no diversions to keep him in London, he left for Chartley the same night. There he was already expected by Paulet for Tuesday 25 January, the brewer having called over the weekend and the letter out already forwarded to London. However, a delay occurred and it was not until Thursday 3 February that the latter received a note from Gifford asking for a trusted messenger to be sent to pick up a packet which had reached him from the brewer. Paulet did as he was asked and Gifford declared in a note that he would arrive on Saturday. He swept in in darkness bringing two packets and two letters. He had also in his possession a cipher received from Curll, Mary's Scottish secretary, which he asked to keep for sending an acknowledgement of the received packet.

Gifford had it in mind now to spend some time in London, and he thought Phelippes might nudge John Gifford into calling for his son's company.[6] Then 'he might deliver these letters to the French ambassador in convenient time for the better conservation of his credit'. While absent from the environs of Chartley, a substitute would take his place and he would leave a 'counter-paper' with the brewer at their next meeting. This disturbed Paulet who could not go anywhere. He recorded his misgivings when writing to Walsingham: 'I will hope the best of your friend; but I may not hide from you that he doubled in his speech with me once or twice, and it cannot be denied that he received these or other packets sooner than he confessed.' Paulet was even mildly perturbed about the brewer whose nonchalance may have grated – 'you shall do well to assure yourself of the honest man'. As it happened Walsingham was not too concerned about a free-floating suspicion of Gifford, but did approve of more scrutiny of the Burton man. This stemmed from the necessity to bring him in further than had been intended. He was to be persuaded with coins that what he received from Gifford should first be delivered to Paulet before being put into the barrel. Also, anything found in the empty barrel was to go first to Paulet before being passed to Gifford (or his substitute), both of whom had to radiate honest endeavour as far as the brewer was concerned.

Thus, the secret post took its definitive form. Gifford received his expected recall to London, and by the time he had arrived the letters forwarded by Paulet on 6 February had been deciphered by Phelippes and resealed, and the whole packet was ready for him to deliver. It contained much of what had been hoped for, including authority for Chateauneuf to hand over to Gifford all the packets that had accumulated over six months; Gifford delivered it on Tuesday 1 March. By then it had been a month in transit and with a compelling elaboration about certain Catholic gentlemen (all a fiction), Gifford at last penetrated the reservations nurtured hitherto. The Frenchman now acted on his written instructions and handed over to Gifford the whole clutch of letters he had long retained to await delivery. This was a weight of work for the overburdened Phelippes, but he tackled it (twenty-one packets) with alacrity and by 4 March he had the first batch deciphered. Since the originals constituted too great a bulk for the barrel tube at one time, Paulet had to arrange its delivery by instalments. There was no immediate hurry for Gifford to go to Chartley, however, because of the substitute who was well regarded as a servant of the Earl of Leicester. Paulet and the increasingly brazen brewer both approved of him, although the latter was not persuaded to bring forward the date of their next appointment. That took place on 20 March.

In the meantime there was general work for Gifford in London. Accepted gratefully by the recusant Catholic community he could report on them and in particular Savage, who had allowed the melody of murder to fade from his mind. In Gifford's company he was pointedly reminded of the vow freely taken in Rheims, and with his vengeful mood stoked up he declared his intention to the priest John Ballard (who incidentally was never a Jesuit as has been averred). A Cambridge MA (Caius College was one of the four Cambridge colleges which produced surprising numbers of Catholic converts[7]), he was a lively, chameleon figure with a cluster of aliases who had fled to Rheims in later 1579, was ordained at Chalons in March 1581 and was sent then to England.[8] Visiting the Gatehouse he made friends with Anthony Tyrell, and when he escaped (something that always raises suspicions), the two travelled abroad. In September 1584 they were apparently in Rome to obtain papal sanction for Ballard's plan to kill Elizabeth; he had become seized with the notion of murder as a political act after the killing of William of Orange. Certainly Walsingham's agents tracked him, and Thomas Rogers for one thought Ballard dangerous. The latter arrived from Rouen in Southampton late in 1584 and linked up with the only known Jesuit in the country, Father William Weston. With a clutch of other priests they became involved in a torrent of exorcisms, with the manifestations and casting out of devils taking place for about eighteen months, and with striking frequency in the period from October 1585 to June 1586. Demonic possession was then a terrifying notion that had an extraordinary power for most people, and the witnesses of the confrontations between demons (some named) and priests included many of the gentry. On one occasion five coaches with gentlemen arrived at Denham House because Ballard was there and they wanted to see what could be done for a servant of Babington who was deemed to be in the grip of malevolent spirits. With Marwood's young and impressionable employer came a cluster of men who became heavily involved in the Babington plot: Robert Gage (of Croydon); Charles Tilney; Thomas Salusbury and Chidiock Tichborne. On the strength of the psychodrama presented there many converts were made (and presumably regarded as potential rebels), narratives written and circulated.* One eyewitness told a sceptical Burghley that he had seen devils like fishes swimming beneath the skins of the possessed.

In April 1586 Ballard was again in Paris and with voluble enthusiasm had meetings with Paget, Morgan and Mendoza. The ambassador's practicality failed to reduce the heat of Ballard's enthusiasm and later, to Savage and Babington, he claimed that a huge continental army would reinforce their domestic effort. Perhaps anticipating a martial role Ballard had re-entered England disguised as a 'Captain Fortescue' but, lacking the discretion of the best clandestine operators, he was tracked by one of Walsingham's agents. It was the disreputable Barnard Maude, whose sleazy plot against Archbishop Sandys (who had sacked him for peculation), cost him a period shut up in the Fleet. In March 1586, when enrolled in Walsingham's service, he kept company with Babington, Ballard, Tichborne *et al.* in the Plough, a Temple Bar ordinary. Nudged by Morgan and then Gilbert Gifford, Ballard was to tour England to arouse again as many leading Catholics as possible; a special emphasis would be placed on the north of England. One house in Yorkshire where Ballard often stayed when meeting gentlemen of the neighbourhood of Newcastle under Lyme, belonged to a member of the Tipping family and James Tipping's brother-in-law had possibly gone to France with Ballard.[9]

As for Gilbert Gifford, he was now needed by Paulet to be available in the environs of Chartley. The reason was that the brewer, in his new position of importance, was taking full advantage of it by behaving in a thoroughly offhand manner – calling for more money and then breaking appointments. Gifford went to sort this out and did so to Paulet's satisfaction. He wrote to Phelippes: 'I am well persuaded of the fidelity of the man.' It was now possible to continue the regular delivery of the rest of the letters Gifford had received at the French embassy. With so many to be deciphered and answered Mary's secretaries, Claude Nau de la Boisselière and Gilbert Curll (or Curle), would take many days over the replies. Since Aldred was calling for his urgent return to Paris, the postal system required a substitute agent. Gifford came up with his cousin Thomas Barnes, to be known to

---

* Tyrell wrote *The Book of Miracles* about the exorcisms.

Anthony Babington with his conspirators

Mary as 'Barnaby' – the man with whom he sometimes lodged in London. Having crisply attended to this Gifford just had time to sit with Phelippes to concoct a letter from 'Barnaby' to Curll warning him to expect a packet from Morgan. The reason for returning to France was that Ballard was in the open and Morgan had discovered that Southwell and Garnet were poised to cross to England. Gifford alerted his employer in London, but their arrival in England from Boulogne was missed because Walsingham guessed mistakenly that, coming from Norfolk, Southwell would want to land there. It was a miscalculation that cost him dear in terms of effort over the next few years.

For a time the plotters found a haven in France, where their collective sense of oppression led them to mull over various options. The keyed-up Ballard told Mendoza, Paget and Morgan that English Catholics were afire to aid Mary, and the assassination of Elizabeth should be combined with a Spanish invasion. Mendoza soberly discribed the proposal as worthy 'of spirits so Catholic and of the ancient valour of Englishmen'. As for the Pope – it was Gregory XIII's declared view that 'whosoever sends her out of the world with the pious intention of doing God's service, not only does not sin but gains merit'. Nor would Mary herself have balked at it, since she was steeped in the brusquely violent ways of the Valois court of her youth. With scores to settle in England Mendoza listened because the proposals were part of a package. He may have been more sceptical than is sometimes supposed, but he still wanted the effort underwritten by Philip II. Late in May Mary began her own defiant contacts with the ambassador, pledging to override her son's right of succession to the English throne because of his obstinate adherence to Protestantism and declaring Philip her successor. Mendoza was naturally hugely taken with this advance and his urgings to Philip were unequivocal, countering his king's own previous hesitations about helping Mary.[10] He recalled that the Guise family were her nearest relatives and had no wish to improve the French position in Scotland and England. His response was measured, though he agreed in July to pay her 12,000 escudos, and he nodded an acceptance of Mendoza's suggestion that Morgan should receive something. Hence a pension from the ambassador's expenses of 40 escudos; if it was paid monthly it was niggardly and if annually, it was paltry.

At the arraignment of the Babington conspirators it was attested that on 26 April 1586, Mendoza and Paget 'had maliciously and wickedly devised how this realm of England might be invaded, and by what means Mary, Queen of Scots, might be delivered, it was concluded that the said John Ballard should go into the realm of England to understand and know what ports and landings might be procured and provided for the enemy's invasion, and to learn by what means the said Mary . . . might be delivered from the custody wherein she was.' All this had been learned from Maude before Ballard sloughed him off and returned to England. There he turned the full blast of his personality again on to the callow Anthony Babington still ruminating, it is fair to suppose, on the exorcisms; did Ballard dare hint that assassination was a secular form of it? Babington dithered, haunted by the thought that little could be achieved while Elizabeth lived. Ballard responded that the 'difficulty would be taken away by means already laid: and that her life would be no hindrance therein'. Savage was named and Babington given much to wrestle with. Of course it was the two Giffords and Hodgson who had persuaded Savage that Elizabeth should be killed, and since Gilbert Gifford continued to press Savage to act it is reasonable to call him an *agent provocateur*.

Chapter Seven

Babington Baited

The family home of Anthony Babington was Dethick, two miles outside Matlock in Derbyshire. He was born in October 1561, the third child of a wealthy Catholic gentry family. As the oldest of three brothers and two sisters, he inherited the family estates from his father Henry (b. 1530) when still a boy, becoming the ward of his mother, Mary Babington (née Darcy) and Mr Philip Draycot of Paynesley (Staffs). On her remarriage Anthony got a stepfather from a well-known Catholic family. His minority seems to have been a comfortable one and the prevailing circumstances of Catholics meant he was educated at home. For a short time he joined the Earl of Shrewsbury's household at Sheffield in that intermediate position which meant that as a gentleman he was not a hired servant, although he might be called upon for errands. The lord of the household was then gaoler and host (also ambiguous) to Mary, and the boy may have been charmed by her at a distance, even once or twice carrying letters, but there was certainly a divide between the free and the restrained under the same roof. Further limitations on these fleeting contacts stemmed from the fact that a good deal of his boyhood was spent at Paynesley, and from this came a youthful marriage in 1579 to Margaret Draycot, his guardian's daughter. The young couple then had a daughter themselves, Mary (who died aged eight years), and they lived a somewhat fragmented family life when Babington was in the country. However, what took him away was London, metropolitan friends and their collective ambitions which excluded wives.[1]

In addition, the young husband had a desire to travel and within a year of his marriage had set out for a lengthy period in France. There he divided his time between the twin emigrant centres of Paris and Rouen, and so got to know further his countryman Chidiock Tichborne. A member of the prolific papist family, he was married too, but lightly opted to leave his wife Jane at home. As has been remarked 'Tichbornes of Hampshire fill the records of the exiled English Catholic seminaries and also the papers of the agents who tracked them to and from Flanders and Rome.' It is unclear if Babington ever ventured to Rome.

On his return to England Babington became a student at Lincoln's Inn, residing in London during term in lodgings near the Temple, although he had a house in Barbican, rented from a widow, Joyce Franklin. While in France he had made a favourable impression on Thomas Morgan (but then so had Gifford), who took him to meet James Beaton, Archbishop of Glasgow and Mary's lethargic representative to their host country. They recommended Babington to her at the end of April

1586, as he learnt from a secret letter she had delivered through a Mrs Bray of Sheffield. This was followed by a visit from the French ambassador's secretary with a packet of letters from Morgan. Inside was one addressed to Mary which he was to have delivered by Mrs Bray again and Anthony Rolston (whose career as a spy and double agent will be touched on again). The route closed, however, when Sir Amias Paulet became Mary's custodian.

Although Babington undertook both the sale of Catholic books for Girault and the orientation of the missionary priests arriving in England, men whose very presence in the provinces so alarmed the government that they led to a counter-offensive, he still hankered to go abroad again to France and also Italy. Indeed, so pervasive was his gloom he considered settling abroad; he had seen other conspiracies fail. It would be nice to think he consulted Margaret Babington, but it was his close friend Thomas Salusbury of Lleweni (sometime ward of the Earl of Leicester) who said that he would willingly accompany him. Early in 1586, as he reflected on the future, Babington was taken aback when he received another packet of letters for Mary sent from Thomas Morgan. With a brief surge of realism he returned them to the French ambassador declaring that he refused 'to deal any further in those affairs'. Unfortunately for him the warm embrace of Italy was not allowed by Walsingham, who declined a request from Sir Edward Fitton that the two men should be licensed to travel. If Babington had simply fled in disguise he would have lost his unentailed estates; that alone would have shackled his movements. As it was he stayed in London and met Ballard, a man whose personal charm always won him friends. He was also always short of money and very likely Babington had to fund his French trip to meet Paget, Morgan and Mendoza. When the latter wrote to Philip II he noted that four men had agreed to kill Elizabeth 'whether by poison or steel'.

Around Easter, while waiting for news from Ballard's talks, Babington moved to Hern's Rents premises in Holborn. With a boldness that suggests indifference to danger (or stupidity), he continued to meet friends in taverns virtually on his doorstep. His circle included some of the cluster once drawn to George Gilbert – Chidiock Tichborne; Thomas Habington; Henry Dunne; Robert Gage (Southwell's cousin);* Robert Barnewell; Thomas Salusbury and Edward Jones of Cadwgan. Babington probably also now became acquainted with another self-proclaimed Catholic (there is little probability of this and no proof), Robert Poley, whose status as a gentleman by birth was later attested but remains suspect. He confused his contemporaries profoundly, sliding through the tenebrous world of espionage, recruited who knows when by Walsingham. However, by 1583 Poley was in Walsingham's household at Barn Elms and then was placed as a spy in the Marshalsea (Southwark), where for appearance he spent half the time in close confinement and had 'the liberty of the house' for the remainder.

His reward for undertaking such an unattractive assignment was the trip abroad to carry messages between Christopher Blount and Thomas Morgan. Then, early in

---

* Gage and Southwell were also related to the Copleys who, through Anne Boleyn, were blood relatives of Elizabeth.

1585, he returned to England for employment as a financial secretary in Sir Philip Sidney's household. By the summer of that year Sidney's finances* were rickety and it seems in every way likely that Poley made matters worse, while he deliberately cultivated a reputation for extravagant hospitality to Catholic priests in his Bishopsgate house which Burghley had set aside for him. Poley's position was bound to intrigue them, especially when it was given out that he heard mass in secret whenever possible. So as Maude followed on the heels of Ballard, Poley inveigled his way into the circle and confidence of the naïve and only fitfully alert Babington.[2] The spy was able to convey news to his employer, either directly or through Thomas Walsingham, almost before thoughts had passed the lips of those few 'green wits' minded to plot again to take the life of the queen.

Towards the end of May 1586, Babington got another packet of letters from Morgan and he put them aside. Then Ballard returned and quickly sought him out to rehearse with zestful confidence what had passed in his talks. With Catholic Europe supposedly mustering against an impertinent enemy (Leicester had landed triumphantly with his expeditionary force some six months before in the United Provinces), Ballard was to take soundings in northern England about the secret views of papists regarding an invasion. Babington listened, but was essentially sceptical, whereas Ballard frothed enthusiastically. Even when John Savage was named as the projected assassin, Babington shrivelled with unease and a meeting with Ballard did not dissipate his reservations. But after Ballard had gone north with his expenses paid, Babington did set out the matter of violence to his friends. Lawful or not Salusbury rejected the notion, and as if to divert his friends from the viciously wayward and personally dangerous development that he saw materializing, he revived the plan for continental travel which had been on hold. As for the necessary licence, if absence from the country was not to be misconstrued, he thought their friend Tindall could solve that difficulty since he knew Poley, and Babington had £400 to put up if that was apparently necessary.

While the approach was made to Tindall, Babington divulged Ballard's thoughts of violence to Henry Dunne, whose response was not enthusiastic. Nothing much better was evoked when he talked to Tilney in his rooms in Westminster. An encounter at the Three Tuns in Newgate Market brought together Babington, Tichborne, Edward Habington and Tilney, with the last two opposing assassination, although kidnapping Elizabeth and threatening her might 'advise her to grant toleration in religion'. For his part, Salusbury, who in the event of a rising had taken upon himself the task of igniting Denbighshire, was trying to involve Edward Jones, and John Travers of Prescott (Lancs) who had known Savage in the Spanish army in the Low Countries. They held back out of residual loyalty or fear, and Jones seems to have been as anxious to win Salusbury from the toils of Babington, as Salusbury himself was to keep the latter from Ballard's insinuating influence. So little progress was made, and so much existential prevarication took place, that Babington slid towards the view that travel might indeed be the best option.

---

* In 1583 Sidney had been granted over £2,000 in recusancy fines, which he accepted while regretting the circumstances.

Mary, Queen of Scots, by G. Vertue. Her long custody in England became increasingly onerous

A word to Tindall who spoke to Poley, and Babington was quickly invited to the court at Greenwich to meet Walsingham.

By the end of May 1586, Walsingham and his aides expected Mary to write to Babington in her Whitsun mail. The strength of the government side against the ramshackle and hesitant plotters was further enhanced by the return of Gilbert Gifford to London. Although not all aspects of his Paris mission had been fully achieved, enough had been done for the immediate future. His cousin Gifford and Morgan had written to Savage, urging him to fulfil the matter of his sacred vow, and these two letters which another of his own were delivered to Savage's lodgings within a week of returning from Paris. Then he went to Chartley to the satisfaction of Paulet, and since the days were lengthening the two key men avoided meetings, especially since Mary was ill and her household occupied through the night. Even before Gifford arrived the halt to letters had ended, Paulet having got hold of the expected packet by 3 June. The size of it seemed to hint it was well worth waiting for, and the brewer himself candidly admitted he had got an extra £10 for his trouble. As Paulet noted, Nau's extended period of time in the house, ignoring midsummer walks or riding, had been well spent. He forwarded the packet express to London for Phelippes to decipher and, by the time it reached Walsingham again, Gifford was on his way to France. Now his intention was to protect his access to the anti-Jesuit English faction by helping Grateley write a short book attacking the Jesuits; to lure his cousin to England and to wring more details of the plot from Morgan.[3]

Waiting for Gifford to return, Phelippes had plenty to occupy him in the grinding business of deciphering at which he was such an adept. Mary's packet had nine enclosures, and a covering letter from Curll to the phantom courier 'Barnaby'. Phelippes deciphered this and on the back of the paper prepared a draft reply. Barnes ('Barnaby') was then instructed by him to go north to Burton taking two letters for delivery. Bringing him emphatically into the operation was a calculated risk and, indeed, no sooner was he on his way than he made an attempt to get in touch with Mary personally, with a misdated letter he omitted to sign. Since the brewer was in an obliging mood everything Barnes delivered reached Curll on the same night – 10 June. On the morning of 21 June an answer to 'Barnaby' was handed over by the brewer to Paulet. If the courier-agent was in Lichfield, eager to serve Mary, what could convincingly account for the delay as the packet went to London to be deciphered and was then returned to be given back to the brewer for delivery? Paulet pressed Walsingham not to be tardy with the packet which contained two letters – Curll's acknowledgement of 'Barnaby's' letter, and a somewhat veiled answer by Mary to the anonymous text. Curll asked 'Barnaby' to forward the reply and to ascertain the writer's name. Phelippes hankered after the same information, while guessing shrewdly that it had been Barnes.

These exchanges, movements and counter-thrusts were going on as Poley made the arrangements for Babington's first interview with Walsingham, who could hardly refuse to see him. Since he sought consent for his departure Walsingham was able to be cautiously civil, but of course he had no intention of sanctioning travel in exchange for their offers of service. The intention now was to fix the young man firmly into the inchoate plot and he would then either be arrested for plotting or forced to turn queen's evidence. Phelippes, in the mean time, was facing the dangers occasioned by the impulsive Barnes who seemed poised to wreck everything by his private initiatives. Retaining Mary's letter to the nameless writer, Phelippes forged a reply to Curll ostensibly from 'Barnaby', who was instructed to deliver it without additions. Mary's letter and the forgery were put in a packet and, to save time, Phelippes suggested to Paulet that the brewer could be omitted for once and the substitute used. Paulet was not inclined to take this up because it was a diversion and he was anticipating a 'greater matter'; nothing should interfere with it. Meanwhile, he sent a small packet to London which he thought was unlikely to be important. This reached Phelippes on 1 July and contained three notes; one was unaddressed, the second marked with the cipher and the third was a covering letter from Curll to 'Barnaby'. The anonymous item was for a tradesman in Nottingham and the other was for Anthony Babington.

The question now was whether the brittle resolve of Babington would hold and what to do if it faltered too dramatically. Leaving the country still seemed to be his best course and, with Salusbury's agreement, another approach was made to Poley. According to Tindall their intermediary would very much like to accompany them himself, but was held back by lack of money. As a Catholic he was bound with two sureties to present himself every twenty days at court. To overcome this Babington offered him £50 at once and indicated he would be pleased to have him as a companion. Poley's response was a message that Walsingham would see him again on 3 July, this time at his house at Barn Elms. This interview was as inconclusive as the first had been. The secretary wanted authentic details of what services Babington thought he might perform. He was also less cordial in his manner, although not hostile and he did say that Babington would have an interview with Elizabeth.[4] Given this the young applicant left in a reasonably optimistic mood, with plans already being formed for the sale of his property in Derbyshire. With all this in mind he returned to his lodgings, while Walsingham, who had set aside the notion of trying to buy him, called in Gilbert Gifford for a crisis meeting, the briefing being conducted by Phelippes.

Gifford had returned from Paris, having helped Grateley complete his anti-Jesuit diatribe. Walsingham was pleased and the text was in print with an alacrity that astonishes. It was about the wandering Savage that Gifford approached Babington in Hern's Rents, but the conversation quickly diverted to Ballard and herein Babington exposed the various hesitations of his friends. He thought now a small sanctioned group of six gentlemen might do the deed. He may even have begun the letter to Mary which set out the terms of the operation that he envisaged. To undertake it with conviction, what he wanted now as an assurance of its legality, and the prospect of substantial military support from Spain. Back came Gifford's retort that invasion was now a certainty, so this was no time to be idling with thoughts of going abroad. As for Mary – she had to know what was being wrought in her name, because, as Babington revealed, she very likely knew nothing and lived on hope. He added that he had letters for her waiting to be delivered, but so far he had not found a means.

The double agent now let Babington know that Mary had been urged to renew her correspondence with him. Therefore, it was likely that he would soon be receiving a letter from her, and when the courier turned up he could send a ciphered response that would set out the whole plan for her. Did he have a cipher? Yes. Then prepare a draft scheme, turn it into cipher and await the messenger. And this is what Babington did when Gifford left London the following day, 4 July, for Chartley, taking with him Mary's letter to 'Barnaby'. Babington wrote a remarkable letter, which, on the wave of urgency induced by his visitor, took him further into a plot from which he had hitherto held back through scruple and a lack of purposeful energy. With 'ten gentlemen and a hundred our followers', Mary was to be freed, while the *'tragical execution'* would be undertaken by 'six noble gentlemen, all my private friends'. Here his surge of enthusiasm outran what he knew to be the case – that only Savage of the six was a declared supporter of the assassination of Elizabeth. Still, he had no option but to suggest such a thing if the full implications were to be clear to Mary and, when she approved, any remaining objections would surely dissolve.

This lengthy text then had to be put into cipher, an exacting task not relished by Babington. With no assistance he had to set himself to do it and eventually succeeded. Then he added a striking and significant postscript seeking Nau's opinion of Poley. Since the government knew it would take him some time to complete, the royal letter from Chartley was held back until Wednesday evening, 6 July, when Phelippes sent George Gifford with the item marked). He was told to wait for a reply and return with caution when certain he was not being followed. It was after midnight that he sidled back and handed Phelippes three separate packets Babington had given him. Phelippes gave most attention to the one signed), and was correct to do so because it contained the detailed outline of what was envisaged. The draft copy went to Walsingham; the original to Chartley taken by Phelippes himself who set out the following night. He wrote to Walsingham on 8 July from Shilton, having run into a courier bound for London, that 'but for the extreme carelessness of the constables and contempt of some of them', he would have arrived sooner at Chartley to stay with Paulet. On arrival his first task was to see to the delivery of Babington's crucial letter, and this was done in the usual manner.[5]

There was a Scottish element in the Babington plot that never really meshed with the rescuing of Mary and the hope of sparking a general Catholic rebellion in England. Robert Bruce was dispatched by the Catholic Scottish nobles in the spring of 1586 to Spain to urge their petition for a subsidy of men and money. Philip thought him too sanguine about Scotland returning to Catholicism, but was sufficiently impressed to send him on to Mendoza and Guise. Extravagant optimism had long been John Ballard's flaw, but early in July even he was subdued by the lack of enthusiasm for revolt in northern England. Back in London he had talks with Babington and eventually suggested that the latter should take over leadership of the whole affair. This was dangerously flattering and Babington admitted later 'I entertained the discourse of it'. Ballard's presentation must have been exceptional since the younger man was much more given to reflection than action. Further, he agreed to take on the task only if Savage 'should surcease from presenting his intention'. In fact he appeared to have done this already, having faltered in his proclaimed intention. Ballard would go to France to find out from

Mendoza what Philip intended. On 18 July the king wrote to his envoy that Mary had risen in his estimation, 'not so much because of what she says in my favour (though I am very grateful for that too), but because she subordinates her love for her son, which might be expected to lead her astray, for the service of our Lord, the common good of Christendom, and that of England.'

Everything and everyone now focused on Mary. To rescue her from detention it was not envisaged that there would be any difficulty in choosing ten gentlemen from a list of Catholic gentry in Staffordshire and Derbyshire, although for the time being only Thomas Salusbury, full of gallant intention, could be counted as certain. When Gifford's name cropped up Ballard repeated the confident affirmations of Paget and Morgan, suggesting that if he could be traced then they might get him also to write to Mary for authority to press on. In fact he did find Gifford for several sessions, while Babington was besieged by Poley. Since that Sunday meeting with Walsingham, Poley had hung about scattering thoughts on what service Babington could do the secretary. In the hope of nudging him aside Babington flourished the latest letter from Morgan and this secured him a brief reprieve. yet within two days he was back with an embarrassingly commanding message to present himself again to Walsingham at Barn Elms in a week. This was perturbing because, as Ballard was now aware, the secretary was bearing down on them and all they could hope was that a meeting might curb his suspicions. There was even the pathetically optimistic thought that he might reveal what he knew. On Wednesday 13 July Babington took a boat with Poley for a meeting with Walsingham; every splash of the oars no doubt increasing his trepidation.

As ever Walsingham was politely unrevealing, seeking to draw out Babington after his own reference to Mary's clandestine correspondence. He said coaxingly that Babington should 'act with confidence' and speak freely. The man who had become Walsingham's cat's-paw was in a bemused state, but the secretary had found a way to test him. Walsingham had already used Thomas Rogers to try to track Southwell and Garnet and, unwilling to rely too much on Poley, he required Babington to take on the task – something not too difficult because Southwell's cousin Gage lodged at Southampton House. If Babington found the two Jesuits and did betray them he could have no other plot in mind. If the Jesuits, on the other hand, betrayed themselves to Babington, then that would be their fault and if Rogers was on hand to effect the arrests so much the better. Babington's return to London by boat was clouded by the strains that led him to question Poley and may even have given a hint of the duplicity he was reluctant ever to recognize. Needing to talk further he descended with his dilemma on Father Weston who knew nothing of the Babington plot, but plenty about Garnet and Southwell, whom for safety he had removed to his own lodgings, probably a house in Hog Lane, Norton Folgate, the property of Mrs Francis Browne.[6] Barely had he installed them than Babington appeared to agonize about his direction and conscience. Did the two Jesuits in another room overhear any of this and abruptly realize that their fate hung in the balance?

Babington still hankered for an escape abroad. To obtain a travel permit he had to perform certain services. How far could he go, he asked, in giving superficial information about fellow Catholics? Weston said simply that once confidentiality was breached Babington was doomed and after some general spiritual advice nudged him out. Weston, Garnet and Southwell promptly fled from London, eluding an off-guard Rogers who was summoned to report to Walsingham on 18 July. Babington delayed saying anything until he came up with a request for fuller authority. This he got peremptorily, and Rogers was told to collaborate with him. On 21 July it was probably Rogers who told his employer that he thought the confessional quarry might have retreated to Henley Park, the country house of Francis Browne, whereas in fact they had raced to the isolated home of Richard Bold.[7] Once employed by the Earl of Leicester, Bold had been converted by Weston and his home, Hurleyford, drew a distinguished Catholic company, including William Byrd. So, while Garnet and Southwell savoured a respite and plans were made for their mission, Walsingham's team was taken up with the final arrangements for Ballard's arrest and for tracing all Babington's associates. Only Poley was absent, having taken to his bed for three days to keep out of view. In this time Walsingham received various letters from his agents including the packet with the gallow mark □ from Phelippes (which meant only that it should be delivered with all haste). In it was the reply of Mary to Babington which Paulet exulted over; Walsingham meant to deal with Babington when Phelippes had returned to London. As for Weston – he was later spotted in London by Rogers and Sheppard, the keeper of the Clink who effected the arrest as Rogers ducked away. Weston spent seventeen years in captivity and was banished immediately after Elizabeth died. He died, almost blind, in Spain.

Ballard was apparently unruffled when Babington recounted just how far Walsingham had penetrated. He seems to have reasoned that governments before had mendaciously represented what was supposedly known so that naïve plotters would feel free to unburden themselves. Much more vexing was Morgan's attitude that Mary should not be implicated in the violent project – a futile piece of gallantry as it seemed. Someone would have to go to France to get a definitive statement of commitment from Mendoza. Mary wrote to him that the envoy chosen by the plotters should be given 'full recognition as though I had sent him myself'. The man chosen was Gilbert Gifford. The proposal to send him under a false identity with a passport made out to Mr Thoroughgood was put to him on Saturday 16 July and he asked for time to consider it. A night proved enough and the next day he revealed his reluctance, pleading urgent business in the country and sketching various impediments. Yet he remained in London until Thursday 21 June, when he presented himself at Hern's Rents. Now he said he would alter his plans and would cross immediately to France disguised as an employee of the French ambassador. This high urgency is odd, though he did go and very likely that night. Was it real or feigned? Was he anticipating arrests and did he fear that Walsingham would have to incarcerate him because he was a deacon along with the plotters?

Chapter Eight

Babington Snared

Babington's churning thoughts on power and action were still being floated before friends. Their meetings were held in ordinaries like the Three Tuns in Newgate Market, the Rye, the Plough or Ballard's haunt, the Castle, close to the Royal Exchange.[1] The fever of desperation prompted talk that was variously extravagant or absurd: an arson raid on the queen's ships anchored on the Thames; kidnapping Elizabeth, seizing Kenilworth Castle (the absent Earl of Leicester had kept weapons stockpiled there), and holding her prisoner until she sacked her ministers and adopted Catholicism as the state religion. To widen the scope of the plot potential sympathizers were sounded, including Edward Windsor, the suspect Lord Windsor's brother. Yet this ardent Catholic said merely he would 'endeavour what he could' – a muted and ambiguous line. Ballard, who had approached Lord Windsor, was evidently the fluent presence who inspired least confidence, and when the plot had been crushed and he begged to have all blame attached to him few demurred. For the time being he intended to lie low since he had likely been tailed on his return to London. This caution was sensible because Babington, under pressure, was envisaging something radical and dangerous. Ballard's plot was to be sacrificed like a pawn in chess so that a grander strategy could be developed.

At this juncture Poley reappeared to insinuate himself with the plotters. He was the contact who caused Father Weston to recoil 'as at an unpleasant smell', because of his obsequious manner. But Babington had so few options that he could not avoid asking him for another interview with Walsingham. The latter was poised to snap up Babington when Phelippes got back to London, so although the outline of 'a practice intended against her Majesty's person' was naturally interesting, Walsingham's response was muffled. He wanted a letter to show Elizabeth before he granted any interview and he took the opportunity to snap at the heels of the clandestine quartet of Douglas, Yardley, Garnet and Southwell, lately arrived from Boulogne. Father Southwell was hiding in the London residence of Lady Arundel and a letter of his, written on 25 July, apparently to the General of the Jesuits, actually passed through the hands of some of Walsingham's agents. Babington was in no position to suppress information, so he rehearsed the little he knew to Poley, then took him to supper.[2] Thomas Rogers found out about this, but having been selected to arrest Ballard on whom he had a lead, elected to stay at home, as he informed Francis Mylles. The two papist supper guests Rogers was expecting had thoughtfully sent a capon and two rabbits, so he guessed they might be bringing

Ballard as well. If he did not turn up attention should be focused on his favoured haunt – the Castle.

Rogers arranged for a young man called Painter to stand in for him, and to watch the supper party from another room. He suggested that Mylles, unencumbered by ciphering, should be at the Royal Exchange at eight o'clock, 'somewhat disguised', to meet someone who would report from Painter. If Ballard turned up he could easily be arrested in the Castle – 'most safe though it have two doors'. If he went instead to dinner with Rogers (known to Catholics as their trusted agent Berden, a man with some court influence), then Mylles would get a message at the Exchange and could, after the convivial meal, have him followed. As it happened Ballard did not appear at either supper, although Rogers did receive Robert Gage, who had recently seen the priest and given him shelter.

Walsingham's overarching control of colliding events was not unbreakable and he was not helped by a surge of agitated interest from Elizabeth. With the brusque authority that was her hallmark she wanted Mary's letter to Babington, disappointing in not being explicit, spiked with a postscript asking the names of her six would-be assassins (hitherto always referred to in a cipher mode that even defeated Phelippes).[3] The secretary thought that to convince even those who covertly sympathized with Mary but advanced nothing, a leading question about the method of murder would be more effecting. 'By what means do the six gentlemen deliberate to proceed?', in cipher:

$$\sigma\!\frown\!\!\sigma\eta \; //ao\varnothing\underline{\Lambda}+++\overline{V}\;\eight\;\Lambda17a\theta a\varnothing\varepsilon na//a\varnothing +++an1\overset{\perp}{\top}afo\varepsilon a\varepsilon$$
$$\overline{\mathrm{VsfV_{\Lambda}}}\;a+++a$$

At the end of the letter came the fake postscript asking to know the names. The problem was that Curll's letter written for Mary in cipher was too neat to allow these telling additions. So Walsingham had Phelippes copy out the entire letter, safe in the assumption that Babington would not be familiar with Curll's handwriting, and he would not know either that only Curll did Mary's ciphering. Arthur Gregory could seal the fake before it was sent to Babington on 29 July. The government kept the original.

The delivery was made, but a reply was not immediately possible so the serving man then retired, having been told he should call again in four days. Babington seems to have had no illusions about his skills in deciphering and he had two items to work on, apart from an anonymous note. The two were from Nau and, of course, Mary; that from her secretary being blessedly short, indicating that Poley was to be trusted, though perhaps a hint of mistrust is to be found in the phrasing. Then Babington had to begin the laborious task of deciphering the long royal letter and this proved a particular challenge to his low threshold of boredom. So much so that when Chidiock Tichborne turned up to see him, he was persuaded to take over the deciphering. While the work was in progress Ballard arrived, and the twists and turns of the next few days suggest that he was deeply perturbed at the way the whole quixotic enterprise was sliding forward. Weeks before, Sir Thomas Tresham of Rushton, a prominent gentleman, had threatened to denounce him, and despite the assertions of Conyers Read that the plot revealed a willingness on the part of

England's leading Catholics 'to rise in support of any invader who came against Elizabeth in the name of their faith', it was horribly clear to Ballard and Babington that this was nowhere near happening.

Walsingham's note to Babington, delivered on 30 July, allowed the recipient to do some investigative shuffling on the intentions of 'the principal practisers'. Concerned about what this meant Babington went to Poley and in their exchanges blurted out that he could bring down the government. The spy wanted to know the means for all that he could not think it lawful. Even so, if Elizabeth was not hurt he was ready to join them and Babington should go on with the coup. This settled Babington temporarily and he invited his interlocutor to Hern's Rents for the following morning. When they got finally to talk the next day as they walked in open fields, Poley offered the view that Babington should disclose everything to the secretary. The apparent naïvety of this disguises the advantage that would accrue to Poley himself; the rogue was in a happy position. They walked then to the Rose at Temple Bar where they found Ballard, Savage, Henry Dunne, Robert Gage and one or two others. Leaving them to go to Hern's Rents, Poley remarked to Babington that it was probably watched. To avoid arrest before the crucial meeting with Walsingham, when he would confess the plot, Babington should spend the night with Poley at the Garden outside Bishopsgate. (This could be the Garden Inn near Fleet Street, or more likely the Gardens, near the further end of Aldersgate where Tichborne had a house.)[4] That evening Poley provided and paid for a supper at the Castle – an expense he had later to justify. For the time being their actual whereabouts was not known to Walsingham and his men, and the disappearance of Babington, following Ballard, caused some collective government agitation. Phelippes was so afraid Babington had bolted that he wondered if he had fled to Staffordshire. If he turned up in Lichfield Paulet could have him arrested, or if necessary Phelippes was ready to ride there himself, so long as Walsingham gave him a bodyguard.

The secretary was worried, but not enough to send his right-hand man on such an errand. He wondered if Babington had been warned by Henry Dunne of the First Fruits office, a sometime follower of Sir Christopher Hatton, now high in Elizabeth's favour. Fleetingly, Walsingham even wondered if the queen herself had let slip something to alert the enemy or if the faked postscript had aroused suspicion. 'I look for Poley' he wrote, 'from whom I hope to receive some light' (3 August). Scarcely had he penned this than Phelippes wrote to him at court to brighten the picture with the news that Babington had remained in London all the time. He had been tracked down to Poley's, but instead of arresting him Phelippes held back because he understood his employer was expecting the stray the next day. However, he did want a warrant to use when necessary for the arrest and the search of Hern's Rents. Walsingham wrote from Richmond: 'these causes are subject to so many difficulties as it is a hard matter to resolve. Only this I conclude: it were better to lack the answer than to lack the man.'[5]

Staying with Poley after 30 July, Babington sent a serving boy to Hern's Rents the following day to direct any friends waiting there for him. The lad soon returned with Savage and Ballard, and a critical decision was made. Feeling that what they had wrought was disintegrating, and that their purpose was maimed, it was agreed that the original framework should be revealed at whatever cost to Ballard, who nobly agreed to the tactic. But while prepared to risk his own life he wanted nothing risked that would threaten Savage, and it was with this proviso in mind that Babington went back to Poley to seek to arrange another meeting with Walsingham. He declared he would reveal in detail as much of the conspiracy as he knew (little more than the secretary by now). In a cipher letter to Mary he wrote boldly, 'We have vowed and we will perform or die.' A nobler spirit might have tried to stop them, but Mary was content for the matter to go forward. Any hopes Babington entertained of winning the approval of Walsingham nearly expired when Poley returned to tell him that the secretary was too busy for an immediate meeting, but would allow him some time on Thursday morning from 8 a.m. Whatever Poley said, Ballard and Babington now envisaged a personal calamity, the whole tenor of affairs having shifted. They both decided that they should reveal everything for, by turning queen's evidence, they could safeguard each other and deliver up only such as Barnard Maude and George Gifford.

This was the conclusion reached on the night of 1 August. The next day they arrived at the decision that Ballard would write to Walsingham, sending the text by John Charnock. Simultaneously Babington would rehearse the whole matter to Poley, pressing him to gain them prompt access to the secretary. In talking to Poley he said there was a design to murder the Earl of Leicester, the favourite of Elizabeth, and then campaigning against Parma's army in the United Provinces. Remove him and Burghley to replace them by Catholics or pragmatists, and Elizabeth would be politically unfettered. She would soon be brought back to Catholicism and Mary, for whom Babington seems to have worked up a dreamy infatuation, would be released to her place in the succession. Before strolling out with Ballard and Savage, Babington left a paper for Poley to read – a copy of some of the principal elements from Mary's letter to him. The spy, who had feigned enthusiastic acceptance of Babington's thinking, was so absorbed in making notes from it that when the plotters returned he was caught. With a flourish (and no doubt a pang) he tore up what he had written, while guileless Babington declared that on Thursday he would himself show it to the queen and Walsingham.

Ballard, Savage and Babington stayed in conference the following day as Poley went to Richmond. When seen he said innocently that he had no idea that Babington was being hunted. He was lodging with him, came the explanation, so that he might instantly be at Walsingham's command. Far from wishing to evade the privy councillor, he was on the brink of revealing all he knew – something Walsingham no longer needed or wanted. He wrote to Phelippes and admitted that though 'Poley hath dealt honestly with me, yet I am loath to lay myself any way open unto him'. All he wanted now was Ballard's arrest 'which I have caused to be done by a warrant signed by the L. Admiral, for that I would not be seen in the matter'. Poley returned to London with wrenching news for the plotters: Elizabeth was indisposed and Walsingham had arrears of Irish business to occupy him all Thursday and Friday too. A Saturday interview did not dissipate a mood of strained unease as they went to join Gage and Dunne that evening at the Castle.

Their state of mind might have been panic if they had known that Mylles, alerted by Phelippes, was watching the house during the day, and when they arrived at the tavern Rogers took over. He followed when they left the premises, and from the shadows saw a serving man call at Poley's to collect a packet. Babington felt so fatigued he had no inclination to do more than add the date, 3 August, in cipher to a letter he had written two days before to Mary. The hidden watchers let the courier pass without a flurry and the next morning were rewarded for their patience when Ballard turned up. He was there even before Babington had quit his bed, lingering in the fitful hope that disaster might still be averted. With the warrant in his pocket Mylles delayed his own appearance until he entered the house and in a downstairs room arrested Ballard for being a priest. The fitfully sleeping Babington heard people entering the house, strange voices, a door closing and then silence. Suddenly his host burst in to deliver the news that Ballard had been taken, but the gloss he put on it was that, in an excess of enthusiasm, an uncurbed subordinate of the secretary had taken it upon himself to act. He thought Babington, now struggling into his clothes, should stay there while he went to the court to find out what was happening. However, Babington was by now rapidly losing faith in Poley's obviously limited power of negotiation and he rushed out to seek Tichborne at his lodgings. Having missed him here he went on to a barber's outside Bishopsgate and then hurried through Smithfield, meeting his friend there, only to find that he had injured his leg.[6]

Babington explained the accelerating disaster and then raced back to Poley's. When Savage arrived he was suddenly fired with the active animosity missing for so long and proposed an assassination attempt on Elizabeth. The ugly proposition, long resisted by Babington, was agreed to in desperation, and he handed over whatever items of jewellery and cash he had on him so that Savage could purchase suitable clothes to give him access at court. With Tichborne lame Charnock was to take his place and he was traced to St Paul's churchyard, agreeing then to the purpose. Returning to Bishopsgate there was still no news of Poley and, racked by fear, Babington penned the famous, haunted letter to him.[7] His other letter, the one directed to Mary and collected for Phelippes, proved rather limp. Having deciphered it and delivered a copy to Elizabeth at Richmond by his own hand, there was no denying that what had been 'so earnestly looked for by her Majesty' conveyed little of weight. Babington had ignored the infamous postscript specially prepared and said nothing of his associates. He was chiefly incensed by Maude's treachery and said he would keep Mary informed of the danger that arose from it as well as 'by what means we have in part prevented'. These were the overtures to Poley and, given the general undercurrent of suspicion about him among Walsingham's aides, it is not surprising that he too was held. (There is always the possibility of course that his arrest was to screen his activities for the government.) Poley's servant, Nicholas Dalton, was sent to the Counter in Wood Street off Cheapside on 6 August, but 'charged to have dealt treacherously', his employer fetched up in the Tower later in the month.[8] With Ballard also in the Counter and Poley gone, there was a risk that Babington might go into hiding or flee. To soothe insistent fears the government needed someone to keep in constant touch with him and their choice was John Scudamore. He was to deliver an explanatory letter that Ballard's arrest had been the result of a spurt of Richard Young's noted anti-Catholic zeal. The advice therein was to remain in company with Scudamore to avoid the same fate, so they went out to take a meal together. Towards its end Scudamore was handed a note and Babington seems to have been sufficiently alert to recognize Walsingham's hand. Rising to pay the bill he ducked out of sight and fled the tavern, leaving cloak and sword on the back of his seat; the jolt may, of course, have been deliberate.

He knew that Ballard had been sharing rooms with Robert Gage so, by now thoroughly agitated, he went there. Savage was there with Gage and was the first to flee while the other two changed clothes. They went then to Charnock's where Gage changed again and then they retreated hastily to St John's Wood, a remnant of ancient woodland that offered dense cover. Later, when asked why he took to the forest, Gage snapped 'For company'.[9] They were joined there by Barnewell and Dunne when the national alarm had been raised. Port authorities were quickly notified and messengers went about the south-east with descriptions. Given the undertow of support for them in North Wales and the north of England, it was judged that they would have eventually to take to the roads. As far as Mary and her household at Chartley were concerned Walsingham rapidly introduced a means of hemming them in. The clerk of the council, William Waad (Wade) had already been sent to confer with Paulet, and they had a meeting in a field early in August. When Waad returned to London formal instructions were sent to Paulet that Mary was to be temporarily moved to Tixall, the home of Sir Edward Aston. There was to be a strict guard to prevent news reaching her and in some measure her circumstances deteriorated because, in her absence, Curll, who was recently a father, and Nau were arrested and removed to London. Chartley was to be searched and every item of paper secured for scrutiny.

By the time written authority for this had been issued on 9 August, the first batch of plotters had been seized. Of Tilney, Tichborne and Savage, the last became the most important to the government because, without recourse to torture, he was induced to write a confession. Poley was also in custody, of course for cosmetic reasons, and writing his long narrative of dealings with Babington. The latter was still at large, but any hope of slipping over to France dwindled with their supplies. At length the fugitives had to move towards Harrow where the staunchly Catholic Bellamys lived in Uxendon Hall. A message reached the family, and Bartholomew and Jerome Bellamy turned up with food and replacement clothing. To complete the disguise they hacked off their long hair and stained their visible skin with walnut juice to reduce their chamber pallor. With the night they scuttled into refuge in the outbuildings of Uxendon, and when a suspicious local constable was persuaded to go away, seemed a little more secure. On Saturday 13 August a priest was at hand to hear confessions and say mass in the little secret chapel. The following day, however, came the sudden swoop that gobbled up fugitives and family; Bartholomew died on the rack and Jerome was executed.[10]

Walsingham had delegated the task of capturing these men, and he soon received a tart comment on the business from Burghley. Returning by coach to London from his country home in Hertfordshire, Theobalds (pronounced 'Tibbalds'), Burghley had noticed clusters of men standing at each alehouse. This was not exceptional, but if they were actually sheltering from rain, what kept them under the eaves at Enfield when the weather had cleared? Struck by this Burghley halted his progress to ask and was told they were waiting to take three men. When asked how three conspirators could be identified, one of the cluster said that one man had a hooked nose. Burghley asked then if there was anything else to identify him and was told no. To Walsingham he wrote: 'Surely, sir, whosoever hath the charge from you hath used the matter negligently, for these watchmen stand so openly in plumps as no suspected person will come near them, and if they be no better instructed but to find three persons by one of them having a hooked nose they may miss thereof. And thus a thought good to advertise you, that the justice that had the charge, as I think, may use the matter more circumspectly.'

Despite this rumble of criticism from his colleague who may have felt a twinge of envy that he had not been in on the matter, the destruction of the Babington Plot was a dramatic coup for Walsingham. The stumbling and fumbling of Savage, then Ballard linking with Babington and his friends, had been prodded into something much more significant with a compelling blend of effort and ingenuity. It did frighten the government for all the haphazard mode of the plotters. Foreign intervention was thought a real possibility, so trained bands were prepared along the south coast, and John Hawkins, then at sea, and Sir William Winter in the Medway, were ordered to be vigilant in their readiness to repell a French landing party. Lords lieutenants in the south of England were told to watch for a possible Spanish fleet. So there was a level of readiness that the radical interventionist grouping in the Privy Council, led by Walsingham and Leicester, thought was always necessary, at a time when the earl was trying to stay the Spanish hand in the United Provinces. Even so, there is a great difference between identifying all this, and saying, as some historians have, that Walsingham was the instigator of the plot. It was known by such as William Camden that through his spies the secretary had learned of almost every stage of it, but that he originated the plot is not merely unproven but also very doubtful.[11]

There was still much to be done and more arrests made. Thomas Salusbury went north for cover, but was captured with his inseparable companion Edward Jones. Thomas Habington proved more elusive, avoiding being taken for a month, while Edward Windsor was free for even longer. His name did not appear on a torture warrant marked down for the rack with Thomas Tipping and Habington until 23 December 1586. His testimony shows that Barnard Maude and Captain Jacques (Giacomo de Francisci) had been active as *agents provocateurs* and, like Poley, they were excluded as trial witnesses.[12] The Catholics realized with anguished horror how they had been baited, and the temporary imprisonment of Poley and the Antwerp-born Italian did nothing to ease their pain. Ballard's actions emerged in a series of examinations beginning on 8 August. By the time of the trial, over a month later, he was unable to walk and even a glimpse of him occasioned a long, incoherent statement from Anthony Tyrell. Babington, not being a priest, was treated more scrupulously and even cleverly. With Savage and Barnewell he was held at Hatton House before the trial, home of the vice-chamberlain, Sir Christopher Hatton, who conducted the crown case heard at Westminster in mid-September. Before that Babington wrote two long confessions, though only the second has survived, giving his full account of the plot and his links to Mary. Walsingham and Phelippes put to him a torrent of supplementaries, and the most unlikely plotter with a truly Catholic impulse to confess, had toiled for his own extinction.

The main thrust of all was finding a legal path to advance the execution of Mary. There was also hectic state activity verging on a terror because Southwell and Garnet had not yet been captured, although Weston had. Even someone as well protected and favoured as William Byrd had his home searched. Nau and Curll were lodged with the secretary in the charge of Francis Mylles. The letters and documents seized at Chartley (the task for which Waad had been paid £30) went to Windsor, where they were pored over by Phelippes. Yet there was nothing in them that could be produced in court for the maximum effect to show absolutely that the plot had Mary's approval. The famous letter from her to Babington never reached him of course, because he received, then burned, the doctored variant prepared by Phelippes. The original was shown to Curll to prompt him to attest that the decipher/recipher was genuine. Mary had had no part in the minutiae of planning, but her desire for the elimination of Elizabeth is not disputed, and her silence on the plot was at once understandable and fatal to all concerned.

The trial, which began on 13 September 1586, came as a great shock to Catholics.[13] It was especially bitter for old John Gifford, who, after the first day's disclosures, sought comfort from Phelippes. He had been stunned to hear the crown clerk read the indictment of John Savage, naming as conspirators Dr William Gifford and Gilbert Gifford. Walsingham had certainly been angered by the latter's 'sudden humour of estranging himself' and, it seems, did wonder for a time if his agent had betrayed him. This unpleasant thought was lingering when Gilbert Gifford wrote from Paris to ask that his retreat from the action should not be taken 'sinistrously'. To win back good opinions of himself Gifford wrote, 'The answere of diverse Catholick English Gentlemen to a certain seditious book veiled with the name of D. Allen.' It sought to persuade Europe that English Catholics were loyal and contented, and was introduced with a letter supposedly 'From a Jesuit in London', addressed to Robert Persons, saying that it was beyond belief that Allen

William Stafford clearing himself

could have defended the renegade Sir William Stanley in print. Persons is cheekily asked to expose such a thing as an impudent forgery. Perhaps it was this literary device that finally persuaded Elizabeth to settle a pension of £100 a year on him. Unfortunately for the beneficiary – who now called himself Jacques Collardin – in December 1587 he was recognized in company with an English whore in Paris, some months after his ordination at Rheims. Arrested leaving the brothel, he was held '*ex carcere Épiscopali*', where in mid-August 1588 he made a confession. The most obvious question that arises from the available printed Latin version is how much weight should be attached to its claims when he tilted his reported actions as an agent to try to satisfy his interlocutors; there is even a claim that he had personally intended to kill Elizabeth.[14] While in prison Gilbert was visited by Henry Caesar, a brother of Dr Julius Caesar, sent by Walsingham to try to find out if Gifford had become a double agent.

For the main Babington conspirators, some of whom were showing outward signs of the excruciating indignities visited on them, the trial was swift. They were condemned to death with the brutal rider that Elizabeth and her ministers could increase the severity of the sentence in any way they chose. The first cluster of executions took place on 20 September at St Giles's; Ballard, Babington, Barnewell, Savage, Tichborne, Tilney and Habington died.* The rope of the noose for Savage broke so that he was still alive as they dismembered his body. Many who watched were shocked to see young men treated so vilely and privy councillors noted the mood. The settled estates of Babington passed to his brothers, while all other goods and lands went to Ralegh as Elizabeth claimed only a clock.[15] Although Edward Habington was executed, his brother Thomas remained in the Tower until 1593. Their sister Dorothy held that priests had been 'the cause of her brother Edward's overthrow'. Leaving the court she went to the family home to take positive steps to discourage yet more priests from seeking shelter at Hindlip – and still later was converted herself. Richard Bellamy would also have been executed, but broke out of prison to escape to Germany, where he was later recaptured. He was handed over in Stade to William Milward, who delivered him to the captain of the *Swallow*, John Postok, for transport to England. He was then held almost continuously in prison, although he was able to buy the occasional period of freedom.

As for Walsingham, recovering from an abscess or boil that had driven him to bed, he was only concerned with Mary's own faltering health might delay her trial or even make it superfluous. The severities Elizabeth had mentally stored up for her rival were not enough to satisfy him and he manufactured another jolt as his dark mood was made more extreme by the suffering and death of Sir Philip Sidney, fighting in Leicester's army in the United Provinces. Among those involved by the secretary was William Stafford, the unruly brother of Sir Edward Stafford, and the latter's wayward Catholic former servant, Michael Moody. Chamber accounts

---

* The fourteen were divided into two groups of seven 'and dragged on hurdles in exactly the same alignment on two consecutive days'. The first group suffered the full penalty while the second only hanged: Salusbury, Henry Dunne, Edward Jones, John Travers, Charnock, Gage and Jerome Bellamy.

The processional hurdles of the type that delivered the Babington plotters to execution are clearly shown

The execution of Mary, Queen of Scots, February 1587. Walsingham's clandestine operations had foiled the royal plotter, and her beheading was his triumph

between 1580 and 1584 show that Walsingham signed warrants to pay Moody for letters carried between London and Paris. But by 1586 he was in squalid Newgate gaol, probably for debt, and there he was visited by William Stafford.

Shortly before Mary's trial Stafford called on Chateauneuf, the French ambassador, to rehearse his woes. He was particularly indignant that Leicester, now temporarily back in England, had shifted his detestation of Sir Edward to him. From this the chat shifted inevitably to Mary and the defiant notion of killing Elizabeth. Stafford's choice for the hired mercenary to do it was Moody, who was then visited in prison by Leonard des Trappes, the ambassador's secretary. It was an ill-advised excursion since Elizabeth was told and ordered his arrest. Burghley, Leicester, Hatton and William Davison, now a principal secretary with Walsingham, were told to interview Chateauneuf, who agreed that William Stafford had put up a proposal. Although he claimed he had spurned it, nevertheless he was confined in his residence until the execution of Mary in February 1587. It was an extremely effective way of placing a barrier between the ambassador and his king at the critical moment when Henri III might have been roused to intervene. As for des Trappes – he admitted being persuaded by Stafford to meet Moody and that when he told the ambassador, Stafford was barred from the embassy. Moody said much the same as Stafford, who had little to gain unless he was put up to it by Walsingham to block the French. The minister and Elizabeth did apologize to Chateauneuf when Mary was dead. Walsingham even trumped her corpse by having Sidney's long-delayed and lavish funeral in London on 16 February 1587. Any weeping was to be reserved for a Protestant hero.[16]

Chapter Nine

More Spanish Practices

The 1570s saw a continual, logical shift of correspondents in foreign affairs from Burghley to Walsingham. In terms of numbers of correspondents the key year was 1576 when Walsingham overtook his colleague. Yet the Lord Treasurer maintained a powerful interest in a manner that, as has been mentioned in connection with Robert Bowes, did not always please the secretary. In 1577 it is possible to get a revealing glimpse of how intelligence matters abroad could impinge on the broader framework of foreign policy.

In that year agitation in the Low Countries was seen temporarily to be contracting. The new governor of the Spanish Netherlands, Don John of Austria, was conciliatory towards his subjects and also Elizabeth. Nearing the end of June, however, it was reported that a packet of letters in cipher, addressed by Don John and his secretary to Philip II, had been snatched in Gascony and forwarded to William of Orange and the Estates General. The task of deciphering them was given to a skilled cryptanalyst previously used by Walsingham, Philip van Marnix Ste Aldegonde, Orangist patriot, and before the end of July what was happening was known both in London (from Dr Rogers) and Brussels.[1] The contents themselves were soon widely available, the Estates having a resumé printed in seven

Don John of Austria, 1545–78

languages; Leicester's copy is in the British Library. It disclosed that Don John's friendly professions were a ruse to mask a deeper belief that if Holland and Zeeland could be regained by force, the conquest of England thereafter would be a simple matter. Although any danger to England was temporarily diminished by the departure of Spanish troops from the Netherlands that year, and Don John's failure to conclude a peace with the Dutch, he was regarded with suspicion spiked with hate in London. The hostility was so great that the triumvirate may have prepared a secret scheme for his murder. Unfortunately the details are skimpy and involve two men with blemished reputations. The first was the Bolognese court musician, Alfonso Ferrabosco (I), who in 1577 was touched by a drama (robbery and murder) in Philip Sidney's household.[2] By 1578 Ferrabosco was trumpeting his loyalty to Catholicism while in service to the Cardinal of Lorraine. The papal nuncio in Paris, Anselmo Dandino, called him 'a spy and complotter' even so. In August Dandino wrote to the Cardinal of Como in Rome that Ferrabosco planned to leave for Italy in the company of Egremont Radcliffe, whose murky involvement in the Northern Rebellion has been noted. After its failure he escaped to Spain, but ventured home in 1575 when he was arrested and sent to the Tower. His release in 1578 was very likely the result of a deal with Walsingham. The Italian did depart carrying money from Elizabeth to sources in Lombardy, Venice and Rome; Radcliffe stayed behind and was arrested in Flanders. He was condemned and then executed in December for 'having purposed to murder Don John'. Since he had only left England again in May it is reasonable to suspect he was commanded by the triumvirate. A political tract by him was published that year; a translation from French, it was dedicated to Walsingham.

Don John and Thomas Stukeley (see Chapter 3) were counted two prongs of the hostile forces that might attack England. A third was James Fitzmaurice, who had been involved in various Irish uprisings, last sighted in Portugal by the intelligencer Botolph Holder. Fitzmaurice's effort, acquiring a vessel manned in Portugal, then landing with one Jesuit priest in Dingle Bay in 1579, was a fiasco, whatever his intention. But Walsingham always took any hints of a possible Spanish invasion of Ireland very seriously, being convinced that the enemy would one day muster something that was a true threat. Hence his attention in 1580 when three English merchants in Spain all sent him intelligence about elaborate naval preparations. And hence, no doubt, Mendoza's call to Philip II in the following year to watch all Englishmen trading in the country. Was he tipped off by someone like Lord Henry Howard?

Traditionally the north coast of Spain was safer than Andalucía for English traders.[3] Even so, those merchants prepared for risks were drawn to the more prosperous southern markets because the return cargoes were more varied and had a wider margin for profit. Holder remained in Portugal, John Donne (or Done) in La Coruña, while Roger Bodenham, who requires some attention as an informed source, was in Seville. The city was then the largest port in Spain and specifically noted by Mendoza for action by the Inquisition, while at the mouth of the River Guadalquivir was San Lucar de Barrameda, where the patron of the merchant colony was the Duke of Medina Sidonia. Bodenham, who could also be found in San Lucar, had a Spanish wife as well as a female cousin in attendance on the

Robert Dudley, Earl of Leicester, 1532(?)–88. Leicester used his agents to strengthen his own position as an invaluable privy councillor, and his alliance with Walsingham reaped political benefits for both

English-born Countess of Feria. A kinsman of Sir James Croft, himself now an enemy of Leicester, Bodenham was a Merchant Adventurer and had first offered his services to Burghley, but he wrote as well to the earl, and from 1581 was regularly sending information to Walsingham. The man's unpopularity with the majority of the English community must betoken something not quite right about him even so, and it has recently been noted that he 'steered an ambiguous course through the muddy waters of Anglo-Spanish intelligence and espionage'.[4]

Clearly, not every Englishman in Spain was a patriot. The unlucky John Donne (not the poet) was denounced as a spy by another Englishman, a merchant's factor living in San Sebastian. Yet Donne's value to Walsingham was not over despite this career hiatus, for as soon as he was released he moved back to England and wrote a detailed report on Spanish shipping in the northern ports. At much the same time the London merchant, Thomas James, was arrested for going to Mendoza's London residence to attend mass, and when released he moved to Spain, spending much of his time there from then on. He tarnished his name further by translating the writings of the bustling Father Robert Persons into Spanish. His brother, Francis James, who had himself once lived in Spain, remained in business as his partner in Bread Street and it was through him that the erratic government spy, based in St Jean de Luz, Edmund Palmer, was paid in the 1590s.[5] An opportunistic double agent, Palmer maintained a career of duplicity for far longer than he should have been allowed.

Years before that curious situation it was from Lisbon that Walsingham had news of a notable development. Not only did Philip suddenly close all Spanish ports to English merchants in the mid-1580s, but in December 1585 an English trader landing at Dartmouth reported a distinct pattern in maritime activity. To find out more Walsingham picked Anthony Poyntz, a sometime student of the Inner Temple who, despite his well-placed family,* had found a troublesome niche for himself on the other side of the law. There had been a clutch of felonies, including highway robbery, and a rather fortunate pardon in 1581. From a spy master's cynical viewpoint Poyntz was raw material; educated, but ultimately expendable.

During the early part of Leicester's difficult expedition to aid Dutch rebels (and incidentally cap his striking career), Poyntz was employed to spy. The beleaguered earl's mistake with him was to part with the hefty sum of £100 before any ventures into enemy lines – a rather typical example of Leicester's misreading of character and purpose. There was also a confusion between Walsingham and his political ally over the sending of Poyntz to Spain, and in any case the latter's departure was delayed when Sir Thomas Heneage (then married to Anne Poyntz, the spy's sister) sent him to England with urgent letters from Leicester to Elizabeth. Doubtless Poyntz preferred this since it involved less effort and less danger, but by December 1586 he had been directed to Paris, ostensibly to spy on Lord Paget and his son William, who was a first cousin once removed.[6] In addition he was supposed to spy on Mendoza, but, with the slick ease of his profession, confessed instead to the ambassador what he was employed for and even flourished a royal warrant for expenses as proof. In mid-December he wrote to Walsingham: 'My sickness hath hindered me that I cannot have so often access to such persons as I would deal with notwithstanding I have been twice . . . with Morgan, and oftener would be if I had my health. I do find him a busy fellow although he be enclosed. I have desired him, that if he have any matters of importance in England that he would trust me withall.' Given Morgan's dealings so recently with Gilbert Gifford, there is something almost hilarious about Poyntz's presentation. He went on, 'The like offer I have made to my Lord Paget, who told me he had good affiance in me and said he thought I would not be the ruin of him . . . I will not overmuch press him lest he suspect me, with Mendoza I will deal in like manner that I may know their friends in England, for doubtless they have good intelligence from some persons of much account.'[7] Guess or not, Poyntz was correct in this.

When Poyntz eventually arrived in Spain it was with a recommendation from Mendoza. But, after a brief visit to Madrid, he returned to Paris and then moved to the Spanish Netherlands in January 1587. It was Sir Edward Stafford who wrote from Paris to Walsingham with news of the meeting between Poyntz and the leading English exile, Sir Francis Englefield. He warned that while in Spain Poyntz had trippingly declared that either through his own efforts or those of his sister Anne, he could secure Elizabeth's death for 4,000 crowns. In fact both sides watched this braggart warily and Philip II put it to Mendoza that 'a very bad

---

* Sir Nicholas Poyntz, his father, had strong Dudley connections.

opinion was held of him here by all the trustworthy English Catholics'. He was left unmolested to see whom he would contact.

Walsingham favoured a more tangential approach to the enemy and his headlong agents faltered. One way was through Philip II's Italian territories, and there his plucky intelligencer was Anthony Standen, whose lengthy service allowed him to build a significant cluster of contacts. The tall blond scion of a Surrey recusant family, early in his career he had served Mary.[8] Darnley's murder and Mary's eventual imprisonment caused him to stay abroad after being sent on a mission to Charles IX of France. Standen managed to acquire various pensions, though how they were ever paid to such a nomad is a mystery. Equally teasing is how he managed to maintain his contacts with Mary who, for a time, was taken up by the thought of James VI marrying the Grand-Duke Francesco's eldest daughter, Eleanor. He was employed by Mary from 1582–5 in Florence, yet immediately was preparing to shift to Walsingham's service, if he had not already done so. During the time up to Mary's execution, Walsingham was never entirely satisfied that he was trustworthy, even if willing to use his material. The adjustment of the secretary's perception came in the winter of 1586 when Standen was visiting Flanders. With Poyntz proving so erratic and useless, Standen had to be ready to take an important position in Spain and Portugal, employing his new false identity as Pompeo Pellegrini.

His methods of gathering information were commonplace; talking to sailors (always prone to fabulation), merchants, travellers and diplomats, some of whom could be bought. One connection he nurtured was with Giovanni Figliazzi, Florentine ambassador to Spain, who observed activities at Philip's court. Standen also thought it worth sending an agent to Lisbon (newly under Spanish control), a Fleming whose brother was a servant to the Marquis of Santa Cruz, the Grand Admiral of the Spanish fleet. His assignee was triumphantly vindicated by the astonishing letters he sent to Standen in Florence with the connivance of Figliazzi. The 300 crowns Walsingham had transferred through the Corsini bank to the spy could not have been better spent.[9] Confirmation of this came when the Fleming obtained an inventory of the admiral's which listed ships, forces and stores needed to defeat England. Since Santa Cruz never belittled the enemy the figures were startling, and with such an item Walsingham was for a time as well informed as many preparing the Armada. When Figliazzi returned to Florence in February 1587, Walsingham began a correspondence that continued for the next few years. It was done at the prompting of Standen who, early in 1588, went himself to Madrid and Lisbon. Six months or so after this he was back in Florence where he found letters from Elizabeth restoring him to favour. His reward for proving his worth as a spy was enhanced by a pension of £100, exactly the sum saved by Elizabeth when Gilbert Gifford was arrested.

Walsingham was immensely fortunate to have another agent who was outstandingly conscientious. A grain and sundries merchant, Wychegerde, orginally from Germany, sent a report on Drake's eruption into Cádiz in late August 1587, though he had every reason to feel aggrieved because one of the ships that had been sunk carried his corn. Only very belatedly did he receive any thanks from a hard-pressed secretary who kept him constantly moving to spy on Spanish-held towns, camps and garrisons in the Low Countries. In one dramatic incident he was seized by marine thieves who snatched his commodities, money and clothes, leaving him to be released in Boulogne in his underwear. Still undaunted he kept Walsingham informed of Spanish successes due to Parma and their problems, doing this by moving through a lawless environment where no one was safe. He plodded through saturated fields, and clambered over ditches and dykes to count Spaniards, forwarding his ciphered reports to London. His head-count allowed that Parma had some five thousand Spaniards, Walloons, Germans and Italians; the previous over-generous guess by Leicester (likely inflated for his own face-saving purposes) had been eighteen thousand. Wychegerde was clearly impressed by these battle-hardened veterans. 'They maintain great order' he reported, 'their chief strength lies in the carefulness of their watch and the prudence of their methods by day and by night.' Ironically, no one in London was inclined to believe his data, though their accuracy was confirmed in Parma's secret correspondence with Philip. Parma's intelligencer Ascanio Cinnafarino was no counter to Wychegerde and no help to Hugh Owen, whose career might have developed like Standen's.

Walsingham did not manage to penetrate Parma's correspondence, but what information he got was augmented by Prince Maurice of Nassau, about whom the young Robert Cecil had recently been so caustic in a letter to Burghley. In entertaining his princely Roman captive, Marzo Colonna, he picked up papal gossip and passed the material to London. News did still seep through from Spain as well, and after the high turbulence of the summer of 1588, Nicholas Oseley was rewarded with a London lease 'in respect of his good service heretofore in Spain, in sending very good intelligence thence'.* In June 1588 someone working for Walsingham managed to filch a copy of a broadside 'Declaration' being printed in English at Antwerp for distribution with the landing Spanish army. Essentially it was an abstract by Cardinal Allen of his 'Admonition' which had denounced Elizabeth as a female tyrant and said that since Philip would free England all should rally to Parma on his landing. As the Armada sailed from Lisbon, Walsingham was bed-ridden, apparently waiting for an epileptic seizure. Hence it was not he, but Burghley who managed to secure a copy of the broadside by Pedro de las Salas, '*La Felicissima Armada . . .*'. Hitherto the Spanish had made real, if unavailing efforts to conceal their plans, to the point that Parma became convinced that the enterprise was doomed the moment that secret emerged. Yet here was this detailed listing of the components of the Armada, men and materials, available in Italian, Dutch and French for obvious propaganda purposes. Burghley ordered an English translation, but used his own Spanish folio edition to note the casualties of the enemy and the ships lost in the serial confrontation. The translation when it appeared was harnessed as a piece of English counter-propaganda, for it served as a striking reminder at home and abroad of what was achieved against great odds.[10]

Burghley was also responsible for 'The copie of a letter sent out of England to Don Bernardino de Mendoza'. A clandestine propaganda piece, it was accurately

---

* Oseley (or Ousley) had watched Malaga smuggling ciphered messages to England in wine-casks. In 1586 he had been under suspicion, but he continued his reports up to April 1588.

identified as the Lord Treasurer's effort in early November 1588 by Marcantonio Messia, an informer for Spain in England. It purports to be a report written by a Catholic layman who laments the failure of the Armada. A fictive device of modern literature was anticipated by Burghley on the title page which declares the text to have been found among the papers of Richard Leigh, a real seminary priest recently executed and so not available to contest the matter. The notion put forward is that the failure of the Spanish fleet was due to a flawed appraisal of English strength, and the sublimely unjustified expectation that English Catholics would rise against Elizabeth. In effect this was Burghley delivering a heavy swipe at Mendoza who maintained in print the somewhat leaky, even bizarre idea that the Armada had been a success. Even as it was being printed, Burghley was sent a copy of another false report by Mendoza and was immediately goaded into a reply. His contempt for the enemy is understandable, for the collective efforts of the Privy Council and the English fleet had achieved more than many at home and abroad had thought possible. It may even have stirred some wonder among the participants for Lord Admiral Charles Howard had previously complained with a sense of foreboding that while Philip II knew all that was going on in England, Elizabeth was unwilling to spend any money to counter this effort.

As a result of the special position he had contrived by his work and success, with unrestricted access to England's great men in politics, Horatio Palavicino was a particular target for spies. Mendoza was keen to tap his expansiveness and to pry further into his correspondence. In 1587 he succeeded again, forwarding abstracts of the more revealing items to Philip. A particularly tart comment therein seemed to express Elizabeth's high displeasure at the monstrous expense of propping up the Dutch through the generally ill-directed and spasmodic efforts of the beleaguered Earl of Leicester, in the United Provinces with his faltering army. The lure of peace terms to her, whatever the antagonism to them among the bellicose faction of the Privy Council, was almost irresistible, so it has been suggested that what fell into Mendoza's eager hands, did so out of policy. The Spanish got closer to Palavicino the following year by squeezing an agent into his household. It was the result of the last gasp effort of the ailing Santa Cruz who had found the submissions of the three Portuguese in the service of the exiled pretender to the Portuguese throne, Dom Antonio, lacking specificity. George Stocker, too, had gone secretly to England, but he was captured and then repeatedly tortured, so that although he made a notable escape to Brussels and a Spanish pension, he was painfully and permanently crippled.

Then Santa Cruz happened upon Messia, like Palavicino and Battista Spinola a Genoese, but unlike them a failure in trade.[11] It was the usual story of crumbling finances leading to espionage. His misfortunes stirred the hope that his countrymen in very different circumstances in England might be compassionate, so he arrived in London in the spring of 1588. Palavicino, and his two business executives Francesco Rizzo and Giovanni Battista Giustinian, did meet him, but they were not enthusiastic about funding him when his business efforts stumbled and his finances took on the aspect of his name. He was courting arrest if he stayed, but lacked the wherewithal to flee; Philip II had therefore to underwrite his efforts, having considered 'it would be well to do something for this man'. He seems to have been proved correct for a time since Messia saw Palavicino frequently and, loquacious in his own tongue, the latter scattered gossip like low-value coins, as well as more useful material that was supposed to remain secret. This was shifted to Mendoza through French diplomatic channels for Chateauneuf had no reason to feel warmly towards Elizabeth and Walsingham, who had bruised his dignity and violated his sense of diplomatic decorum. In May 1588 Palavicino voiced aspects of secret English plans to counter the Armada army. The following February an attempt was made to mislead Messia deliberately, when military preparations for the Counter-Armada to Portugal were acknowledged but claimed for other destinations. Whether Messia was convinced is in doubt because he had already seen a report in Palavicino's home about the best landing places in the country.

For Mendoza the observations and comments of this well-positioned agent on English public attitudes to the war were especially valuable. Because he held Messia in such esteem he continued to dole out funds to him. But the improvident spy was never able to consolidate his own finances, and when, in February 1589, Palavicino sprang upon him a plan to send him to Spain as an intelligencer, he could not refuse to go. To satisfy Mendoza simultaneously he hired two Genoese, Scipione Borgoni and Eliano Calvo, to take over his London work. Ostensibly Messia was in Spain to arrange the ransom and return of Armada prisoners – men lucky enough to have survived the nightmare of shipwreck on the Irish coast, followed by the brutal pursuit of Sir Richard Bingham. His new intelligence task as a double agent was to investigate Spanish attitudes to their defeat and the likelihood of a follow-up. So Messia inched along the espionage tightrope, contriving to serve two masters until, on the eve of his return to London, he died.

Mendoza's resourceful efforts were hampered by deteriorating eyesight and he risked a new surgical technique to deal with his cataracts. His principle advantage was that money could buy almost anything, and there were plenty of English Catholic refugees desperate for money in Paris and the Low Countries. Prior to the Armada they had shown their gratitude by giving estimates of English naval strength, port facilities, armaments and so on, expressing their profound hope that Philip would win. Especially useful to Mendoza were Lord Paget, Charles Paget, Charles Arundel, the Earl of Westmorland, Thomas Throckmorton, an agent of Philip II's since 1582, and Thomas Morgan. (Both Paget and Morgan have been viewed with suspicion by Catholic historians.) Other sources were Pedro de Zubiaur, who had become friendly with Sylvanus Scory, a merchant called Copcott and William Bodenham, a ship-owner based in Dunkirk. There were also many anonymous sources in England (mostly in ports), as well as in France, to add to the ambassador's store of knowledge.[12]

Chapter Ten

Death of a Spy

The embassy in Paris during the 1580s with its resident, long-serving ambassador, commanded much attention in London. Not only was it a channel for information required for diplomacy in peace and war, it was also a narrow window on to the hectic, random activities of the many exiled English Catholics who forged links with the strongest Catholic powers, as well as Scotland and the papacy. Walsingham and his aides were constantly alert to the tense jumble of challenges and plots put up by exiles variously cursed with sustained personal rivalries and raw grudges. There were English (and Welsh) rebels in France and the Low Countries, disgraced activists who had fled the threat of prison, torture and the gallows; and there were also the reluctantly disaffected who clung to dim hopes of a royal pardon and an accommodation with Elizabeth. Among their hosts was the powerful and busy Duke Henri of Guise, committed to crushing the French Huguenots, with Philip II as his pay master.[1] Guise was also projecting a plan to invade England in which he intended to take part and, although it foundered in the autumn of 1583 when given away by a terrorized Francis Throckmorton, it sprang up again with the Babington Plot which was meant to spark a Catholic rebellion in England to chime with an uprising in Scotland. There, a friend of Guise, Esmé Stuart, sieur d'Aubigny, had become a dynamic role-model for the youthful James VI. This Frenchman's ascendancy 'at once suggested itself as a possible instrument to recover the British Isles for the Holy See'. So did the energetic activity of the Jesuits in Scotland in the first half of the 1580s.

Although it was comparatively easy for London to control secret agents in Paris (easier than Edinburgh certainly), there were ruptures among the principal projectors of foreign policy and those sent abroad to act for them. Hence, Walsingham had to allow for the obstructive truculence towards him of Sir Henry Cobham, ambassador until 1583 when he was replaced. Things began more equably with his successor Sir Edward Stafford, who had been clearly briefed and waited to develop his own notions on espionage. His high self-esteem and unresolved desire to control all intelligence matters in Paris taxed Walsingham's patience and led to some cool, even gruff, exchanges. By the end of 1584 the principal secretary wanted a responsible, loyal agent of his own in the city to bypass an ambassador who could not be jettisoned. The arrest of Thomas Morgan there that year led to the dispatch of William Waad in March 1585, with a mission to secure the extradition of Mary's agent for plotting. Waad failed in his representations to the

French court and paid for his temerity in seeking a Catholic's expulsion when, on the return journey to England, he was assaulted by the Duc d'Aumale, acting for Guise.

When Thomas Rogers (alias Berden) was sent over by London he delivered his reports indirectly, skirting the embassy. Horatio Palavicino, who received them, also paid him. Because of these clear-sighted submissions, the Walsingham-Leicester grouping on the Privy Council increasingly regarded Stafford as a liability – at the very least unsound. Viewed so and clearly alert to it, the ambassador was too much inclined to rely on his own employees like his secretary William Lyly (the elder of the two brothers of that name – the younger was at school with Christopher Marlowe in 1579–80) and his finance assistant, the recusant Michael Moody. Stafford found it natural to expostulate to Burghley, who himself had a lengthy connection with Lyly's older brother John, the playwright in service to Burghley's son-in-law, the Earl of Oxford. The envoy was undoubtedly riled that as a diplomat he got less attention, as he claimed, than double agents like Charles Paget who 'hob-nobbed with French politiques', William Parry and Gilbert Gifford.

The ambassador's uneasy frame of mind was not helped by veiled hints (possibly from Palavicino) that his confidence was actually being betrayed by both William Lyly and Moody to Thomas Morgan. In the event, Moody was eventually dismissed and by January 1587 he had fetched up in prison in London and there remained for three years. Yet Stafford went on doggedly deflecting talk of Lyly whom he declared (rather unconvincingly of a secretary), 'knoweth no more of me and my doings . . . than the Pope of Rome knoweth; nor dealeth with any papers of writings of mine'. But Lyly remained under suspicion and in the autumn of 1585 he was sent back to England to be examined by a committee representing the Privy Council. Nimbly avoiding the pitfalls of such scrutiny he disguised sufficiently well the extent of his dealings with the engaged exiles that lack of evidence prevented any case being brought against him. Stafford went on bemoaning his absence and, reluctantly, in January 1586, Walsingham agreed to let Lyly go back to Paris. However, to offset any threat arising from this, be began doctoring material for Stafford in the firm belief that the envoy would be selling to a foreign bidder in order to pay off his rising gambling debts. It was a justified precaution because in April Stafford accepted a payment for communicating material to Charles Arundel. The money was from Guise, and Arundel's Spanish contact was Don Bernardino de Mendoza. He was at last linked to the imprisoned Mary, and on 20 May she began her vital and risky series of negotiations with him. Her sometime realm was also stirring with Catholic sympathies and, in that spring, Robert Bruce, a secretary then of James Beaton, exiled Archbishop of Glasgow, was sent by the Catholic nobles of Scotland on an important mission to Spain.[2] Philip II thought him too sanguine in his hope of bringing Scotland back into the papal fold, but impressed by his ability and good faith, sent him to Paris again to talk to Mendoza and Guise.

Into the clutter of unstable allegiances centred on Paris, Walsingham needed to send a new resourceful spy – Bruno having removed to Germany and around midsummer 1586, Roger Walton arrived to worm his way into the confidence of Father Derbyshire and other leading Catholics. If there was a whiff of Rome about a spy so much the better, and it was this, I believe, that led to the employment of the young Marlowe whose contact with the younger Lyly may have been the clinching element in the decision. By accident or design he must have made the acquaintance of covert Catholics within Cambridge University, where on a scholarship to Corpus Christi he had taken his BA and was now preparing for his MA. An unfamiliar face to the myriad watchers on the roads, Marlowe could travel with special letters, and with other students who were absconding in increasing numbers to Rheims and other European universities. But for him I believe it was to Paris first (he was fluent in Latin and might have picked up some French from Huguenot refugees in Canterbury), to spy on the embassy. His brief could have been to monitor movements in and out, while eavesdropping on the conversations of Stafford, Lyly and anyone of note who called there, just as Bruno-Fagot had done in London. By then, of course, Charles Arundel was back from Spain, where he had apparently convinced a wary Philip II that he was not a double agent, and he was now engaged in 'working on Stafford to get his assistance'.[3] Just about concurrently there was the London intrigue of his brother William Stafford in tandem with Moody – a plot that engaged the interest of French diplomats, including the ambassador Chateauneuf, who should have been more wary. The underhand routine devised may ostensibly have proposed the murder of Elizabeth, but it was much more likely Walsingham's devious way of disarming two ambassadors at the time of Mary's execution in February 1587.

By mid-July, when Marlowe was safely back in England earning praise and support from the Privy Council and even Elizabeth, William Lyly was writing to Walsingham to express satisfied relief that the secretary was now willing to accept his declarations of loyalty and his pressing desire to be of service directly to the minister. Lyly consolidated his new position after the arrest in Paris of Gilbert Gifford (apparently prompted by Stafford) by getting access to the agent's papers and transcribing many of them for London.[4] This hitherto unexplained switch for Lyly from suspect to associate was perhaps the result of Marlowe's efforts. His absence for months from college almost cost him his MA, but he was able to muster prompt support from the Privy Council in the form of a resolution to the university Senate. In many ways deliberately unrevealing, it still deserves scrutiny: 'Whereas it was reported that Christopher Morley [*sic*] was determined to have gone beyond the seas to Rheims and there to remain their Lordships thought good to certify that he had no such intent, but that in all his actions he had done Her Majesty good service and deserved to be rewarded for his faithful dealing.' This was written about a young man whose life was to be notched with public incidents. Yet at this time the queen did not want someone who had served his country 'defamed by those that are ignorant of the affairs he went about'. The plural 'affairs' defines a mission with at least a dual purpose. The Senate knew nothing about this, but then someone tossed out a simple guess that, like so many, he had been lured to Rheims. If it did come to light now that he had made his way there to spy we would have confirmation of the suggestive details to be found in his late play, *Massacre at Paris*. In it Marlowe showed a real familiarity with the League viewpoint in the section dealing with the murder of Guise.[5] Still, at this time the government decried the notion, and the playwright got his hastily conferred degree. Leaving Cambridge for London, Marlowe had (or now made) two contacts of immediate and lasting consequence.

Thomas Walsingham (b. 1563) was then on the fringes of the government. The son of a cousin of Sir Francis he had had intermittent employment from him and now was increasingly a man of some social standing in their home county of Kent. Even so, it is doubtful if he was responsible for recruiting Marlowe for clandestine work; that can be assigned to Waad, whose autograph is on the title page of the British Museum copy of Thomas Watson's *Amyntas* (1585). Born in Bishopsgate, London (*c.* 1540–5?), Watson was educated at Catholic-haunted Winchester and then Oxford, like his contemporary Richard White of Basingstoke, who after his BA in 1559 had quit England for study abroad and then teaching at Douai. Although a Catholic, he remained a loyal Englishman and demonstrated strong patriotic feelings. Watson first went abroad in 1569, which coincides with the failure of the rebellion of the northern earls, and he remained in exile, yet in 1572 when he was in Paris he formed some sort of link with Francis Walsingham, during the latter's time as ambassador. Watson moved about as a student of languages, civil and canon law, and reading a good deal of continental poetry. He was at Douai from 1575–7 (but not continuously), and after returning home he kept company with such well-known closet Catholics as the Earls of Oxford and Arundel. Evidently, Watson abandoned his personal attachment to Catholicism, and in 1581 (the year Waad joined Walsingham's staff) he went in the entourage to Paris for treaty negotiations by the principal secretary between the end of July and September. In 1585 (or thereabouts) Watson's most interesting memory treatise, *Compendium Memoriae Localis*, was published, and in that year he married Anne Swift, a sister of a retainer in the Catholic household of the Cornwallis family, now resident in Fisher's Folly in Bishopsgate, purchased from Oxford. Watson was employed as a learned tutor; he was already a man of the theatre and a poet in Latin and English. Yet today many would regard this shadowy figure as chiefly significant for intervening to save his friend Marlowe's life in a street imbroglio. It happened in September 1589 in Hog Lane, Cripplegate when Marlowe was set upon by an incensed William Bradley, the son of an innkeeper. When Watson arrived on the scene he sustained a minor injury before killing Bradley with a sword thrust to the right thorax.[6]

Neither man saw any reason to flee. They were arrested by the constable and taken before the litigious Sir Owen Hopton, Lieutenant of the Tower, who consigned them to Newgate. The processes of the law were rather more protracted than if the ailing secretary had been able to intervene. As it was, Marlowe fetched up in the loquacious company of a John Poole whose uncurbed habit, even after several years in prison, was to speak whatever seditious thoughts came into his head. It is possible to suppose that the playwright found this engaging and that later he remembered a conversation in the gloom about the petty treason of counterfeiting. This action was still punishable by death under the treason law of Edward III (1351), and it was conjured into a disguise of his real purpose when Marlowe was again apprehended – only this time, late in 1591, it was in Flushing. The town and garrison were then under English control, having been put up by the Dutch as security for English loans and involvement in the war against Spain: 'Both sides expected to find perfidy everywhere', and the governor, Sir Robert Sidney, spent much of his time collecting, sifting and forwarding news and intelligence.[7] One of those with whom he had reluctant contact was Michael Moody, freed after approaches to Sir Thomas Heneage, and then Burghley, some time during the summer or autumn of 1590. During his prison term he had encountered not only Poley, but also James Tipping, who had given hospitality to the Babington plotter John Ballard – a contact that cost Tipping a whipping. As soon as he was released Moody chose to offer his services to anyone likely to pay, juggling the wants of employers.

In the autumn of 1591 Moody was writing to Essex about hangings – a not infrequently used code-word for military equipment – the elated earl having been sent with a small army to assist Henri IV against Philip and the league. Within a few weeks Moody was in Flushing (prior to Marlowe) and he wrote to Tipping, then Poley, requesting the latter to visit Gravelines 'to speak with Charles Paget'. Years before Gravelines had been betrayed by its French governor to the Spanish, so Poley did not comply and he wrote to Moody 'under your Honour's mark' (this could be Heneage still or Burghley and Robert Cecil) to rebuke the agent who talked too openly, wrote too many slack letters and visited Flushing too often. Burghley and Cecil who controlled the queen's Scottish policy, not only heard from someone there about the irrepressible Moody, but Cecil followed up a lengthy report from another spy, John Ricroft, by writing a summary that set down his own suspicions about Moody. It was through him that Parma's most trusted counter-intelligence agent, Hugh Owen (see Chapter 15), slid forward a compelling but certainly bogus offer of service to the queen, something that caused Sidney a few problems. He had already rejected friendly overtures and presents from Owen, but Elizabeth recoiled at unsupervised contacts and it took Burghley to deflect her. Now Sidney rejected the offer made through Moody, and the queen was irked that, as it seemed to her, an opportunity had been missed to capture Owen. Burghley thought to satisfy her that enough was being done and, suspecting that Owen was also linked to Patrick Sedgrave with whom Sidney was dealing, he ordered Moody to approach the latter with something that would close the trap on Owen. The honourable Sidney fidgeted at dealing with Moody and was made even more uncomfortable by the just suspicion that Owen intended his ruin and the betrayal of Flushing to the Spanish.

The effort to entice Owen, never rich from his endeavours, was linked in some obscure way – so it seems – to the apparently whimsical counterfeiting charade involving Marlowe. He had fetched up in Flushing at the time when Poley was preoccupied with visiting Berwick, the centre for the organization of the English secret service in Scotland. In 1592 the Privy Council instituted an investigation of the circulation of counterfeit Scottish coins in England. While abroad Marlowe was in company with a goldsmith called (confusingly) Gifford Gilbert, as well as the apostate Richard Baines who had studied successfully at Cambridge, before shifting to Rheims and then ordination at Soissons a decade before this. It was he who laid the accusation against Gilbert and Marlowe of counterfeiting, and they were separately examined by Sidney without any denial of the charges, save that they claimed it was all a test of skill. So – had Marlowe been instructed to remain silent in the event of a hitch, in order not to undermine Sidney's position and confidence? Once in custody Marlowe and Baines seem to have whipped up a little trick of their own invention to divert the threat of summary justice and it worked. They accused each other of intending to go over to the enemy (Owen perhaps?) or

Rome. The counterfeit coins were intended to be Dutch and English – Dutch coins could be used in England – though the one Dutch shilling they had struck was so obviously pewter that the real purpose seems to have been something else altogether. A perplexed Sidney therefore went no further in his investigation, and instead shipped home the culprits under guard, after Marlowe had cited two lofty noblemen to give testimony on his behalf: Henry Percy, Earl of Northumberland and Ferdinando, Lord Strange. The son and heir of the Earl of Derby, he was of particular interest to the Cecils, since some exiles wistfully regarded Strange as another potential husband for Arabella Stuart.[8]

It was Burghley at this time who was especially anxious that the spy Anthony Standen, in Spain from December 1591, should report any practices between that country and Scotland, and who was so employed. And it was Standen himself, writing to Anthony Bacon in April 1592, who gave some sketchy corroboration of the way money matters intruded into politics. His Spanish pension had been stalled – a not infrequent experience for an Englishman in Spanish pay – but this time due rather to a shortage of cash. No treasure fleet; no pay. Interestingly, the information he garnered was communicated both to Burghley *and* to Essex. As before, Standen reported on ship sailings, the recruitment of soldiers, and dealings between Spain and Scotland. In one of his letters he noted that a promised sum of 200,000 crowns was to be sent to Scotland when the opportunity arose. He also noted that his fellow spy Anthony Rolston, who would travel via Calais to Flanders, would report in more detail on Scottish matters, particularly the distribution of the money. Standen saw the 'giddy neighbour' Scotland as a danger point, and it was a view not lost on Burghley for all the kaleidoscopic calls on his time.[9] The long chains of underhand machinations linked London, Flushing and Brussels, visited by Poley for Heneage in March 1592. In the following month a broker called Robert Rutkin was interrogated in London about his correspondents, including Moody, who was living now in Brussels or Anvers. With the agreement of Heneage and very likely the Cecils, Rutkin was given letters by Poley to be forwarded to Moody, and by May it was Cecil who was writing to Heneage to say that Burghley wanted to know more about Rutkin. The old man also wanted to talk to Poley, and unless it was a repetition in error, noting it twice suggests urgency. Towards the end of the month it was Robert Cecil again who wrote his wonderfully understated comment that Poley 'was no fool' – all the more weighty because Cecil was a supreme realist in such matters. This was probably the point at which Poley made the important shift from working under the control of Heneage to directing English espionage in the Low Countries for the government. A career hike to a pivotal position that stemmed from the approval of the Cecils – in particular Robert, who had been made privy councillor in August 1591. He disliked Thomas Phelippes, who had been treading water since the death of Walsingham, and there was no willingness to employ him on important affairs.

Phelippes, however, needed espionage as others craved the modish, expensive item, tobacco. So he looked to the Earl of Essex for employment at a time when the courtier-soldier seemed the only likely patron of men shrugged off by the Cecils. Although nephews of Burghley, Anthony and Francis Bacon were two such; gifted men in broader ways then Phelippes, yet they had received only slights tempered by vague hints. The reason was the diminutive, ill-formed Robert Cecil, whose public career was underpinned by his devoted father, but which went on unspectacularly until Elizabeth was convinced of his worth. At the same time, through 1589 and 1590 there had been no particular evidence that she was favouring Essex instead. Indeed, in June 1590 Essex had been forced to sell Keyston Manor (Huntingdonshire), in order to repay, as required, a royal loan of £3,000. Back in England after military service – his great advantage as it seemed over his rival Robert Cecil – Essex considered with his friends how to improve his position and hence jostle the immovable Burghley and his rising son. The return of Anthony Bacon in 1592 from his long sojourn in France meant that Essex could turn his attention to espionage, with the knowledge that, if successful, it was a direct route to Elizabeth's high approval. Indeed, in August 1592, as Poley prepared for a lengthy trip to the Low Countries, Francis Bacon was cooing over the pleasing notion of a visit to his home by Phelippes who had no liking himself for Robert Cecil. Elizabeth soon decided to test her courtier's intelligence skills and, on his first day as a privy councillor in February 1593, the earl wrote jubilantly to Anthony Bacon about her praise for passing the test she had set – writing a draft instruction on an intelligence matter to a fictitious agent in France.[10]

Robert Poley's first cipher has been assigned to 1590, and within two years he had become as indispensable as Phelippes had been, making more frequent letter-carrying journeys and also undertaking supervision of agents.[11] In June 1592, and then September, he was in Berwick, Anvers and then Dover. This latter journey took him twice through Canterbury at a time when Marlowe and Paul Ivey, the fortifications engineer and periodic intelligencer, were both in the town. This just may be a coincidence, but given their employment histories, probably not. By the end of the year Poley had to make two consecutive trips to Scotland because the country played a definite part in the deliberations of the traitor Sir William Stanley.[12] The first visit was extended to two months and included a period at the court, but these trans-border forays have never received much attention, despite the deep distrust that infiltrated Anglo-Scottish relations after the failure of the Armada. Scottish Catholics felt incensed that Philip II had been persuaded to mount his grand attempt on the south rather than the north, and the earls who had originally proposed an attack on England through Scotland remained insistent that the notion should be tried. In the summer of 1592 the meddlesome Earl of Huntly was up to his old tricks again and there followed a startling discovery. A Scottish Catholic, George Ker or Carr, leaving for Spain, was found to be carrying mysterious blank sheets of paper as yet only signed by a handful of his fellow nobles. When tortured he revealed a project guided by the Jesuit Father Creighton by which Philip II would send an army to Scotland as previously envisaged, prior to invading England. The Spaniards hoped 'to have Scotland as their back friend', and the discovery of the 'Spanish Blanks' caused an anxious flurry in London. Poley's second journey to Scotland was made in January 1593 and, towards the end of that month, Ralegh wrote strongly to Elizabeth on the machinations of the Scottish Catholics. He was trying hard to rebuild the credit lost when he secretly wed Elizabeth Throckmorton and, although not received at court for another five years, his analysis of the influence of Spain at the Scottish court did not lack vigour. He was certainly extremely hostile to James VI as a possible succession candidate, that most controversial matter having erupted into the public domain when it was raised in the Parliament of 1592–3 by Peter Wentworth (jailed for his temerity).[13]

In that parliamentary session the drama in Scotland of the 'Spanish Blanks' was handy for exploitation by a London government wanting a vote for subsidies. Even if the prospect of a summer (1593) invasion did recede, the Privy Council continued to pay close attention to anyone crossing the border. To advance the claim of James, it was Anthony Bacon who, with the knowledge and consent of Essex, opened a correspondence with several agents in Scotland. A hint by Elizabeth that she knew about this came when she remarked that Anthony Standen – now one of Essex's followers – was reported to her as being too pro-Scottish, when what he had written to Bacon suggested the opposite: 'they are a numerous and valiant people; and generally (I except none of them) our mortal foes'. Essex may have winced when Elizabeth made her loaded quip, but a campaign to destroy Ralegh as a direct consequence and by any means does not seem likely. As it was, James VI had weighted the arguments for and against invasion. Then, despite the clamour of Scottish Presbyterians and diplomatic representations from London, he took no further serious actions aginst his own wilful nobles. To the fury of the English envoy none of them even lost their estates. No wonder then if an English intelligencer like Marlowe, mentioned unexpectedly in regard to Scotland, was looked upon with suspicion. There were significant tensions in Anglo-Scottish relations with James VI himself ascribing the intrigues of the neighbouring government to the Cecils. His hostility to them was increasing, while his relations with Essex and those about him grew in affability.

The English government, with its nagging internal rivalries and uneasy groupings, did still feel beset by domestic and foreign problems. As a result it was made suspicious and harsh, lurching to suppress the slightest deviation wherever it could. Religious radicals felt the full weight of Whitgift's pursuit of them. Sly calumnies also filtered through from that sharp Jesuit propagandist Robert Persons, who deftly managed to set in motion a push against a great enemy like Ralegh by marking him down as the leader of a group of free-thinkers and so-called 'atheists', including Thomas Hariot (astronomer and scientist of colossal learning), Walter Warner, Robert Hu(gh)es, George Chapman and, of course, Christopher Marlowe. Even so, it is now time to reject the often repeated view that it was his 'atheism', referred to by such as the late Robert Greene (d. 1592) and by Gabriel Harvey, that set Marlowe at odds with the Privy Council and, in particular, the Cecils. Nor is there much point in energetically trying to yoke him to the fly-poster campaign in London at that time – an effort that was blemishing the city with round attacks on immigrants, especially those exiled from the Low Countries and northern France. Such hostility, grounded in economic prospects, had a tenacious hold and in early May 1593 the government's attention was drawn to a rhyming ultimatum placed provocatively on the wall of the Dutch churchyard, Broadstreet Ward. Official fear of the uncontrolled utterance was as usual strong, and an order of 11 May required the round-up of those suspected of writing and distributing the libels. One of those caught up in the sweep was the playwright Thomas Kyd, who for a time (*c.* 1591) had shared premises with Marlowe.[14] It proved to be a lamentable connection for lamentable connection for the former scrivener, because on a search an apparently incriminating text was discovered. It was a manuscript of material drawn from John Procter's *The Fall of the Late Arrian* (1549), which had no appeal to the lay reader and was not even banned. However, its drift was immediately noted as if it was heretical and, catching the mood, Kyd at length squirmed to disclaim it and shift it on to Marlowe who must have revealed something of his thoughts in previous conversations.[15]

By the time Kyd was tortured, Marlowe was dead. In desperation Kyd wrote two undated letters to the Lord Keeper, Sir John Puckering, in which he dredged up his former friend's 'monstrous opinions', claiming that Marlowe 'would persuade men of quality go unto the King of Scots, whether I hear Roydon is gone and where if he had lived he told me when I saw him last he meant to be'. Unlikely if Marlow followed Ralegh's anti-Scottish views. Burghley and Cecil already knew that Anthony Bacon and Essex were in contact with agents in Scotland, and that agents in Scotland had had contacts with the Duke of Parma. What they wanted to know was the nature of Marlowe's politicking and who better to find out than their head of operations, Robert Poley, saturated in Scottish business from his recent travels there. But at this time he was abroad in the Low Countries, from 8 May 1593, ostensibly to carry letters to the Hague, and it was nearly three weeks before he returned to put Marlowe on the spot. Until that time Marlowe was not held under arrest and he did not seize the chance to flee abroad. Until 18 May he was staying at the country home of Thomas Walsingham at Scadbury near Chislehurst (Kent). This was known to the Privy Council when the document was signed requiring Henry Maunder, a messenger of the queen's chamber, to go there for him, and Marlowe responded to the call for his presence without demur. He entered his appearance on 20 May, and the requirement to report daily to the council at Greenwich palace with the queen until licensed to cease was no more than had been required of Anthony Munday in 1588, when unspecified charges were made against him. The delay in dealing with Marlowe, whose name does not appear on the records of the Privy Council meetings held at Greenwich on 23 or 25 May, nor that at Westminster on 29 May in Star Chamber, was caused by Poley's absence.

The encounter between Christopher Marlowe, Robert Poley, Ingram Frizer (then in the service of Thomas Walsingham) and the enigmatic Nicholas Skeres took place in the premises of a Mrs Eleanor Bull (née Whitney) in Deptford. Let us now bury for ever the entirely incorrect notion that she presided over a tavern, or something rather more squalid like a disorderly house. Eleanor Bull, a widow, was a rather well-connected woman, known as 'cousin' to Blanche Parry (d. 1591) (herself for many years a gentlewoman to Elizabeth, and every likely related to the Cecils), who may have kept an 'ordinary' – an eating house for gentlemen, 'very often a gambling house'. Evidently she was trusted, with the meeting probably set up by Robert Cecil to substitute for the daily routine of Marlowe registering his appearance before an official. In this case Poley was the official when the men met together at 10 a.m. It would require exceptional naïvety to believe that the spy met the erstwhile spy only for a day of convivial chat and a few hands of cards. In a secure house Poley was required to try to establish for Cecil and Burghley what sort of contacts Marlowe had had with the Scottish court and its agents, as well as perhaps whether it was ever going to be possible to employ him in clandestine matters again. Poley was clearly the man with the challenging brief to find out as much as possible while they were 'in quiet sort together'. Thomas Walsingham, who knew Poley from the time of the Babington plot and who was moving now into the orbit of the Cecils, could hardly turn up to support Marlowe. So he sent along Ingram Frizer to represent him and Skeres went too. Although listed in the inquisition as a gentleman resident in London, Frizer was a venal individual – the equivalent then of a 'loan shark' today. With Skeres he had already been involved in some financial sharp practice that left their victims rueful of involvement with them.[16]

So who killed Christoper Marlowe on 30 May 1593, and why? The succinct answer, the official answer, is that it was Ingram Frizer who was responsible. The account of the event and a little of the circumstances is in the inquisition (a document) of the post-mortem inquest held by William Danby, coroner of the Verge, with the assistance of a properly constituted jury of local men, on 1 June 1593. The inquisition is unusually detailed, as if in expectation of interest in the victim, and was found by a notable document sleuth – Professor Leslie Hotson – in the Public Record Office in 1925. It states that Marlowe, after a day in company with the threesome that took them from the hired room into the garden and then back into the room again, sprawled on the only bed therein after supper was served at about 6 p.m. He and Frizer began arguing about paying the bill, and no doubt in a sardonic aside about one who gulls an innocent but declines to pay a few pence for meals, Marlowe set in train the mischief that led to a bloody denouement. Sitting between Poley and Skeres at the supper table (according to another version playing backgammon), Frizer took two light blows on the head from his own dagger wielded by Marlowe, and using the handle to inflict the modest injuries. Frizer grabbed hold of the dagger to defend himself, 'in fear of being slain' and Marlowe was stabbed in the eye to a depth of two inches. Apparently he died instantly and modern medical opinion now holds that the wound occasioned an air embolism. So there was no death-bed scene of recrimination or Christian forgiveness, and no summoning of a surgeon; simply a shriek, gasps and a heavy thud as Marlowe hit the floor.

Since the poet was dead, it was early evening and Poley was a privileged government agent, he probably declined to call the watch, preferring to put the corpse on the bed to await the coroner. The delay of a day in the setting up of the inquest need not be ascribed to anything sinister, simply Danby's absence. Perhaps he had followed the court to Westminster and needed to come back along the river. His jurisdiction (the Verge) was a circuit of twelve miles radius from the body of the sovereign and he took precedence over a district coroner.[17]

There are lacunae in the inquisition, and conspiracy theorists have furiously exploited them to deride the verdict of self-defence. Certainly Marlowe was dead and not spirited away to write the plays of Shakespeare in collaboration with the Countess of Pembroke; an eccentric conceit even in a field littered with absurd notions. Could it have been a political assassination, as some have argued? Marlowe had surely been a spy, but only a quite minor participant in the complex mesh of secret agendas and covert explorations. The testimony of Kyd about

Marlowe and Roydon is barely more than suggestive, and the infamous Baines note or libel listing the playwright's philosophical errors was seductively shocking but hardly original. An accusation against George Gascoigne made to the Privy Council, when he was admitted as a burgess to parliament, declared him to be 'a notorious ruffian and especially noted to be both a spy; an atheist and godless person'. Still, Baines did name Richard Cholmley as one who 'hath confessed he was persuaded by Marlowe's reasons to become an Atheist'. Thoughtful of him to come up with the name of somebody already under a cloud and being sought by the government; someone who had vanished for the time being. A political murder of a playwright, a cause of animated gossip and rumour when the government only had to shut him away to neutralize him? The playwright's activities in the spectral world of high diplomacy may have appeared dubious, even verging on treason if viewed in the most lurid light by a suspicious government, but assassination rather than incarceration seems to me too sinister even for that gloomy decade. Still, it is worth noting that, because Poley had been there, the government smothered direct references to the killing, and although there may have been quiet talk in the taverns the references in print were either few, bland or Aesopian. The man who had stormed the theatres to become the most popular and highly-regarded dramatist of his time was placed in a winding sheet of silence; no funerary poems or commemorative anthology. Even his admiring friend Thomas Nashe cloaked eulogistic comments in 'The Unfortunate Traveller' (1593) in the pseudonym 'Aretine' which Gabriel Harvey used to pillory Marlowe's heterodox views. Harvey knew nothing about the circumstances of Marlowe's death, which is remarkable because his diminutive brother, the Revd Richard Harvey, was rector at Scadbury. As for Thomas Walsingham, did the 'liberal affection' he had had for Marlowe so easily transfer to the presumed killer Ingram Frizer who maintained contacts with the Walsingham family into the next century?

Place the verdict of the inquest held by Danby with sixteen jurors on hold, ignore the murder conspiracy theory and consider what is left. The death was commonplace, stabbings happened all the time, but add a little nuance or a swerve to the events and something emerges as a possibility. There was an abrupt eruption (no matter what the cause), and the aftermath was dealt with coolly and logically. Frizer appeared before the jury as a gentleman in service to another gentleman – a man well placed in Kent to use his local influence to squash any minor consequences that might embarrass the government. A spy murdering a spy might be startling and savage, but an argument over pence leading to a sudden flurry of arms and a knife, a stabbing in self-defence, was within the imaginative range of the jury men. It is remarkable how soundless and shadowy the normally boastful and pugnacious Poley was in this delicate situation. The reason, often remarked but never scrutinized, was that his return at a gallop from The Hague was never openly acknowledged by the government. An unfocused reading of the warrant signed by Heneage for Poley's expenses on 12 June is of little use in establishing his movements, since the document has him continuously out of the country from 8 May to a vague date early in June. Yet he did not make two journeys abroad punctuated by the Deptford drama, as some have averred. Poley was in England for the critical period between late May and 8 June, when he presented the letters he was carrying at the court now at Nonsuch. The warrant glides over this time-lag in order to keep his name out of the business 'being in her Majesty's service all the aforesaid time', and to make the £30 he was paid seem unexceptional.[18] Another matter of timing, the sudden appearance of the rancorous Baines note, has also caused historians to puzzle over its date of delivery, but this was not likely to inhibit someone highly placed who could use it to advantage. The catalogue of Marlowe's supposedly brazen political insolence and blasphemies no doubt reached someone on the Privy Council about the time Frizer stabbed him (perhaps it had even been flourished under his nose), but the copy of the shock-horror only went to Elizabeth on 2 June – the day after the inquest. It is no great feat of imagination to see her eyes bulging as she read; as intended, indignation destroying any intention to enquire further into his fate, despite his fame. The man was dead, buried on 1 June – so much the better if he had thought what the note indicated. She probably thought (as she was to do about Bruno), that he was 'a dreamer, a criminal and an atheist'.[19] Within the month Frizer was freed from custody to live, as far as we know, a blameless life in Eltham. And who nudged the queen's response by controlling the movement of documents, a matter of the utmost importance as he knew already? Who else but the man never seen in Whitehall without a clutch of official papers, Poley's employer for the next few years, following this minor post-mortem sleight of hand – Sir Robert Cecil.

Chapter Eleven

The Mild Intelligencer

By the last decade of the sixteenth century two of the three most important initiators of spying as a government resource were dead. The now markedly ageing Burghley alone lived on, struggling intermittently against the mental and physical torpor that has recently and bluntly been characterized as senile decay. The men who initially replaced Leicester, then Walsingham, in secret service matters were much less prominent and had less authority – what the Elizabethans characterized as 'port'. Though Sir Thomas Heneage (later a short-lived husband of the Earl of Southampton's mother) was vice-chamberlain, Thomas Walsingham had no court appointment, despite his family connections. The result was an interim faltering in the efforts of the spy masters and their motley employees, although some of the very familiar men were still being used.

With the direction of espionage in the doldrums, despite the observed necessity for it, the year 1592 was a turning point because it saw the return to England from France of Anthony Bacon. This chimed with the abrupt and dynamic interest in spying of the soldier and would-be politician, the Earl of Essex. The stepson and political heir of the Earl of Leicester suddenly felt challenged by the quiet, compelling presence of shrewd Sir Robert Cecil and was determined to outflank someone so physically unprepossessing, but always informed and hard-working. The young earl, for his part, was one of the most lavishly gifted of Elizabeth's courtiers, a soldier, something of a scholar and a poet. His campaigning in France with Henri IV against Spain had alerted him to the uses of espionage, but like his stepfather, Essex could not do the sustained work of heading and controlling a spy organization, however rudimentary, on a day-to-day basis, so he needed a strong secretariat that was able to work confidently. To establish this branch of his household he looked for the wide-ranging expertise of someone with a myriad of contacts at home and abroad, someone also with the time and inclination, and he chose Anthony Bacon, nephew of Burghley and older brother of Francis Bacon.

Anthony Bacon was born in 1558, the year when crown servants like his father and many of the commonalty could breathe a collective sigh of relief.[1] Since Nicholas Bacon emphatically prospered serving Elizabeth, he could afford to send his two sons by his second wife Anne Cooke (sister to Mildred, mother of Robert Cecil) to Cambridge. At fifteen and thirteen, respectively, the boys went to Trinity College and after three years they were admitted to Gray's Inn as befitted the sons of the Lord Keeper. It was only a brief halt for Francis, who was very soon sent to

France in the suite of the new ambassador, Sir Amias Paulet. Anthony Bacon did not travel until 1579, shortly after the death of his father and at the suggestion of uncle Burghley. Then, having nudged his nephew out of the country to become an observer and reporter on French affairs, he lost interest in him. With Robert Cecil to protect and nurture perhaps this was unavoidable, but it was uncivil and short-sighted. Walsingham slid into the overseeing position vacated by his colleague, and Anthony Bacon became one of his most useful gatherers of information and intelligence material. Although an unsatisfactory and lazy correspondent on private matters which bored him (like finding the means to stay put in France), Bacon did write frequently to the secretary, whose own replies were not always prompt. Still, to compensate for this and lack of payment, Walsingham's tone in his letters was always cordial and smoothly encouraging.

In 1580, Walsingham took into his employ a young Puritan called Nicholas Faunt, and almost immediately he was sent abroad to discharge material to English agents and to gather intelligence. In Paris in August, Faunt met Bacon and they established a friendship that was to last for many years. While abroad they were mostly separated by the requirements of work; Anthony moved on to Bourges, while Faunt with some reluctance stayed in Paris. His unease sprang from a discordant relationship with the then ambassador, Sir Henry Cobham, hostile as he was to anyone with links to Walsingham.[2] Faunt's aggravations were only resolved when he was able to move on to Germany and Italy, with some time being spent in Padua. Both young men prepared intelligence reports for the secretary, and Bacon still delivered the same material to Burghley. After Bourges he travelled to Geneva, where he lodged with Theodore Beza and his wife Candida. The Protestant theologian was also known to Faunt, since when he visited the city he stayed with a neighbour of Beza's. By the middle of March 1582 Bacon had moved again, this time to the warmth of Toulouse, but Faunt was required back in England as Spanish pressure increased government activity.

As far as his absent friend was concerned, Faunt was slightly neurotic and sentimental, hoping that Bacon would also return to England. But the slow traveller ignored this line and moved through other towns to Bordeaux in January 1584. Whatever the politique tilt of what had once been the capital of the English – controlled province of Guienne, Bacon was still an intelligencer and in danger because of his Huguenot contacts. While in the city he was also in contact with Henri de Montmorency, ostensibly a Catholic, yet who had unexpected privy dealings with their enemies. The Frenchman wanted to contact Elizabeth and Leicester, so he gave two letters to Bacon, who also wrote to the earl and then sent these items to Francis Bacon to deliver. In October 1584 Leicester responded and included the approbation of Elizabeth. News of this seeped out and within a short time Bacon was in trouble, and news of it had reached Faunt. The denunciation came from an exiled English Catholic, as well as two Jesuits who declared his presence to the *Parlement*. He was saved from torture by the intervention of Marshal Matignon, who eventually succeeded Michel de Montaigne as mayor of Bordeaux.

Faunt expected Bacon to shift his abode back to Paris late in March 1584, but instead the agent chose Béarn. This area of south-west France was under the control of Henri of Navarre. That summer the Duke of Épernon, a staunch Catholic favourite of King Henry III, arrived to try to persuade the Huguenot ruler to become a Catholic. It was a consideration given greater depth and meaning by the death of the last possible Valois claimant to the throne of France – the Duke of Anjou, sometime suitor of Elizabeth, who expired in July 1584. Henri of Navarre as yet had no inclination to do what was proposed, and so the league, in conjunction with Philip II, named its own candidate. Henri III, as nominal leader of the league, was forced to send troops against the man whom he most favoured as his successor. Bacon and Henri of Navarre were simultaneously in Béarn and must have met since the former was charged to find out what was going on. Early in the following year he was in Montauban, a Protestant stronghold, where he became well aquainted with Navarre's councillors. It was there, in the summer of 1586, that he was the subject of a startling and even grave accusation. It was that he engrossed a very young male servant in acts of sodomy – a historic first in the prodigious annals of such activity in the British secret service.[3] Naturally, Bacon was greatly exercised to prevent public news of this reaching England and apparently he was successful because there are no accounts or allusions to the case in English documents. Whatever his intention, however, he could not suppress the matter in Montauban, despite powerful French friends. Fortunately Henri of Navarre was looking for increased English help, not the humiliation and punishment of an Elizabethan agent. At every level of French society it was possible to find relationships that transgressed the law which declared sodomy a capital crime, if it could be proven to be repeated.

Informal testimony against Bacon was taken in August 1586 and Henri intervened on his side in the autumn. Yet the surviving reports date from the following year, and the elasticity of the charges hints that Bacon had a well-placed and tenacious enemy. There is substantial evidence that she was Charlotte Arbaleste, Madame du Plessis, the wife of the chief advisor to Henri of Navarre, Philippe de Mornay, sieur du Plessis-Marly, sometimes known as 'the pope of the Huguenots'. Bacon's difficulty was inevitably compounded by a mild misogyny; he tenderly avoided even his own mother as much as possible when in England, and later in his career was a strikingly reluctant courtier, shrinking from contact with Elizabeth. Since he was only emotionally bestirred by young men, Bacon had thoughtfully declined to marry one of the daughters of Madame du Plessis, although it might have provided him with an advantageous cover. His error was to have allowed the notion of marriage to arise, and he discovered at considerable cost to his peace of mind how stubborn and strong-minded this mother could be. He was confident he could always outmanoeuvre his own parent, but Madame du Plessis was even more formidable than Lady Bacon.

Philippe du Plessis had established his family in Montauban in 1584, while holding a series of important consultations for Henri. To his embarrassment his wife then became enmeshed in an angry dispute with the minister of the church in the town over the application of sumptuary rules. Like any high-ranking woman of fashion in her day, she favoured wigs, hair-nets and strategic wire supports in the dressing of her hair. These were locally then regarded as ungodly items of vanity, and she and her daughters were twice banned from communion. The result was an unseemly row with Madame scorchingly defending her views and seeking Bacon's support for her stand. No doubt with a sign of bemusement he failed to give it and, with a certain indiscreet levity, he told minister Bérault that he was on his side. It was an amused attitude to female absurdity that cost him dear in his activities as a spy and a seducer. With his wife seething, Philippe du Plessis was dutiful and supportive, and whatever his private feelings it was probably his intervention that led to the second hearing of witnesses against Bacon.

Once again the royal historian Claude de la Grange heard the testimony, and the preparation of the written record was undertaken by the royal notary, Antoine Vacquerie. The first witness was a recently employed servant of the Bacon household, who said that he had often seen the Englishman in company with a page, Isaac Bougades, even sharing his bed with him during the day. Indifferent to those around who could observe their intimacy, they would kiss and fondle each other, with the older man cheerfully handing out sweets and money when he had it. But had Michel Frutier (from Geneva) simply wanted to shock Paul de la Fontaine when he recalled Bacon enjoying anal sex with Bougades? Indeed, was the not very robust Bacon physically capable of the effort involved? As for Bougades, he claimed stoutly in his own defence that other men excused sodomy, including a Monsieur Constanier of Montauban, a churchman, and Beza, the Genevan theologian – a claim which sounds as if it came from Bacon himself. The circumstantial evidence was then added to when Fontaine claimed that Bougades had himself tried penetrative sex with an inexperienced and younger boy page, David Brysson (or Boisson), unsurprisingly making the boy yelp with pain. Fontaine declared he had learnt of this from David and also his own father, Jean de la Fontaine, another household employee. The older man had apparently protested to Bacon about debauchery, but he ignored the comments, as he did normally with any unpleasantness or correction.

The following morning Jean de la Fontaine gave evidence on the lines of his son's testimony. He claimed too that he had urged Bacon to sack Bougades, but that it was the passive boy David who had been dismissed. On that afternoon Brysson was required to give evidence and said that, after working as a servant in the house for some eighteen months, he had been taken by Bougades into a gallery under the roof, where his breeches had been dropped and Bougades tried to sodomize him. Since he had been the house apparently untouched for a year and a half, there is the suspicion that he intended this: many serving boys prostituted themselves. However, his cries of pain were heard and Frutier appeared. Bougades had bribed him to stay silent with a black hat and, when the boy was dismissed, Bougades had sought him out to hand over a little money, with the reasonable injunction in the circumstances that he should say nothing. The two Fontaines then signed the transcription prepared by Vacquerie, but the unlettered boy was excused.

Henri of Navarre was not a man to be shocked by any sexual behaviour. Catherine de Medici's *escadron volant*, young beauties of the court who used sexual wiles for political purposes, like Anne d'Aquaviva, as well as Henri III's notorious male companions, the *mignons*, were part of French politics. But as far as Bacon was concerned evidence that the offence had been repeated might have led to his execution, despite Henri's shrug. Nor was the accused well placed to extricate himself from the clinging taint that threatened his ruin. Having lost the support of some highly regarded French Huguenots, he was forced to approach Catholics like the Bishop of Cahors, a town some thirty miles from Montauban. With his exceptional improvidence and with poor communications to England, he was mightily in debt and hence could be placed under pressure in ways he might have liked to avoid. The bishop was induced to loan him 1,000 crowns, but the quid pro quo was that he had to ask for the release of two Welsh Jesuits, Powell and Merideth. Writing to the Earl of Essex years later the bishop agreed so that he could get a safe conduct for Tom Lawson, his Catholic friend who had taken the place of Ned Selwyn in his household, and one may believe in his affections. As it happened, Lawson might, with hindsight, have preferred it if he had not succeeded. Although he was able 'to convey and deliver safely to my Lord Treasurer's hands certain advertisements very important for her Majesty's service and dangerous for myself', Burghley promptly had him arrested and he remained in gaol for ten months. Bacon regarded the unfortunate as the victim of the mortified Philippe du Plessis and his own testy mother, Lady Anne Bacon, who was constantly perturbed about her absent son and his relationships.

Early in 1588 one of Henri of Navarre's councillors, Monsieur du Pin, wrote to the ailing and distressed Walsingham about Bacon. His tone was somewhat aggrieved since, in his seeking of contacts, the English agent had ignored du Pin, who was also bemused that an intelligencer should now be involved in a lawsuit. This seemed to violate du Pin's sense of propriety and he wanted Bacon recalled, providing a passport to speed up his return to England. But stubbornly Bacon stayed put, because he was not only constrained by the lawsuit, but also ill. In March he wrote to Walsingham praising Lawson, though this availed nothing when the young man arrived back home. By 1590, after the cancellation of his debt, Bacon was free to leave Montauban. He chose to return to Bordeaux and though ill again with the crippling disorders that painfully hampered him, he was eventually able to liberate the talented and long-serving Anthony Standen. Once again we see that first name which is the bane of the historian dealing with this complicated subject.

Unlike some Englishmen, Standen, whose work until 1588 has already been sketched (see Chapter 9), was able to avoid service in the Armada fleet. This clearly suggests that he was still valued as an agent for Spain, though the emphasis by then may well have been on his French contacts. When the Cardinal of Lorraine was assassinated on Christmas Eve, 1588, in an act that prefigured the political chaos of the following year, Standen and Anthony Rolston remained in Paris for months, until they were forced to flee to the Spanish court late in 1589. The Spanish pension was renewed and, along with the other Anthony and Father Persons, he was supposed to return to France, each to report from a different city. Yet in the spring of 1590, just as Walsingham was dying, Standen was actually in Italy, preparing to leave for Spain, where he was spotted by James Young in the company of Rolston, Hugh Owen and Thomas Fitzherbert.[4] The latter's Catholicism had, of course, wrecked any possibility of a career in law and in 1580 he had directed his energies to helping the clandestine mission of Persons and Campion. After a further spell in prison following the latter's execution, Fitzherbert was released to live in France and, given his rather friendly letter to Walsingham at the time, one wonders if the secretary had sketched the idea of using him as he did the hapless Babington. As it was, in Paris Fitzherbert was secretary for English letters to Catherine de Medici and he was also in contact again with Persons; being named by another spy as the 'secretary to the Jesuits' party'.

In August 1590, still unaware of his employer's demise in England, Standen moved to Bordeaux. He may have convinced an uncertain replacement for Walsingham that this was a good position from which to keep track of the Spanish fleet being prepared for action against Henri of Navarre (now King Henri IV of France) in Brittany; more likely the town was selected by Philip II for him; Fitzherbert was assigned by the king to Rouen, and Mendoza was supposed to expedite their despatches to Spain. After a buoyant career and much luck, Standen now ran into trouble. Two days after arriving in Bordeaux he was recognized by a French spy normally based in Spain and, following his report, the authorities of the town arrested Standen, believing him to be a Spanish spy.[5] Unable to communicate his predicament to anyone, Standen's gloom lifted a little when he heard that Anthony Bacon had arrived to stay. Unfortunately the hope this inspired was premature because, as we know, Bacon was too ill to do anything. Standen's own writing privileges were only restored in April 1591, when, using the alias André Sandal, he wrote a brief and altogether cryptic note because he had no cipher. The following day, 8 April, he followed it with a more revealing missive which he asked Bacon to burn. His hope was that Bacon would muster what influence he had in defence of a fellow countryman; could Elizabeth be galvanized to help?

Clearly not, since Standen was still not free in June. He was doubly unfortunate because he could not pay his prison debts and consequently had no hope of being shifted to the conciergerie where he would have had liberal outside access. Yet, in spite of restrictions he managed to carry on some clandestine work, with informants outside (hard to evaluate) and possibly inside the gaol. In June 1591, therefore, he wrote to Bacon about the number of Spanish ships in San Sebastián, information from someone in St Jean de Luz that might disperse any rumours Bacon had run into. By now Standen was writing so freely that someone in authority at the prison must have been his conduit, either allowing the passage of letters or conveying them secretly to English messengers. On 29 June, as he told Bacon, he had written to Burghley bravely complaining that the English government was being altogether too dilatory in working for his release. Also he warned of a plot (source unknown) to kidnap Bacon, believing him to be under surveillance, so that if he sailed for home an attempt would be made to intercept his boat at sea. Apparently it was planned that Bacon should be held hostage to force the release from English captivity of Don Pedro de Valdés, sometime captain of the Andalusian squadron of the Armada.

Standen too now longed to return to the country he had quit so many years before; he was anxious to end his roving. Anthony Bacon, however, showed little enthusiasm for ending his retreat, ignoring the ever-frantic calls of his mother, and the more measured beckoning of the government. The length of time he stayed abroad may have been caused in part by acute nervous embarrassment at the thought that his sexual peccadilloes might have been revealed. In the mean time

Standen came out of prison, a result of his own efforts, with some bolstering by Elizabeth and Burghley, and while waiting for his passport he worked to consolidate his position by giving practical help to the gout-stricken younger man, writing and deciphering letters. When Bacon's servant, Edward Yates, was seriously injured in a town scuffle, it was Standen who sought redress for the victim. Bacon's trust in him was unhesitating at this time, perhaps brought on by relief that there was someone to act for him in dealings with the Bacon family. It was this trust that initially underpinned the later development of Essex's clandestine network. For example, Bacon sought Standen's opinion of Rolston before offering employment, and one wonders about Standen's candour over someone he knew well from past contacts.

Before leaving Bordeaux, Standen prepared for his eventual return to England by writing to Burghley and also Francis Bacon. The first was a prospective employer, so Standen outlined current political affairs in France, Aragón, Valencia and a Rome agitated by the death of Pope Gregory XIII. This caused Burghley to bestir himself and he responded by stating what sort of intelligence he wanted, with the emphasis, as ever, on military preparations by land and sea; this chimed with Elizabeth's somewhat exaggerated respect for Spanish sea-power. Standen moved on in December to act as a peripatetic agent for Bacon and, moving south towards St Jean de Luz, he was able to test his new disguise as 'Monsieur La Faye'.[6] It worked well enough with some travelling Englishmen, but it must have been a challenge to persuade anyone that he was a rich merchant. It is possible he borrowed more money from Bacon before he made the long-delayed return journey to England. Writing to his brother Edward Standen later in the year the spy referred warmly to Bacon – 'this noble gentleman of whose bounty I have so largely tasted'.

During the period that Standen spent in Spain reporting to Bacon, it was Tom Lawson who acted as courier and deciphered the correspondence, and with his cheerful disposition he diverted Bacon when his spirits were low. After Bacon's return to England in early 1592 he had soon to retreat from London to escape the plague, and in the autumn came the unsettling news that Lawson had fallen ill in Spain. Standen wrote soothingly of Lawson's general demeanour and his loyal efforts to put Bacon's business first. As for his own personal dealings with Rolston, he urged Bacon not to reveal them, being sensitive to a possible misinterpretation by the English government of two Catholics meeting abroad. There was too much scope for thoughts of conspiracy and that would have been particularly embarrassing for the slippery Rolston, who was procrastinating over whether to return to England. Persecution of Catholics continued even as Standen sought to engage Bacon's new influence with Essex as a mechanism to promote toleration. With Rolston shuffling his feet and holding back Scottish news, Standen wrote to Bacon in cipher about the Scottish representative at the Spanish court, Sir William Semple, the betrayer of Liere (near Antwerp) to Spain. Although James VI had not been a party to this a decade before, he did choose to retain Semple as a diplomat and Standen's scorn was freely expressed.

A year after his arrival in Spain, Standen was still analysing aspects of his plan to return home. To reduce the hazards he decided to travel under an alias and then to present himself to Burghley when he reached London. This deference to the old man was well understood by Anthony Bacon seeking to cultivate his uncle's interest and goodwill. To assist Standen's reception he passed to Burghley the latest letter giving news of a small Spanish fleet with 2,000 soldiers and a large quantity of arms. It was leaving San Sebastián to aid de Lussan, the governor of Blaye, north of Bordeaux on the Gironde and now besieged by the Huguenot Marshal Matignon. In a personal note Bacon eloquently defended Standen from harmful imputations – necessary because Burghley was often testy about the use of Catholics as spies. (If he had known more about Rolston he might have been less pleased.)

Chapter Twelve

The Lopez Conspiracy

When the youthful bachelor King of Portugal, Dom Sebastian, died in the battle of Alcazar (al-Qaṣr al-Kabīr), in 1578, it was a demise 'heavy with consequences'. His only heir was his elderly and consumptive great-uncle Cardinal-Infant Henry, the last surviving son of Manuel I. When the ailing sexagenarian himself died there was certain to be a dispute about his successor, because the house of Aviz disappeared. Considering the situation and anxious for his country Henry gallantly asked the Pope for a special dispensation to marry. The request was refused as unseemly, and it left Dom Antonio, the illegitimate son of Duke Luis of Beja and his converted Jewish mistress Yolande Gomez (known as 'La Pelicana'), as the principal Portuguese claimant, ahead of the Duchess of Bragança, the daughter of one of Henry's brothers. In 1565 Dom Antonio had become a knight of St John of Malta, and within a decade characteristically owed the order's treasury over 35,000 scudi from the income of his priory at Crato. Perhaps his connection meant something in 1582 when the knights allowed English merchants free entry to the island while on trading voyages to the Levant. Henry detested Dom Antonio and when the latter claimed his parents had eventually married, a special tribunal was set up by the king to assert the prior's bastardy.

When Henry died early in 1580, it soon became clear that the succession would be settled by force. Since Dom Antonio was the only active opponent of Philip II, a son of Henry's sister, his spokesman in England beseeched Elizabeth to give him her support in return for commercial concessions. In May 1580, for example, Juan Rodriguez de Sousa was told to offer a fortified vantage point on the West African coast as security for military aid, and to protect the Portuguese Azores from Philip. As usual the queen was cautious and Mendoza, then in London, exploited her reluctance to get involved by warning that she should not 'offend a King who had so strong an arm and so long a sword'. Despite receiving some French and English help, Dom Antonio was routed at Alcantara by the disgraced Duke of Alva – recalled on the emphatic prompting of Cardinal Granvelle. The fugitive claimant nursed his wounds in northern Portugal before exile, which had him travelling to England, France and the United Provinces. The piecemeal sale of the Portuguese crown jewels made this possible and even allowed him to put forward funds for the stillborn English expedition to the Azores and two later French efforts that also shrivelled to nothing. By July 1583 Santa Cruz had subjugated the islands.

In England, Drake and Hawkins had done most of the Azores preparations, acting on a plan advanced by Walsingham. It was very likely worked out with Leicester – both men having collaborated in council for some years and both having profited from Drake's global circumnavigation.[1] Mendoza, of course, had diligently sought to thwart them and with Dom Antonio's arrival in England in late June 1581, he was instructed by Philip to press Elizabeth to surrender or expel Dom Antonio 'and paint in vivid colours my displeasure if she refuses'. One of the Spanish ambassador's principal agents for spying on the pretender was another Portuguese, Antonio de Escobar (alias Sanson), while directly employed by Philip for the task was Antonio de Viega. In 1587 he sent Gaspar Diaz, one of the Montesinos brothers, to Spain with proposals for the assassination of the exile. For security reasons Mendoza, then envoy in Paris, kept Montesinos in the city while Viega's letters were forwarded to Philip. The diplomat had no liking for his unexpected detainee and was relieved when he decamped to Venice. Viega also wrote up intelligence material for Mendoza, using the pseudonym Luis Fernandez Marchone, serving alongside Escobar and the Flemish-speaking Manuel de Andrade.

London offered a somewhat wobbly sanctuary to a modest number of Iberian Jews. In theory they were Christian converts, and since Dom Antonio was half Jewish, these exiles generally favoured him. This was important to his faltering cause because some were wealthy merchants, active in business and with pan-European contacts. Unfortunately for him there was also jealous rivalry among his adherents, and generally hard times caused dissensions and defections, with some fearing he would eventually come to terms with his supplanter. In March 1588 even Dom Antonio tried to flee from England, and according to one report he was detected when the Lord Admiral Howard recognized the pretender's pet dog on board the vessel of a Captain Edward Prynne, who had been Dom Antonio's main English agent; he went to prison and Dom Antonio was forced to return to London.[3] In London, one of the most prominent of the Christian Jewish community of some ninety Marranos and son of Jorge Anes of Valladolid, was Dunstan Anes (otherwise Benjamin Jorge or Gonzalvo Jorge), a freeman of the Grocer's Company since 1557, and also purveyor of groceries to the household of Elizabeth. Moreover, he was the principal London representative of the Marrano Spice Trust in Antwerp, where he had many friends and relatives. His daughter Sarah was married to Doctor Rodrigo Lopez, living in the parish of St Peter-le-Poer with their five children. Lopez attracted many clients and was also a house physician for St Bartholomew's. In court circles he was well known, especially for his contacts with the Earl of Leicester, whose ardent patriotism was untainted by xenophobia; Walsingham from 1571 and later Essex. Eventually, in 1586, Lopez joined the group of trusted physicians called to deal with Elizabeth's ailments, so perhaps he sweetened his garlic-laden breath before attending her. Or had Sarah modified in England the traditional Jewish–Iberian mode of cooking meat in oil with onions and garlic?

Evidence of continuing royal favour did not recommend Lopez to a grumpy Gabriel Harvey. He thought the doctor 'one that maketh a great account of himself as the best' – the sort of huffy view that Harvey's enemies would cheerfully have attached to him. Having been bundled aside when constantly seeking preferment with Leicester and chronically short of money, Harvey was scandalized that Lopez 'by a kind of Jewish practice hath grown to much wealth'. The sniping is familiar and the content incorrect; Lopez had a large family and was not rich – indeed, it was because of his perception of need that he became a double agent. His plan was eventually to quit London for Antwerp, thence to move to Constantinople where there was a large, tolerated Jewish community, including, since 1492, many from Spain. A covert Jew (and for confirmation of this a knowledgeable Elizabethan spy might have watched the Lopez house for lack of smoke from the chimney even on a midwinter Saturday), Lopez had his practice; a monopoly of the import of aniseed and sumac, as well as the 'Lopez-leases' – grants by Elizabeth of some of the estate holdings of the Bishop of Worcester. From his income he sent funds to poor Marranos in Antwerp and exported whatever capital he could for the envisaged flight to the eastern Mediterranean.

His countryman, Dom Antonio, was another of the immigrants fortunate enough to be taken up by the Earl of Leicester. The latter's particular interest and sympathy curiously chimed with that of Sir Edward Stafford who detested the earl. Unfortunately for Dom Antonio, despite their regard Elizabeth remained generally aloof and her policy towards him rather enigmatic. The problem was that she was more than willing to shunt his cause aside in order to maintain a rickety peace with Spain. When this did collapse with mutual recrimination, the pretender's career as an exile reached a peak with the appearance of the Armada which he had nervously anticipated. With the fighting he had his greatest prospect for successfully exploiting the vital myth that his people would rise in arms to his call. Walsingham, as we have noted, was ill, and Leicester died early in September 1588, so it was Drake who presented the plan to Elizabeth, one that was a response to the repeated pleas of Dom Antonio.

Drake wanted a Counter-Armada to concentrate on Lisbon with its well-protected harbour.[4] The reason was that it was expected that such an effort would prompt the much-vaunted rising of the Portuguese. It would also allow for the destruction of the Spanish fleet remnant – Drake intending to command the navy, while the military operations were to be entrusted to his peppery friend Sir John Norris, the ruthless professional soldier, once loathed by Leicester. The appeal of the whole effort was to be underpinned by finance from a joint-stock company with Elizabeth as a major shareholder after investing £20,000, and supplying some of the fleet and munitions. The Dutch were also interested and for his part Dom Antonio committed himself to repay the cost of the preparations once he was secure in his country. The enterprise, which was actually bigger than the Armada, was to be ready to sail in February 1589.

In fact it finally sailed on 18 April, and the planning flaws that had required the royal tranche to be raised from £20,000 to nearly £50,000 continued. To begin with, Drake put into La Coruña for two weeks instead of sailing to Lisbon directly; result, pre-emptive executions of some of Dom Antonio's likeliest supporters. When he reached the Tagus he landed forces under Norris that had suffered food shortages and illness, so that the march to Lisbon became a great travail. Drake's fleet was overtaken by sickness and the difficulty of outwitting the land fortifications so that he never reached Lisbon. Hence no rising – 'The Portuguese would not revolt until the English took Lisbon; and the English could not take Lisbon until the Portuguese revolted.' Early in June the fleet sailed off with Dom Antonio and the remnant of Norris's troops.

Such a raw failure, a largely ruinous effort, wrecked Dom Antonio's prospects. It was also a calamity for others, including Lopez, who had not only lost money in the venture, but had forfeited goodwill. He had been persuasive about its viability; the huge scale of the wasted effort left many investors like Essex aggrieved. Lopez now needed to show the utmost discretion if he was to emerge unscathed. In fact, it is possible to see now that the first, almost imperceptible jolt that presaged his ruin came late in July 1588. Remarkably, despite the bristling presence of two great fleets in the English Channel, a courier from Dom Antonio to his Paris aide, Antonio de Escobar, arrived in the city. Manuel de Andrade, always referred to as 'shabby', a comment on his clothes or his morality, chose this time to go to Mendoza to sell his services, probably anticipating a great Spanish victory.[5] Andrade suggested he should retain his current employment, but supply copies of the correspondence assigned to him for delivery. On an exuberant note he added that he would kidnap Dom Antonio or even poison him, and although Mendoza was bound to reflect on such an offer he gave no formal response. Instead, Andrade was to plunder the correspondence so that the Spanish were well informed about Drake's plan for the Counter-Armada. All went well until a day in the spring of 1590, when Andrade was arrested in London following the interception of a letter to Mendoza. By then Dom Antonio's reputation was in tatters and his post generally scorned, so Andrade had fallen back on the kidnap notion, made more meaningful because Dom Antonio was about to visit France.

Andrade was soon released after Lopez had approached various members of the Privy Council. Unless he was acting at the prompting of someone else, it is difficult to see why he would have bothered. The man behind it was surely Walsingham planning a death-bed enterprise with a man who had work to do before he secured a total free pardon. The dying secretary, with a flourish, created some hollow peace negotiations as a cover for Andrade to enter Spain as a spy. Both countries were now facing increasing difficulties in obtaining information about war preparations. If Andrade could enter and leave Spain without experiencing too many difficulties the Secretary would have been satisfied. It seems to have worked well enough, although Walsingham did not live to measure the success. Andrade was received cordially enough when he arrived late in 1590 (or early 1591) to be interviewed by Don Cristobal de Moura, adviser on Portuguese affairs. After consultations with Philip II it was decided that their subject should return to England with a little money and a ring valued at £50 for Lopez. He was instructed to say that Spanish negotiators would wait until Andrade could show an official letter of credence from the English government. Also, he was to do some routine intelligence work by reporting anything of interest.

After shipwreck and other adventures Andrade got back to England by July 1591. But now Burghley was overseeing foreign policy at the direction of Elizabeth, and he had no inclination to employ Andrade. He was sceptical that such a lowly individual should be taken seriously by the Spanish court, famous for its dignity and deference to high birth. Burghley evidently believed that if Andrade had been accepted it was because they had divined Walsingham's last secret intention. Thereafter, and for the next eighteen months, Andrade survived on doles from Lopez. However, in April 1593 Burghley consented to use Andrade again and he was sent on a mission to the Netherlands, possibly to trawl for details of Stanley's murder plot. By June he was loitering in Calais and two months later was still trying to nudge Burghley into sending him money by gruesomely ill-chosen hints about selling out to Spain. The clumsy presentation was loftily ignored, but by then Andrade was trying to rescue his career from the doldrums. Even without official backing, for who was there to approach, he and Lopez decided to revive, if they could, the earlier peace negotiations with Spain. A curious private initiative, it had its inception in Lopez's desire for a truly large sum of money, something approaching the worthless bond for 50,000 crowns he held from Dom Antonio. If this life-enhancing sum was to be pocketed, it had to come from Philip II, and it could be that he alluded to the matter in conversation with Elizabeth.

From time to time Lopez had a Portuguese exile, Esteban Ferreira da Gama, staying in his house.[6] Both men strained at their lack of money and Ferreira was anxious to return home to enjoy his forfeited estates. To this end he wrote to de Moura through an intermediary offering his submission as a subject of Philip II, and he took Lopez into his confidence because he hoped the Spanish reply might be channelled through him. On a quick trip to London Andrade must have been told about this, as well as the distinct shift away from Dom Antonio of his son, Dom Manuel. When Andrade returned to France he had several commissions and these became meshed with the activities of a youthful Portuguese employee of Essex, another ruined follower of Dom Antonio called Manuel Luis Tinoco. Essex was still profoundly interested in Portuguese affairs in the larger European context, and he identified a possible substitute for the lightweight Dom Antonio in the Duke of Bragança, hoping that with some nurturing he might become a rallying point for anti-Spanish forces. The chances were not great, but Essex was not prepared simply to let an opportunity pass. Unfortunately, with the impulsive carelessness that was the hallmark of Essex's political naïvety, he gave the mission to Tinoco, declaring his aim in general terms, but allowing him to cobble together a method of carrying it out. Even Tinoco recognized that as a nonentity he would have no weight with the Spanish, and if he managed to get back to Portugal there was the acute problem of carrying out his work.

His moderately ingenious solution was to coat-tail Ferreira da Gama; this should ensure that his initial contact would not be frosty. His intention then was to disclose the remainder of Dom Antonio's supporters and to sketch some adventure involving his country. When he approached Ferreira and Lopez they accepted his collaboration because of his links to Essex, which might splash an official gloss on what they had spatchcocked. Tinoco left England on 26 July 1593, carrying the formal letter of submission from Dom Manuel, one of the pretender's ten children. Arriving in Brussels Tinoco sought to contact the Count of Fuentes and Secretary Ibarra of the archduke's administration. They received him with alacrity because they had already seen or been in contact with Andrade, whose peace effort with Lopez had them mesmerized. What mattered was peace and Philip II had evidently given them instructions that if the cause could be resuscitated it was to be given detailed attention. This was a crucial revision of his previous attitude and probably stemmed from the removal of Walsingham – until then he had himself preferred the possibilities of spying. With effective spies as rare as successful coups against Elizabeth, it was a new realism that drove Philip to hope for success in negotiations; even so, as the prescient Burghley had judged, he did not regard Andrade with warmth. Fuentes and Ibarra must have been alerted to the hope of finding a more reliable link with Lopez, whom it was known had many links to the ruling élite of England. So when Tinoco arrived they were pleased, since he appeared to be acting with, or for, Ferreira da Gama, who was in close touch with Lopez. After an interview Tinoco was swiftly sent back to England with a message for Ferreira; it accepted his offer of service and expressed the wish to deal further with him and Lopez (but not Andrade).

In late August or early September Tinoco arrived back in London. With barely time to gulp a meal and exchange his horse he left for Brussels the next day, scarcely any the wiser about what was happening. He had simply been told that Lopez and Ferreira da Gama would consider the Spanish proposal as outlined and send their reply by yet another courier. In fact, Lopez was out of town and this was Ferreira's response, immediately conjured up because Tinoco could not safely linger. Nor did Ferreira want him to, since peace negotiations had become a mysterious and defiant force utterly at odds with what Essex espoused. So Tinoco was told little and shunted out of the country. Shutting out Andrade was logical, but it left Lopez more exposed and, with the connections on his peace component, Ferreira's own position was altering. If taken up in England as genuine then he and Lopez became men of consequence in the diplomatic realm, but if not, or if the personalities involved were rejected by the Privy Council, then he and Lopez could expect a very frosty response. After some further deliberations together they went ahead, recruiting a new courier called Gomez d'Avila. He was sent to Brussels in mid-September with the promised answer – a qualified acceptance with two reservations. First, that Lopez would receive 50,000 crowns (in effect paying off the bond of Dom Antonio, which was a horrible reminder of failure). And secondly, that the letter of credence from Burghley would have to coincide with a Spanish equivalent available for scrutiny in Brussels. Hence, if the Spanish put up the money before the credentials, Lopez and his associate could loot the pot and disappear. Or, if the credentials did reach Brussels, they could then go to Burghley with a much less tenuous operation and a chance to negotiate a peace.

Suddenly on the 18 October, Ferreira da Gama was arrested in London.[7] The ostensible cause was that his earlier exchanges with de Moura, offering his service to Spain, had been revealed. No one in the English government paid much attention at first because arrests were routine and in any case the matter of Portugal had been marginalized; Ferreira was handed over to Dom Antonio, then lodging in Eton. However, simultaneously instructions were given that all incoming Portuguese correspondence should be stopped at ports and any suspicious items forwarded to Essex, the privy councillor with responsibility for Portuguese affairs. This sieved out several quaintly worded letters from a Francisco Torres in the Spanish Netherlands to a Diego Hernandez in London. Ferreira blurted out that Torres was in fact Tinoco, and then added that Lopez was a partner in a scheme to reach terms with the Spanish. When the courier Gomez d'Avila returned to England nearly three weeks later, he too was arrested, but it was found that the greater part of his correspondence for Ferreira was unimportant. Except that one letter, drafted by Tinoco, from Ibarra or Fuentes, because of its enigmatic wording, caused considerable suspicion and perplexity.

5 December 1593: 'The bearer hereof will tell your Worship the price in which your pearls are held; and will advise your worship presently of the uttermost penny that will be given for them; and receive what order you will set down for the conveyance of the money and wherein you would have it employed. Also this bearer will tell you in what resolution we rested about a little musk and amber, the which I am determined to buy; but before I resolve myself I will be advised of the price thereof. And if it shall please your worship to be my partner I am persuaded we shall make good profit.'

Not only was this in Portuguese, but the nuggets of jargon could mean virtually anything. If Phelippes was called upon for an opinion it is doubtful if he could do more than guess what the 'pearls' were. If it meant the peace negotiations, then what was being indicated was that the Spanish would pay the price Lopez and Ferreira da Gama had set for their services. 'Musk' and 'amber' might stand for Dom Manuel and Dom Antonio, but with a reference back to Spain for a final decision. D'Avila knew little, other than what he had mastered to brief Ferreira – namely that a large sum of money would shortly be sent over. Lopez, in the mean time, had seen his partner snatched and so he went to Elizabeth to rehearse the case for Ferreira's release. He added that he and the prisoner 'had already laid a good foundation' for peace, but instead of being gratified Elizabeth growled about meddling, and the interview ended inconclusively. Perhaps Lopez had said too much or even too little. Suspicions about his degree of candour increased when Ferreira da Gama, still in custody and ignorant of d'Avila's arrest, smuggled a note to Lopez begging him to prevent the courier's return 'for if he should be taken, the Doctor were utterly undone without all remedy'. Lopez affirmed that he had tried to do this. both notes were intercepted but not communicated to Essex for some time. In an increasingly tense mood Ferreira tried to bribe the young man called Pedro who was assigned to watch him. He offered (though probably did not have) a considerable bribe for a message to be carried personally to Ibarra in Brussels; his greatest anxiety now being the Spanish letter of credence and its whereabouts.

At the beginning of December Tinoco was en route from Brussels with the Spanish reply. He halted at Calais before the crossing, and learnt that Ferreira and d'Avila were under arrest. What to do? He applied eventually for official permission to enter England, approaching Burghley, not Essex, because he was reasonably certain now that since its inception his mission had undergone a striking metamorphosis. It will be recalled he had left England in connection with Essex's probe into the notion of the Duke of Bragança ultimately replacing Dom Antonio as the leading claimant to the Portuguese throne. He was now returning in connection with certain negotiations to which he believed Burghley was party, and he was well enough informed about the personalities of the Privy Council to know of the divisions between his erstwhile employer Essex and the Lord Treasurer. The possibilities of misunderstanding were endless, and when he was arrested in

Dr Rodrigo Lopez plotting to poison the queen

England and presented for questioning to the earl, Tinoco must have been a very frightened man. He said little beyond the obvious and that though he was the source of the Torres letters to Ferreira, the latter was actually in a position to do important service to the state if released and allowed to communicate with Lopez.

After this effort Tinoco sought a private interview with Sir Robert Cecil and talked about his real mission, handing over two letters to Ferreira which he had hitherto held back. They were puzzling to Cecil, though the one from the Count of Fuentes to Ferreira is more revealing and utterly demolished the hopes of Lopez and Ferreira. There was to be no reward and no recognition until after the letter of credence had been produced. There would be no Spanish letter of credence either until Lopez and Ferreira had produced theirs. So there was a deadlock and it would even have been useless to go to Burghley to tell the story so far, because they would have to confess to months of covert dealings with Spain, and there was a strong possibility that they would not be believed. They had no proof because the Spaniards had never committed themselves. In fact, the Fuentes letter led to more questioning, with Essex now predictably seized by the thought that something significant was afoot and had to be laid bare. Tinoco, therefore, was threatened with torture and he said now that Andrade had told him that Lopez had been a Spanish agent for many years, and that Andrade had once brought him a ring which he described, from Philip II. This statement was made on 23 January 1594. Almost simultaneously there arrived from Eton copies of the notes between Ferreira and Lopez intercepted nearly two months before by Dom Antonio's efforts. Lopez was now arrested because the juxtaposition of circumstantial material pointed to his involvement in something serious. His house was searched, but no incriminating papers were found – only the ring whose possession he denied, claiming he had had it but had allowed Sarah to sell it.

On 24 January 1594 Lopez was questioned by Burghley, Sir Robert Cecil (who had taken on many duties of the principal secretary without yet holding the office) and Essex. With the most senior councillor well informed about the background, he does not seem to have thought Lopez guilty, although perhaps culpable in some cloudy way. Essex was much more inclined to believe Lopez guilty of infamy and had him removed to Essex House for further examination. On the following afternoon there came the famous interview between Elizabeth and Essex at which she upbraided him for meddling. He was predictably incensed and retired to Essex House for two days of sulking. So why did he refuse to believe his own physician? In part, no doubt, he was pawing the ground because the story had been elicited by Burghley. Further, the breach with Lopez had grown after the doctor had proved unwilling to supply Essex with a private fund of secret information and had disclosed the matter to Elizabeth.[8] In addition, it has been averred that in his cups Lopez unwisely revealed that he had treated the earl for a venereal infection; then and later such a thing 'did disparage his honour', although his unchaste private life was talked of by many. But principally Essex was still mortified that the promotion of Dom Antonio's cause and his association with it had sent his own finances into a severe dive from which he struggled to recover for some ten years. Finally, there was the matter of Bragança, a clandestine initiative kept from the council and the queen, who, when she found out, directed her anger at the culprit who sauntered into territory she regarded still as very much her own. So, if any consequences stemmed from this, Essex was determined to deflect them.

For two days nothing happened. Then on 28 January Essex scribbled an abrupt, almost fevered note to Anthony Bacon, who otherwise seems to have remained aloof from the matter. 'I have discovered a most dangerous and desperate treason. The point of conspiracy was Her Majesty's death. The executioner should have been Dr Lopez, the manner poison. This I have so followed that I will make it as clear as noonday.' Such was the vehement lurch prompted by outraged vanity and a disordered imagination. He said there was a conspiracy so there must be one, but now he needed new evidence and that at a gallop. It came from the forgotten and disparaged Andrade. His career was in limbo following his side-lining in Calais, and the fact that he had been bundled aside by Tinoco and Ferreira in the opaque peace initiative. Andrade depended on spying for his living, so if the Spaniards neglected him perhaps he could be employed for something more wayward than peace negotiations. Andrade's indiscretions were reported even before his chance meeting with Tinoco when he rattled on about a commission to assassinate Antonio Perez, the envoy of Henri IV, given a special place in the esteem of Essex. And if Andrade was desperate, so increasingly was Essex; a boast from the lowly Portuguese that he had persuaded Lopez to poison Elizabeth might in retrospect seem unlikely – to the earl it was a godsend.

The hapless doctor had been held in custody by Gelly Meyrick, Essex's household steward. By 5 February he had been shifted to the Tower, according to Standen writing to Anthony Bacon, and a second interrogation was concluded before the earl and Sir Robert Cecil. Certain aspects of the matter even unsettled the young imperturbable, and it is no surprise that, by the end of the month, with a greater show of alacrity than heretofore, Lopez was put on trial at the Guildhall. The prosecutor was that unpleasant, urgent bully Edward Coke, Solicitor-General, before a special commission of fifteen judges, including Essex, his brother-in-law Lord Rich, Sir Thomas Heneage (for whom Anthony Munday was a spy at this time), and Robert Cecil. Without counsel to defend him Lopez, who said he had 'confessed' to avoid the rack, was inevitably found guilty of spying for Spain, seeking to promote rebellion in England (how and when?) and planning to poison Elizabeth. The lurid gossip of London was that the doctor had been repeatedly racked to obtain a confession, possibly by Richard Topcliffe. Yet Cecil, in his letters, the contemporary historian William Camden and other sources deny torture. Such was the public interest that five official accounts were published, including one by Francis Bacon, hoping to promote his own career. Lopez's accomplices came to trial on 14 March.

The expected executions were delayed by a reluctant sovereign still unconvinced that a man who had attended her ill could have wished her ill. Even so, a plea for his life from the Duke of Mitylene in the eastern Mediterranean failed and Lopez was eventually executed on 7 June 1594. Tinoco entertained the crowd by fighting with his executioner, while it seems that the fluent Ferreira da Gama may have been saved so that he could go on a mission to Morocco; Dom Antonio (d. 1595), it has been noted, had a son Dom Cristovão, who was being held virtual hostage in Fez. Elizabeth's hesitations did assuage some of the misery of the Lopez family. Sarah kept her late husband's estate, normally forfeited, living on with her family in Mountjoy's Inn, Holborn, while according to some sources Elizabeth kept the Spanish ring as an enigmatic symbol of the Portuguese connection. Nor were the somewhat peccable activities of the father permanently visited on his schoolboy son Anthony, for after briefly losing his scholarship to Winchester, he had it restored in 1595.[9]

Chapter Thirteen

A Semi-Official Secret Service

By the 1590s the political authority of Burghley was massive and seamless; he had not faltered in office for over twenty years. What disconcerted two of his nephews, Anthony and Francis Bacon, was that, despite their manifest gifts and willingness to work, as had been evidenced in the past, he made not a scintilla of effort to advance them as they surely deserved. All they got from the relationship were grave nods of insipid encouragement, which only left a teasing expectation of something more substantial and rewarding. Years before, when sententiously reflecting for Robert Cecil's benefit on the ten precepts he cherished for a successful public life, the Lord Treasurer warned about giving jobs to relations or friends – 'they expect much and do little'. Yet in office this wry admonition lapsed and Burghley

Sir Robert Cecil, 1563–1612. Political heir to his father, Burghley, the deft hunchback administrator (later Earl of Salisbury), realized the advantage of an effective secret service late in the reign and had the means to fund it

employed a clutch of relatives, including four nephews by marriage through his first wife's family, and Catholic gossip had him striving to have his first-born son, Thomas Cecil, made Lord Deputy of Ireland in 1592. His resistance to the blandishments of the Bacons may have had something to with shielding his diminutive hunchback son Robert Cecil from direct comparison with his cousins – perhaps he feared that they would shine and his hope for the future would be overshadowed, as he was physically by the Earl of Essex. It was to the latter that the Bacons therefore attached themselves, hoping to float careers, but thinking of the Apollonian aristocrat as a stopgap. So they sought to maintain friendly contacts with the Cecils, and there was sometimes trading of contacts and information. For example, in 1593 Anthony Bacon's dealings with Dr Thomas Morison, Essex's aide in Scotland, were strengthened by Michael Hickes, one of Burghley's principal secretaries.

The secret service of Essex required liberal funding, when privately for the Bacons it was a time of perpetual financial squalls. All the time his open-handed brother had been abroad Francis Bacon had been living on borrowed money, much of it coming from a willing source – Nicholas Trott, a barrister at Gray's Inn, who in turn borrowed from his mother and brother. Yet no sooner had Anthony returned than he too dived into Trott's resources for £600, and when the repayment of the loan was due he had the gallant effrontery to ask for another £1,400. The borrowing, spending, pleading and later railing, went on for years, with the pitifully hilarious consequence that in September 1597 Trott asked Anthony Bacon for a £5 loan which he promised to pay back in eight days. To prop up his tottering balance of expenditure over income, Bacon had to sell land, and the urgent need to do so at a time of bad weather and harvests meant a reduction in the sale price that businessmen, like Alderman John Spencer, were prepared to pay. When Spencer backed away from a second purchase, Bacon approached Thomas Phelippes, now in Essex's employ also, for a loan of £1,000 a year. It may help explain the ruinous debt of Phelippes to the crown some years later.

Though he had to defer to Essex, whose ideas were not always well focused (*cf.* his Brangança probe) and who conspicuously lacked the political guile of Robert Cecil, Anthony Bacon organized a useful secret service. It was flawed because Essex was not especially good at assessing the material submitted, and because it worked best in Italy and France, rather than Spain and the Low Countries. Moreover, it was somewhat limp because, despite his long service as an intelligencer, Bacon was lacking energy in his direction of the spies. It seems curious now that a man whose failings as a private correspondent while abroad had irked many people, should have committed himself to the task of organizing a spy network that ran parallel to that of the sagging affair of the Cecils (actually Burghley). It seems doubly odd when it is recalled that Bacon only infrequently met his employer, being often bedridden, and relying on couriers and personal messengers.

The head of Essex's secretariat was Edward Reynolds, and his closest colleagues were the brilliant young academic Henry Cuffe, Henry Wotton and a Mr Temple, with Anthony Bacon in an autonomous position. In addition there were two other important aides, Thomas Smith, clerk of the Privy Council and Arthur Atey, inherited from Leicester. When Essex was absent, it was Reynolds and Bacon who held the reins, but as far as hiring agents was concerned, that was left to Bacon. Both Essex and his spy master expected active participation from the agents and those who submitted stale news were rebuked. Because Bacon spent so much time in bed, even when illness did not require it, he acted as archivist of the Essex group with new files and copies of letters. Many of these were in code, so they demanded extra attention. Bacon deciphered, sent the material therein to Essex and on his instructions prepared answers. It is perhaps a little unfair to picture him as an idler, because he was prepared to copy poorly written material when his illness gave him respite. Also, he oversaw the preparation of abstracts to give Essex the most potent items and wrote comments on what he submitted. Sometimes he did feel exploited, as when he was instructed to translate in French and then cipher the instructions given by Elizabeth to Essex for his agent in Scotland. Bacon complained to his brother about the time wasted on this effort and that much labour would have been saved if he had drafted the letter himself for Essex to sign.

By delicate filtration only the most pertinent matter was submitted to Essex, who clearly impressed Elizabeth with his secret service. It was he who finally decided what letters or despatches were presented to her by Thomas Smith or Sir Fulke Greville. Both Bacon and Reynolds tried to maintain a smooth flowing operation, but their intention could be undermined by the genuine slackness of Greville, who was slow to return the papers. As far as Smith was concerned there may have been a deeper motive, since there is a suggestion that he was also a client of the Cecils. Reynolds knew very well that the longer the papers were in circulation, the greater the likelihood that a surreptitious coin would be able to buy a copy. The renegade Spaniard Antonio Perez certainly thought security was failing, abjuring the earl to burn all letters he wrote to him. Bacon eventually grew weary of him and was positively cheerful when he went back to France.[1] There Bacon had, of course, built up a wide circle of friends and contacts. One of the most important at a critical time for Anglo-French relations was Jacques de Goyon, sieur de Matignon, a close associate of Henri IV from his days as King of Navarre. Seeking to promote a correspondence between Matignon and his employer, he described Essex in most flattering terms. At the same time Bacon was being reviled by an enemy in France, but not as one might expect, a Frenchman.

Bacon had only been back in London a few months when he received a warning from John Blagge, the servant of Alderman Peter Houghton. Sent from Bordeaux, it drew attention to the calumnies against the spy master of a man called Raffe Ridley. He was an English agent who had become an 'envious adversary' and according to the informant was on his way to London to create mischief. Apparently Bacon had nursed Ridley when the latter was ill and had even asked Francis Bacon to recommend Ridley for employment. Now he sniped at the good Samaritan, calling Bacon a 'bastard' and a 'sodomist', and trumpeting the accusation that the spy master was intending his murder, along with that of another agent, James Peacock. Blagge intervened because Bacon had been kind to him in Bordeaux. He expected Ridley to find London lodgings in the Fenchurch Street home of his own employer Houghton. Furthermore, Ridley had a letter from Anthony to his brother Francis, which was now to be disclosed to the Privy Council. The contents are not known, but were clearly expected to damage

Anthony Bacon's reputation. Since Ridley was employed by the council to undertake various duties in the French town, including dealing with Bordeaux's administrators over ordnance supplies from England to Huguenot armies as well as French wine exports to England, he expected his clamour to be attended.

To add to Bacon's woes – his return to England coincided with the infamous outbreak of plague that summer – he learnt while in retreat at the family home of Gorhambury, that a close associate of Philippe du Plessis had arrived in London. Benjamin Aubéry du Maurier arrived with the ratification of the treaty in which Elizabeth promised martial aid to Henri IV, and secret letters from the king about his contacts with Rome. Even if du Maurier had not already met Bacon he must surely have known the reason for the process of law in Montauban, and they even had a mutual acquaintance in Beza. Perhaps Bacon was just being paranoid in thinking du Maurier hostile to him, for even if the Frenchman was not homosexual, it is hard to see what he would gain from humiliating the highly placed aide of the queen's favourite courtier and sometime companion-in-arms of his own monarch. Indeed, there is no clear evidence that the process in Montauban was known to more than a handful of people.

Against a background of some gloom and hostility Bacon went on to prove his capacity for loyal friendship by championing Anthony Standen. Burghley was shown Standen's latest intelligence on Spanish military activity. The exiled spy was also tracked by two double agents – Chateaumartin and Andrade. He travelled in disguise, yet when he reached Calais he was recognized by some Spaniards who had met him before. To his consternation a letter he had prepared for Nicholas Faunt was stolen from the sailor he had paid to deliver it, and the Flemish thief translated it into French and mischievously sold it to the departing Spaniards. Since it contained references to Rolston, Standen was afraid that a fellow agent would be hunted down in Spain – a clear indication that the Essex network had no notion of Rolston being a double agent. Still, the commendably humane Standen wrote to warn him to leave Spain for France, while he made the crossing to England in June 1593. His reception was mixed: Elizabeth and Burghley naturally cautious; Anthony Bacon delighted. The return of a spy, after twenty-eight years of exile and then clandestine employment, was bound to arouse curiosity mixed with some unease, and Standen himself may have overvalued the significance of his home-coming to spying and diplomacy. He was still candid about his adherence to Catholicism and his crucial efforts for England had lost something of a patina of worth, because they had always been done out of the country. There was also the ticklish present dilemma of how to satisfy Essex with initial courtesies without alienating Elizabeth and Burghley. He did eventually condescend to respond and Standen was summoned to court by Michael Hickes. Since this was currently in Kingston, and Standen was in Twickenham, he planned rather neatly to dine at an inn where he knew a messenger from France was resting and it brought him a scoop. From the court he was able to write to Bacon on 30 July that Henri IV had been to mass at St Denis, and had met the dukes of Guise and Mayenne to discuss a truce. Many people had suspected the steadfastness of Henri's Protestantism in the light of his country's political turbulence, and confirmation came several weeks later. The question that agitated the English government was whether he would now make peace with Spain.

As for Standen, he was received by the queen when Sir Robert Cecil presented him. Her first and certainly unwelcome requirement was that he should write an account of his long years abroad.[2] Standen went back to Twickenham to solicit Bacon's help, but he was crippled with an attack of gout. Standen therefore left him in peace, and went first to Berkshire to visit his brothers and then to the New Forest for a period of quiet slog on the text. When he completed it and had recovered from illness, he returned to court in November 1593 to an unpleasant reality. Elizabeth, on a personal whim, had decided she disliked him and Essex was told not to discuss affairs of state with him. It was an uncomfortable position exacerbated when Cecil directed him to leave the court. This roused Essex, who had to intervene to reduce the loss of face for his hireling. Standen was allowed to remain, goaded by the possibility of advancement, shrinking from the threat of being spurned; his leading enemies seemed to be the Cecils and they were hard to trump. All through the next year Standen haunted the court. In April 1594 he made an attempt to oust the Garter King of Arms, whom he conjectured would be disgraced by a disorder in the queen's chapel. Even though his grab for office was rejected, several years later he still chose to present himself as a candidate for Clarenceux King of Arms. Being a man who thrived on activity and movement he chafed, even when circumstances offered a pleasant diversion. In January 1594 he wrote to Bacon that on Twelfth Night he went to a playhouse and danced until one o'clock in the morning, while entertaining a party of Germans for Essex. Getting back to his lodgings so late in vile weather intensified a cold and also brought on a 'small fit'.

Fortunately for his morale Standen could be useful to Bacon. By October 1594 Bacon had passed on letters from Rolston, still in Spain apparently, to have them sifted for Essex. Acting as a go-between Standen kept the invalid spy master informed about gossip as well as weightier matters. He seems to have acted in a public relations capacity, which was necessary, since for many at court Bacon was a phantom. As Standen wrote: 'I have had many and many speeches about you with personages of import of both sexes, and it should seem none of them have been thoroughly informed of your parts and quality, although they have heard something superficially.' Ruefully, Standen at this time might have said much the same about himself, and the trail of career disappointments continued when Essex allowed the entry of Antonio Perez to his service.[*] The sometime spy's position seemed very shaky, when suddenly he saw an exiled Spaniard swept into the higher reaches of English public life. Nor was he able to dabble usefully in the complicated ambiguities of the Lopez business (it seems hard to resolve to call it a conspiracy when the events are reviewed). Standen had to muster what hope he could that the fantastical Perez, with his exotic allure, would soon fade. Goronwy Rees who knew a good deal about English twentieth-century espionage, wrote of the spy Guy Burgess 'the very word *secret* was a call to battle, a challenge which he never failed

---

[*] Essex's employment of Catholics among his advisers was noted by Robert Cecil and later led to a firm accusation: 'Your religion appears by Blount, Davies (Sir John) and Tresham (Francis). . .'.

to accept. He hunted out secrets like a hound after truffles.' In a number of compelling ways Antonio Perez, sometime Italian secretary to Philip II, might have been his model.

Born in 1540, Perez had had a favoured childhood and was educated at universities in Spain and abroad.[3] At the age of twenty-eight he had achieved extraordinary promotion within Philip II's hugely swollen bureaucracy, dealing with the Portuguese correspondence, and then became an important figure in intelligence work. However, like so many of his contemporaries, Perez was not satisfied with handling one set of secrets. The sense of duty that bound him to the king ebbed and he made contacts with Philip's unbalanced half-brother, Don John of Austria. His sudden death in 1578 led to the discovery of Perez's duplicity and he was arrested in July 1579. After some years of imprisonment and intermittent torture, he escaped and fled to his homeland of Aragon. In 1591 he decamped to Béarn to the protection of Catherine de Bourbon, sister of Henri of Navarre, and a lady well known to Anthony Bacon. To boost his credit and his welcome, Perez claimed to have valuable documents in his possession (Guy Burgess never threw away a letter), though years excluded from power must have drained them of much value.[4]

In April 1593 Perez arrived in England at the behest of Henri IV and, after lodging briefly at the French embassy, he left London to travel to various country houses to avoid the plague. In July, when another representative of Henri arrived to ask for more troops and a loan, Perez made himself available to the mission which was a political flop but a social success. Yet, when Jean de Ferrières, the vidame of Chartres (chief lay officer of the bishop), and his son returned to France in October, the feisty Perez stayed behind. At Sunbury he met both Dom Antonio and Dr Lopez, who thought it useful to glean anything he could on Perez in the hope of selling it to Spain. He did it by engaging a domestic servant to spy on Perez, who finally settled at Essex House in March 1594. We know the partial consequence of Lopez being indiscreet within hearing of his Sunbury acquaintances.

Fluent in Italian, Spanish and Latin, Perez with his breadth of contacts was undoubtedly a useful, if eccentric and occasionally risible intelligencer. Although still a Catholic he was trusted by some and underscored his value to Essex by insolently scorning his rivals, most notably the Cecils. There was some venom in his smirking hostility to Robert Cecil whom he called 'Roberto il Diavolo'. Cecil's aunt, Lady Bacon, found Perez just as repugnant and stormed at Anthony for his dealings with him. In addition she was incensed by what she saw as unseemly closeness between her other son, Francis, and the renegade. He was a papist with a dispensation to say mass in his rooms and Lady Bacon was a Puritan. In a letter to Anthony she reckoned, with a considerable insight, that Perez 'will use discourses out of season to hinder your health'. Anthony might not have been inclined to admit it to his well-meaning, albeit narrow-minded mother, but the personality of the Iberian cuckoo did become tedious. His booming voice could fill a chamber, and on the page his flamboyant prose could be equally tiring. By July 1595, when Perez left for France as an intelligencer for Essex, he went leaving a high-water mark of derision as the original interest in him retreated. He took with him a wardrobe of the earl's livery, a bodyguard and secretaries.

Edward Wilton thought him 'exceedingly timorous', and if the stories told of Philip II's unabated animosity were true and did not stem from a desire to inflate bogusly his position, then he had every right to be. As it was, Henri IV was cajoled eventually into providing him with a bodyguard, while Godfrey Aleyn was employed by Essex to spy on the spy. In October Jacques Petit, a page to Bacon, was sent to France with letters from his employer and the earl, and instructions to Aleyn to report back to England if Perez became too loquacious. Given the subterfuges commissioned by his betters, it is not entirely surprising to find Aleyn succumbing to the temptation to show off about his clandestine work. He copied letters between Essex and Perez, and forwarded them to his father John Aleyn, who had been a messenger for Sir John Bowes. He corresponded as well with Lord Zouche, ambassador to Scotland in 1594. Routine scrutiny of the mails revealed Aleyn's peccadillo and Henry Wotton went over to France to bring the miscreant back. With his father he was sent to the Clink to reflect ruefully on his folly. From its squalid surroundings he penned appeals to Essex and Bacon, while Perez raged against him. Eventually, this anger decayed when he imagined Aleyn blabbing indiscreetly. In the mean time he began a series of reports that looked at the circumstances and personalities in the French court. Even more usefully, having probed some intercepted correspondence, he was able to warn Essex in November 1595 that the Spanish were planning another assault, but failed to identify Calais as the target. He bemoaned the low-key response in London believing England should seize the initiative by attacking Spain. This took him a step away from the official French position – that France and England should combine for a European war effort. He wanted a direct challenge to Philip II whom he called 'the disturber of the earth'.

In April 1596, as Essex was taken up by the preparations for the Cádiz expedition, Perez arrived back in England. He came this time with Dom Manuel of Portugal, the Duke of Bouillon and a party of about fifteen, who sought a signed treaty between England and France, with English troops being sent immediately to aid besieged forces in Calais. Perez was himself having to lay siege to his sometime patron, but Essex, swamped by demands on his time, was able to stay aloof. Perez was put out and turned to Bacon, ill and overworked suddenly. Anthony soon became quite oppressed by this additional list of woes about which he could do very little. Perez was bemused because for months his intelligence efforts had been shaped to the earl's requirements. This rejection was very likely caused by the queen's dislike of a pederast. Late in May he returned to France; in January 1597 when he was made a royal councillor in France the connection with Essex's secret service was partially severed. Robert Naunton was deputed to have dealings with him in Paris, while supposedly tutoring Essex's cousin, Robert Vernon; it was a task that sapped his strength. Finally, Perez's connections with England were severed by James I in 1604 as the peace negotiations with Spain made him redundant.

Chapter Fourteen

'Secret Spialls'

Although Burghley assiduously fostered the development of his second son's political career, there was no likelihood of high office for Robert Cecil in 1590. When Walsingham died in the spring there was a most interesting episode. It has been suggested that Robert Cecil was responsible for the swift and secret pounce on the late secretary's London home, when many important and revealing papers were seized. There are other candidates for the organizer of the raid, with Burghley in a superior position ahead of Sir Thomas Heneage. Thomas Walsingham, the Earl of Worcester, or even Sir Christopher Hatton, conceivably anxious to eliminate any hint of political indiscretions. If it was indeed Robert Cecil who filched the archive, then for such an adept political man he took a surprisingly long time to master the mechanisms of espionage. For a man of great acumen, he found his initial involvement in secret service matters was faltering, somewhat in contrast to the efforts, usually well received, of his sparkling rival at court, Essex.

With the sudden death of his stepfather Leicester in 1588, the young earl became the most compelling figure among the younger generation, having perpetual access to a somewhat brittle-tempered and ageing sovereign. His high-spirited and beautiful sister, Lady Penelope Rich, also found a diversion from a wearisome marriage in court politics. She became, for a time, an intermediary in a secret correspondence initiated with James VI of Scotland, the man widely favoured by many to secure the throne of England without violence. Letters were passed via a young member of the Douglas family in Edinburgh – Thomas Douglas, the sulky nephew of Archibald Douglas, the king's representative in London. They were in cipher, but one so simple that it is not at all remarkable that a contemporary informer could penetrate it. The correspondence was known to Burghley because Thomas Fowler, once employed by Leicester as a spy, was now being retained by the Lord Treasurer. In October 1589 he had sent Burghley a list of names and code names: Elizabeth (Pallas); James VI (Victor); Essex (Ernestus); Lord Rich (Richards); Penelope Rich (Rialta = the Exchange).[1] Fowler thrived after this, living in Islington and becoming lord of the manor of Barnsbury. He was knighted in 1603 by the new ruler and then had no option but to serve on the jury of knights that condemned Ralegh in the rigged state trial that ultimately allowed for his execution in 1618.

Very soon after the leak of his sister's epistolary efforts, Essex was actively involved in the war in France. During the siege of Rouen Robert Cecil employed a

French spy to shadow his martial contemporary, but Thomas D'Arques was soon spotted and jailed. On his release he was promptly taken by the Spanish agent in Rouen working for Mendoza, who required him to visit England to contact Andrade, the Portuguese double agent then living with the Lopez family. When D'Arques arrived, he was arrested for a debt of £20, a hefty sum that remains something of a mystery. Was it a trumped-up charge or had he already received money from Cecil, but failed to satisfy his pay master? As it was, he wrote begging letters from prison to Cecil, but found his position sliding when the Dutch ambassador, Noel de Caron, denounced him as a spy. Although interrogated by a man with a public reputation hardly less ferocious than that of the baleful Topcliffe, D'Arques revealed nothing directly to Richard Young, but allowed his tongue to loosen in private exchanges with a desperate cell-mate Benjamin (possibly John) Beard. He denounced anybody, including his own family, in order to win his freedom. Young was apprised by Beard of the whereabouts of the Frenchman's papers and so D'Arques remained in prison. Freed many months later, he was quickly rearrested by a suspicious mayor of Southampton, perhaps because his interest in English shipping was too pronounced.

This time the spy fetched up in the Gatehouse at Westminster (where there may have been two prisons), because it was mainly for political prisoners, and control of the premises was shared by the Privy Council and the Bishop of London. Again he wrote to Cecil stressing his accomplishments, but there was no response and, unable to pay for his keep, starvation threatened. At his lowest point he could only accept Cecil's offer of freedom, made on condition that he went back to Europe. In Brussels in the mid-1590s he collected material which was passed to Palavicino who paid him. Two months later the merchant heard that four men in Antwerp had been arrested as English spies and concurrently D'Arques vanished.[2] Given his past record of ineptitude and blunders, it would not be surprising if he was one of the quartet. At that time Antwerp resembled post-Second World War Vienna, awash with spies, counter-spies, lies and double-dealing. Many seminary priests were also briefly in the city, waiting for passage to England. Father Creswell said that a Jacques Ghibbes had carried people (for a fare of 40 shillings) and letters to England for years, and had sent reports to continental Catholic authorities of all the covert activities of their enemies.[*][3] Coming from Brussels or Louvain the men in transit would meet at the house of Adrian de Langhe in Black Sisters Street. He was the city postmaster who, since 1582, had managed the correspondence of the priests with England, and was also a skilful forger of passports. These were usually prepared in the hand of Sir Thomas Baskerville, and to try to stem such activities the Privy Council used investigators at home and abroad. In Antwerp the work was likely done by an astute agent and sometime servant of Worcester, called variously Sterrell, Robert Robinson and H. Saint Main. Thomas Morgan, the impoverished Welsh recusant gentleman, once close to Mary, actually lived in de Langhe's house,

---

[*] Ghibbes (or Gibels) was also identified by Poley as a carrier in a report written for Sir Robert Cecil in 1602. The retired secret agent named several carriers of packets, including a Genoese merchant, Filipo Barnardo (*sic*). Actually, Barnardo was in Cecil's employ too.

harbouring a secret loathing of the Jesuits, and Sterrell bribed one of his letter clerks.

The English priests not only foregathered in the city, but used it as a mailing depot for letters to their immediate superiors and Rome. In 1592 Thomas Payne, a haberdasher, and James Taylor in London were receiving letters for forwarding. Most of the arrangements seem to have been made by Dierick Hendricks, a merchant living in Blackfriars, whose brother lived in the rue Perpot in Antwerp and managed the continental side of the traffic from the sign of the Golden Horn.[4] To try to wreck this clandestine routine, the English side were willing to pay, and they were additionally assisted by the fact that, once they reached the Low Countries, ciphered missionary letters were sent through the ordinary posts. All the letters assigned to the royal post there were kept a day for weighing in both Antwerp and Madrid, so by bribing one of de Langhe's clerks with 28 ducats a month, Sterrell was able to scan the letters. If necessary he could also purchase at a special rate the misdirection of an important item. Sometimes the opposition themselves scored a hit. Richard Verstegen once reported to Robert Persons that a packet had reached Antwerp containing the confession of Anthony Tyrell, numbering fifty sheets, plus other material for Walsingham's secretariat. However, Persons had no very high opinion of either Verstegen or apparently Hugh Owen, saying they were 'very unfitting persons if money be given them for it' (meaning information). Verstegen was paid by Philip (the cause of Persons being so grouchy?), and his despatches to Spain were sent through Richard Hopkins, his 'ligger in Paris'.[5] According to Anthony Copley, Verstegen's clearing-house was very comfortable, so he must have been well paid when others begged for a pittance. One such was Copley himself, who only got a pension with the aid of Owen, and in 1590 had the temerity to return to England without permission, to the shocked bemusement of Topcliffe.

Verstegen's ancestry has been a matter of dispute, but it seems he was born in London of an old Guelderland family that had migrated to England during the reign of Henry VII and used the name Rowlands, obviously derived from his grandfather, Theodore Rowland Verstegen. He studied at Oxford but took no degree and after a brief period in London operating a secret press discovered by Recorder Fleetwood, he avoided prison by removing to Paris to begin writing his first book on the English persecution. Learning of its contents, Sir Edward Stafford prevailed upon Henri III to have Verstegen imprisoned. In danger of extradition he was saved by the papal nuncio and also Cardinal Allen. Verstegen then went to Rome, where he finished and published his book in 1584. When he took up residence in Antwerp with his wife he published more. *Declaration of True Causes* (1592) is especially revealing of his scorn for Burghley, who he maintained had succeeded in making Elizabeth believe that her throne was in jeopardy because of the spread of Catholicism. 'For it is he, that neither of conscience, nor any other cause, but merely for his own ambition – hath wrought the mutation and change of religion whereof such wonderful inconveniences have followed.'

Intended as the *Declaration* was to discredit Burghley in the eyes of his sovereign, it was well received by his enemies in England, especially by the grouping around Essex. The Lord Treasurer was stung and since he could command an eager nephew, Francis Bacon, he commissioned him to write a response. Bacon had also been rebuked by Verstegen and so he fashioned a reply in which the talented exiled poet, artist, archaeologist and controversialist is accused of actually attacking Elizabeth through the severe criticism of her chief minister.[6] Perhaps the most considerable aspect of Verstegen's polemic was that in provoking such a response it revealed Burghley's unease at the condition of the England he had helped to create for decades; the country was suffering in the 1590s and matters stood to get worse. Verstegen's treatment of Elizabeth was somewhat less severe. As for her possible successor he was an ardent supporter of the Spanish group, so his standing with exiles who favoured James VI declined. Exasperation with him increased with the publication of *Conference on the Succession*, which he knew would be offensive to everyone except the Spanish faction. He also acted as an agent for more orthodox items recently printed, supplying them to Hans Wowtenel, a Fleming living in London at St Faith's, Farringdon, who travelled often to Antwerp.

As for Tyrell, the son of a notable Catholic family in impoverished exile, he arrived in London in 1576 in a desperate attempt to beg £10 with which to continue his studies. He was arrested and imprisoned, but soon released as a mark of respect for his father, Sir George Tyrell. Anthony Tyrell then entered the English College, wherein he encountered Solomon Aldred, the sewing spy, as well as Grateley, Gilbert Gifford, Nicholls and Paschall, all then or later agents of Walsingham. Tyrell became a priest in 1581 and was directed to missionary work in London, where his presence was betrayed by Nicholls. Yet he managed to escape from the Gatehouse in 1582 and the suspicion arises that this was done with the collusion of the authorities. He was then tracked to Rome by the spy P.H.W. in the company of John Ballard. Five years later he was back in London doing his missionary work before being imprisoned again, this time in the Wood Street Counter where he was allowed liberty of the gaol before examination by Richard Young. By psychological pressure Tyrell was brought to another change of direction and, after making an oath on the Protestant Bible, he was conditionally released. The price exacted was that intermittently he had to return to the gaol to spy on Catholic prisoners. His routine done there he was moved to the Clink where Father Lowe thought him suspicious.

In the febrile atmosphere of beleaguered piety Tyrell confessed to Lowe, yet was still used and even allowed to say mass in the prison. As a result of his actions many Catholics were seized and Lowe, Adams and Dibdale executed. When summoned to a Catholic house to explain his situation Tyrell went and found his interview was to be conducted by Father Lewis Barlowe, whom he had once betrayed. He was given a chance to repent and apparently in a paroxysm of spiritual perturbation was reconciled to Catholicism again. Fearing discovery he fled from London and no one could find him until Walsingham got a letter from Leith denying the truth of Tyrell's confession. Agents went in pursuit, but again he reached Rome and there wrote his confessions. For a time he reined-in his private demons, but the poise was destroyed, and he began to long for the liberty of a layman, money and excitement. He chose to return to England where, as expected, the authorities took a stern line. To secure his position again he became a Protestant minister and married.

Sir Robert Sidney, 1563–1626, was always
uneasy in his necessary dealings with the
secret operators who swarmed through the
Low Countries and northern France

Almost equally erratic was Michael Moody.[7] Last sighted in the Low Countries
living in Brussels or Antwerp, he edged again into the espionage picture in 1591.
Then Robert Cecil was contacted by an agent called John Ricroft who reported
talking to Moody. Ricroft suggested that although Moody was proving wearisome
to his masters in England, he should not be spurned. Unfortunately his record of
the spy's activities is so opaque that all that claims the attention now is that with the
recommendations of a 'Mr V', Moody was soliciting a portrait of Lady Arabella
Stuart from the great English portrait miniaturist, Nicholas Hilliard. 'Mr V' was
surely Verstegen and he was a close associate of Hugh Owen known then to be
prompting the Stuart-Farnese marriage. Owen also stalked the English governor of
Flushing, the upright Sir Robert Sidney, offering presents as inducements,
including two small tables and a pair of bracelets for Barbara Sidney.[8] The former
might have been useful for Penshurst, but this compromising advance had to be
shrugged off by forwarding the items to Burghley. This helped Sidney duck more
than routine demerits from Elizabeth for dealing with Owen unadvised.

In February 1592 Sidney wrote to Burghley that Moody had suggested that, since
he was governor, he had the authority to deal with Owen who could be drawn to do
Elizabeth some service. Sidney naturally saw Owen as exceptionally duplicitous,
'an ill man to the state', and he wanted no more contact with him for fear of
fumbling the matter. Yet, in Elizabeth's sour view, he did just that when an
approach might have led to Owen's capture. No doubt Sidney was as confused by

her attitude as we are; Machiavellian statecraft was not his forte. As for Burghley, he suspected links between Owen and a fugitive Irish priest called Patrick Sedgrave, who was also courting Sidney's attention. Again, Sidney was extremely candid about the priest, but still managed to irritate Elizabeth by meeting him and then letting him go because he had promised a safe conduct. Moody may have been set by Burghley to try to nudge Sidney into trapping Owen, but the governor decided to mark time because of his suspicions, which included the thought that there was a plot to betray Flushing to the enemy. His reasoning and instincts seem to have been correct, because in April, several months before he was arrested, a Reinold Bosely (or Bisley) wrote to Cecil declaring that, while employed abroad on the queen's affairs (obviously as a spy), he had learned that Owen and Sir William Stanley had planned a coup against the English stronghold. They had lined up William Whipp, once a Sidney servant, to obtain an impression of the town keys, while simultaneously Owen tried to suborn Lord Burgh into surrendering the Brill.[9] If England had been stripped of both cautionary towns the effect on Philip II's attitude to Stanley's invasion plans might have been strikingly altered. Stanley eventually retired somewhat bitterly to a Carthusian monastery, having failed to improve his position when a Spanish pensioner. He died in 1630.

In the mean time Moody (who had a clutch of aliases) was showing signs of being restive as a double agent. There was still the controversial (if sagging) matter of the projected Stuart-Farnese union, and he too received instructions through Robert Poley to keep watch on the exiled Francis Dacres, self-styled Lord Dacres. In particular, Moody was supposed to unravel the efforts being made by Dacres, Norton and Westmorland for an invasion of northern England. Any military adventure was likely to be headed by Stanley, whose defection to the Spanish cause had not expunged all traces of family attachment. A cousin of the Earl of Derby and his son Ferdinando, Lord Strange, Stanley, together with Robert Persons, had been seeking closer links with the latter since 1590. In the spring of 1591 the bustling Jesuit sent two emissaries on a mission to England to discover whether it was practicable to support Lord Strange as a possible successor to Elizabeth. (The claim of the Stanleys, it will be recalled, came about because in 1555 Derby had married as his first wife, Margaret Clifford, granddaughter of Henry VIII's youngest sister.) The two men sent used the aliases John Snowden and Thomas Wilson.[10]

John Snowden was actually John Cecil, of a Worcester family with no Catholic leanings; his brother died fighting the Spanish in the Netherlands. Born in 1558, Persons has him as a relation of the ruling Cecils. What is confirmed is that this graduate of Trinity College, Oxford, had gone abroad early in the 1580s and at some point acquired a doctorate in theology from Padua. In 1587 he joined William Allen's household when the latter became a cardinal, yet by the following year, with the alias Juan de Campo, he was in touch with Walsingham. Allen sent him to Spain to assist in the foundation of Valladolid and he remained in the country until the end of 1590. He met Medina Sidonia in San Lucar, the duke being ordered by Philip to book passage for the English priests in merchant ships. In the spring of the following year he was in Lisbon and in May he turned up in England, handing over two letters from Persons to Sir Robert Cecil. He proved somewhat offhand, saying in a letter of 10 June to Burghley that John Cecil would do good work if he avoided the suspicions of his fellow priests. According to a Catholic historian, one of the letters was probably forged by Robert Cecil, since it was not in the Jesuit's hand. Even though he never formally apostasized, John Cecil did supply political information, as well as data on priests abroad. He went back to Spain and in September 1591 returned to England with Thomas Wilson (the alias of John Fixer) and four other priests.[11] All were captured before landing, probably by prearrangement, and at some point Cecil and Fixer made a claim that they were instructed by Persons 'to seek entrance with my Lord Strange, and cause Catholics to cast their eyes upon him'. This was bad news for Strange, especially when Topcliffe was reported as saying that all the Stanleys were traitors. Thomas Barnes (alias Robinson) wrote to Phelippes from Brussels in June 1592 that Strange and Cardinal Allen had links.

John Cecil was questioned ('examined') but not imprisoned, and he turned up in Rome in 1592 before being sent by Allen to Scotland. Rumours of his duplicity reached the cardinal and in October Cecil sent him a long apologia. He remained in Scotland until 1594, when he set out for Rome and was 'captured' at sea by Drake to provide a cover for his dealings with Sir Robert Cecil. When allowed to leave England he went to Madrid, sending Burghley some extracts from Pedro de Ribadeneyra's *Del Tratado de la Tribulacion*, which had been written to assuage the distress of the nation for the loss of the Armada, with encouragement to mount a second attempt. There was also material from the *Relacion de Algunos Martyrios*, written to convince the nation that Philip II's *reputación* (sovereign prestige) was still vital and unshaken.[12] John Cecil was no ordinary mercenary spy; he had developed a larger notion of a 'National Catholic' sect and to underpin this he was prepared 'to work the dissolution or diminution of the Seminaries'. In fact, for missionary Jesuits like Southwell the activities of Cecil and the murky Fixer were a calamity, since they pointed to his involvement in high treason along with Sir William Stanley, two of whose sons were among Lord Strange's retainers. They were also a dismal headache for Allen, who seems to have discovered what Cecil and Fixer were about late in 1591, telling Persons in January 1592 of the betrayal, while pondering a response to a threat to the entire exiled community. The English Catholics, even an agent like Hugh Owen, had enemies in the Spanish Netherlands as well as Spain, and a scandal would have shattered a fragile confidence so slowly achieved. Allen's anxiety had been to get the two intelligencers out of England, as was revealed by another captured priest, James Younger, who had been in Valladolid with them, and in time he admitted he had been empowered to offer Fixer a post as chaplain to the cardinal.

By May 1595 John Cecil was in Prague writing to Cardinal Caetano of Spanish plans to land in Scotland as a preliminary to an invasion of England. He then shifted back to Scotland's intelligence orbit and, like the Scottish spy Robert Bruce, found himself denounced in 1599, when in Paris, by the Scottish Jesuit William Creighton. Both men now favoured resistance to Jesuit claims for Spanish candidates to succeed Elizabeth. Consistent with his 'National Catholic' ideas, John Cecil was apparently happy to see the entwining of two groups of Catholic patriots into a transborder party which, after 1595, gained strength, favoured peace, loyalty to the English crown and eventually the succession of James VI. The English Cecils may not have been so ardent, but that was where their policy would end. As for Fixer, the tall, swarthy linguist, who as a seminarian had apparently exploited opportunities for seduction and blackmail – he was sidelined and, for a time chaplain in a priest's house in Lisbon, he sent despatches to Sir Robert Cecil. Persons secured his arrest in 1601, but in 1607 Fixer was spotted in Madrid by Sir Charles Cornwallis, the resident English ambassador, and the sometime intelligencer was still in Spain (under some sort of restraint?) as late as 1613.

Chapter Fifteen

Spy Master v. Counter-Spy

Even when Sir Robert Cecil had individual agents dotted around Europe, he had no inclination to seize the direction of espionage from his revered father. In the early 1590s he held no public office, though he joined various commissions, like the one established in 1592 to separate plunder from the great Portuguese carrack *Madre de Deus* from the plunderers, so that the queen and investors would not feel aggrieved. He was always very preoccupied with business for the Privy Council and Burghley prudently did not spur him to rival Essex whose prodigal style brought him the services of many cast down by the death of Walsingham and 'the sweeping poverty of the times'. At this time Robert Cecil was not rich (indeed he was probably partly reliant on his father still), so he calculated that presently he could do without the efforts of even Thomas Phelippes, whose passion for espionage verged on the neurotic. As it was he cast about for material to send the man many tipped to be the next principal secretary, and late in 1591 he deciphered one of Moody's letters as an *amuseguêle* for a man he disliked. It was Phelippes who continued to employ Thomas Barnes, who lodged at one time in the Golden Ape at Tournai to report on travellers coming from Brussels and Louvain, or from Bar-le-Duc and Pont à Mousson by the Ardennes road.[1] Phelippes also held on to the services of William Sterrell while he could, although he became expensive, claiming that he needed at least £140 a year to live in Antwerp. Increasing debts meant the removal of the latter agent to England, where he sought employment by Worcester. He approached Cecil as well, drawing attention to his previous work, before going back to the Low Countries on a mission for Phelippes. The task was to look for signs of a 'design' against Elizabeth and in 1592, as details came through of Stanley's war aims, Barnes also went. My view is that Barnes and Sterrell were the same person, and Marlowe was also there for a purpose linked to this threat. It was Phelippes who secured the release from prison of Bosely in September 1593, at about the same time that the Dutch released Poley, who had run into trouble in Middelburg.

Men like Sir Robert Sidney in Flushing who sent Marlowe and the others home for examination, remained fastidiously aloof from espionage. It carried a taint as far as he was concerned that could sully his honour, and so he had to rely on proxies and goodwill. A spy like Edmund Palmer, who also traded in St Jean de Luz while working for the Cecils, also pitched in with insistent grumbles. He claimed his situation was dismal and that for five years Walsingham had only paid his expenses. Apart from them being nearly £50 in arrears, he was also irked and soon complained that Essex's agent in Bayonne, Anthony Rolston, was paid more. Palmer drifted back briefly to the orbit of the Cecils in 1596, but never achieved what he held he deserved. Juan de Velasquez, governor of Guipuzcoa, bluntly called him 'an outright knave' – a view confirmed by Palmer's devious money-making scheme in the Iberian peninsula. By visiting London he compiled information on English traders involved in smuggling to Spain. Returning to St Jean de Luz he found a Spaniard willing to risk touring ports in southern Spain and Portugal to determine the merchants so occupied. He would then denounce them and seize their goods in the name of the new King Philip III. Remarkably, considering the claimed subsequent losses to traders, and consequent bankruptcies, Palmer was not murdered nor even totally excluded from Robert Cecil's expanded network of agents, for he continued to report spasmodically until 1604.[2]

Trade was the key to the continued employment of the consul of the English merchants at La Rochelle. Chateaumartin protected English commerce for a fee of 1 per cent of the value of all English traffic, and further acted as an intelligencer for Walsingham for expenses and an annual payment of 1,200 escudos. The money was paid to him by Palavicino and it was under his instruction that an agent was sent to Madrid. From whom and to whom the Frenchman allowed the notion of a negotiated peace to penetrate is not clear. Certainly Burghley did not utterly reject the possibility and he put to his agent Elizabeth's desire to correspond with her sometime brother-in-law. It must have been wretched for the Cecils to discover eventually that for years Chateaumartin was a double agent and in 1596 was planning to betray Bayonne to the Spanish. Philip II thought so highly of him that for a time he willingly paid out 100 escudos a month, though he knew the Frenchman sold his services to England. Persons thought that Chateaumartin died at his post in the cold that winter, while as far as the English were concerned it was more than merited if he was indeed executed by the town governor of Bayonne.

This was a turning point for the Cecil secret service which hitherto had operated by fits and starts. It was also an important time in the dynamics of the Privy Council; Robert Cecil and Essex managed to rein in their mutual antipathy for a time. The rivalry in all its convolutions was damped down by the commission and execution of a major military project against Spain, the first such since the expensive fiasco of 1589. The Cádiz venture called for a huge investment in time and money, particularly by Essex, agog at the possibilities he envisioned, and designated joint commander with Lord Admiral Charles Howard. The earl was taken up by the narcotic dream of a great victory, because he hoped that a military success would boost his power at court and so weaken that of the entrenched Cecils, who naturally remained at home. There were risks in this thrust. Because of his headlong enthusiasm for a scrap, he might be maimed or killed (though even that might have had a morbid attraction to a melancholy man), and as Henri de la Tour d'Auvergne, Duke of Bouillon, pointed out in April 1596 while in England for Henri IV, absence from court for a lengthy period would give his rivals a positional advantage. He added with a sagacity that eluded Essex that even a success would incite envy and not even Elizabeth would be immune. She had annexed the failure of the Armada and likely would do the same for any English victory in Spain. And so it proved. Essex defended his plan and thought the envoy partial, because Henry IV was desperate for help in defending Calais against Spain. In fact the Gallic viewpoint was substantially correct. Calais fell in mid-April, adding to the bustle to challenge this latest threat, but the expedition itself was a flawed effort (albeit striking to observers) and, while it went on, Sir Robert Cecil was finally made principal secretary. The Cádiz raid was a huge shock to the Spanish who seem to have had no inkling of it.

With this long-anticipated advance he no longer had any reason to delay in coordinating and deploying a broad secret service that also had some depth. The availability of official funds also gave a new impetus and he was soon confronted by a striking instance of how necessary such an effort was. In mid-November there was an invasion scare and reliable information was hugely important because no one knew if this was indeed a quaintly timed repeat of 1588. Cecil cast about for someone with wide-ranging contacts and a ready fund of cash, before concluding that obviously Horatio Palavicino was his man; the taint occasioned by his private dealings with Stafford had long since been removed. Cecil wanted first to know what was going on in the Spanish Netherlands now ruled as joint-governors by the Archdukes Albrecht and Isabella. Were landing craft and transports being assembled? Was there any noticeable effort to assemble infantry? What was happening in Calais now it was in Spanish hands? Also it was going to be necessary to get a spy into Spain to collect data on naval activity, and since a new face might easily be remarked Palavicino singled out the trusty Paul (or Paolo) Theobast for the commission.

Long resident in London with his wife and children, Theobast had been employed in a modest way as a trader, as well as factor for some Dutch traders. He was given £40 in advance for expenses and travelled via Nantes. By April 1597 he had settled in Spain and there remained until early the following year for an effort that concentrated on the ports of La Coruña and El Ferrol. His back-up was the oddly named Hans Owter, apparently an Englishman with an alias and based at Santiago de Compostella. There were also three agents in Lisbon: Peter Gerard; Balthazar Peterson; and William Resould. The latter was a London merchant who had been a factor in Spain twenty years before. He had subsequently been to Morocco, and in the 1590s had been linked to illicit trade with Spain involving Robert Savage and others. The Savage family had many contacts with Robert Cecil, so it is no surprise to find Resould an intelligencer with the alias of Giles van Harwick. In April 1599 he reported to London on the activities of the controversialist Father Joseph Creswell, warning that he had excellent intelligence of everything happening at the English coast. Resould wrote frequently, sometimes once a fortnight, and went on doing this until mid-1602. His yearly retainer was 400 ducats with 100 ducats for travel paid through Edward Savage, the London merchant.

Palavicino's rapid survey of the Channel ports was undertaken for him by the improbably named William Spiring. However, proof that it was no pseudonym exists, for Francis Spiring, originally Frans Spierinck, was responsible for weaving the famous Armada tapestries from designs by the Haarlem painter Henrik Vroom commissioned by the Lord Admiral Howard, now Earl of Nottingham.* The agent

---

* There are tapestries by Spiring at Knole.

Richard Hawkins, imprisoned in Spain for many years

assigned to Brussels and the court of the archdukes was one Massentio Verdiani, whom Palavicino assessed with a certain sceptical realism, while figuring he was a potentially useful gamble. He reflected that in such operations an employer had to spend money and inevitably some was frittered away by the incompetent; the brief employment of the useless George Weeks who was paid a hefty retainer underlined the truth of this view. Verdiani received £60 for travel and could expect 6 shillings a day when at his post. Actually getting him there took some time, because his approach to Brussels was a leisurely detour through France and Lorraine. He began the scenic loop in Antwerp and cheekily complained about lack of money. Palavicino cautioned their employer: 'Think whether you will entertain him and risk the second arrow after the first.' In the middle of the following month Verdiani was at last in Brussels, but still untroubled by the concept of sustained effort – useful reports from him were slow to arrive. Having eventually established himself as moderately trustworthy, he was then sent to Spain in the late autumn, where he roosted in Seville alongside the agent named 'Andover' who sent all his letters to a merchant in Waterford for forwarding.

Before his brief diplomatic excursion to France for negotiations in January 1598, Robert Cecil had a document drawn up that gives useful details of his network, and by now it seems reasonable to use the word.[4] It not only names those employed, but also the payments made to them and by whom. Thus the Peter Gerard based in Lisbon had a salary of 400 ducats a year paid via a London merchant called Tobias Tucker. Peterson (who may have been Dutch) was recruited by the Dutch-speaking George Gilpin and paid 500 ducats a year after a preliminary sum of £140. In a later account for the period July 1599 to October 1600 it is clear these amounts were not exceptional, for in that time Thomas Wilson (John Fixer? Another of that name?) was paid £150 and Francis Lambert £109. The notorious Palmer, who remained in St Jean de Luz, was paid a total of 500 ducats. His letters were directed to London by Thomas Honyman, the merchant whose services to Cecil became more valuable as the Anglo-Spanish war lengthened. Interestingly Honyman suggested discussions on trade to Juan de Velasquez in late 1595, and it is clear from a letter that this was not their first exchange. However, it may simply have been a useful cover for his real intention – the gathering of information for which he was immediately paid £50, while acting as a paymaster for two other agents.

It bears repeating that war and trade were the usual shaping forces of Robert Cecil's secret service in the period 1596–1603. In the Low Countries his principal organizer was a Captain Ogle; in the Spanish Netherlands, apart from Verdiani, there was George Kendall who recruited the ineffectual Weeks, and Lawrence Bankes in Middelburg. Cecil's chief agent in the Hanse towns of northern Germany was Stephen Lesieur, an able man who did work as well for the Merchant Adventurers in Prague, where a decade before Dee had been ensconced. Further afield he had an ambiguous informant in Henry Lello, now following in the footsteps of William Harborne in Constantinople. In his 1598 memorandum Cecil noted that there were 'friends' in Scotland, Holland and Zeeland, Italy, Germany, Denmark and Sweden. Even a prisoner in Spain like Richard Hawkins, son of Sir John Hawkins, could correspond with Cecil through various secret 'drops'. He had been captured in an action off South America and after some three years' detention in Lima was sent to Spain to be held in Seville for years. Yet in these unpromising circumstances he showed an ability to sift material in order to give an effective presentation of what was important. Since he was better at this than someone like Cecil's French servant Julian Place, who was sent to Spain in 1600, a suspicion arises that the secretary did not clamour for his release. There was also apparently a demand for a ransom of £12,000, which suggests the Spanish were after punitive damages against his family. When he was finally freed early in the seventeenth century after the combined intervention of Sir Thomas Myddelton and Cecil, it is consistent that Hawkins became a very public advocate of opening up America to trade – the idea that had become the *idée fixe* of his family and which did eventually engage Cecil's attention.

Given the geographical spread and expense of what had evolved into a single secret service under the precise control of Cecil, Elizabeth continued to press for value for money. Indeed, in May 1599, Hugh Owen, the counter-spy of the archdukes, prepared a report stating that the English government was not then satisfied with the level of intelligence work being done in Spain. Owen noted that their new stance was to send 'persons with French names', hence Place and

Lambert.* His source in England was obviously well informed and possibly even within Cecil's own secretariat. My candidate for the culprit is Simon Willis, who dealt specifically with intelligence matters and was later dismissed abruptly when Cecil wanted his own secret correspondence with James VI to remain just that. Whomever – he turned down an offer of 1,500 felipes a year because the effort was too risky. This should rule out Phelippes who was always breathtakingly short of money, but withal loyal, despite the correspondence with Hugh Owen.

Owen was a Welshman as adept in the organization of secret operations as Walsingham. He faced even greater difficulties with determination and with less chance of success. The son of Owen ap Gruffydd of Plas Du was born in 1538 in the old manor house in Llanarmon parish, not far from Pwllheli.[5] His mother, Margaret, was the daughter of Ffoulk (Fulke) Salusbury of Llanwrst. His older brother, Thomas, heir to the estate, was high sheriff of Caernarvonshire in 1567–8, and there were other brothers of whom the exiled Robert requires some immediate attention. Hugh and Robert were the youngest and had to seek their opportunities well beyond the confines of Wales. Hugh certainly went into the service of Henry Fitzalan, Earl of Arundel (d. 1580) and these two brothers were probably educated in his household, although Arundel was childless. Neither seem to have gone to university, but in 1560 Robert received the living of West Felton, near Oswestry in Shropshire. In 1566 Hugh went with Arundel to the Diet of Augsburg and may have travelled with him to the medicinal baths of Padua. The earl had resigned from the sinecure post of Lord Steward in 1564, and there were fleeting signs that this high-ranking Catholic was slipping from acceptable political paths. When Mary, Queen of Scots, erupted into England thinking to secure her own safety, Arundel became the acknowledged leader of the faction that supported her. In 1571 Hugh Owen became a participant in the Ridolphi plot (see Chapter 1), with the task of arranging relays of horses (by no means easy) for Mary's flight abroad. By October Burghley knew of his involvement and warrants for his arrest were prepared. After lying low in north-west Shropshire, which had Arundel loyalties and numerous recusants willing to risk giving him shelter, Owen made his way to the Spanish Netherlands. In January 1572 he was in Madrid with letters for Jane Dormer, Countess of Feria, and Thomas Stukeley, still thinking of trying to spirit Mary to Spain.

Robert Owen was also in Europe, having been deprived of his church living.[6] He took himself to Douai to study law, but kept in touch with his brother Thomas, who supplied both the exiles with some funds. Leaving Douai in 1573, Robert travelled to Rome, then back to Paris armed with recommendations to the papal nuncio in 1576. After this there is a career gap, while Hugh was building a career in intelligence. In November 1572 he received 150 ducats and, when he returned to the Spanish Netherlands, a pension of 20 ducats. A hitch in payment was always likely and he did have to beg the intervention of Sir Francis Englefield before it was paid. In December 1574 the extradition to England of the brothers was formally demanded under the terms of the *Intercursus Magnus* of 1496. Since neither of the

---

* The son of Don Pedro de Valdez came to England disguised as a Frenchman.

Owens had been convicted of rebellion, however, the demand could not be pressed. Both men remained in touch constantly with Arundel, recusant friends and former parishioners, as well as their own family. In 1575 these necessarily clandestine links were denounced by an Oswestry man and investigations were made by the Council of Wales and the Privy Council. Owen's servant Parry was alleged to have travelled to England frequently with concealed letters, on one occasion eating a letter when he imagined himself close to capture.

When the Privy Council blocked his lines of communication, Hugh Owen had to work indefatigably from his lodgings at the sign of St Michel in the Brussels cheese market. Among his associates there were two men with excellent business contacts. One was his compatriot William Myddelton, of the well-known family who had declined to give up the old faith. To maintain his spiritual freedom, he gave up his business in London to re-establish it in the Spanish Netherlands, where he settled with a Flemish wife. Like the Owens he nurtured links to his family against the grain of separation. Sir Thomas Myddelton was, after all, one of London's richest merchants, and ironically it was he who acquired the vacant Plas Du in 1626. There was also the polyglot Richard Verstegen, who had set up a printing business and whose home was a meeting place and post office for recusant Catholic exiles. In addition there was Charles Bailly, another Fleming by birth, but this time Scottish by descent, who had formerly been in service to Mary, Queen of Scots. As we have seen (in Chapter 1), he was imprisoned for intrigues in her cause in 1571, and on being liberated went to Flanders to join up with Owen. Besides, being a good linguist he could pass himself off as a Dutch merchant, and ciphers for the group fell under his remit.

Owen's work in the camps at Liège or Namur and his careful letter carrying to Paris or Allen at Rheims, eventually convinced the Spanish commanders that he was to be trusted. The Duke of Parma was thoroughly convinced around 1580, and the need for a network was growing. It was on an errand to Rheims in company with Robert Persons that the two men were nearly captured by a sortie of English troops from Mechlin. In 1584–6 Owen, Persons and Cardinal Allen formed the privileged trio to whom Philip II entrusted to sole dealings with Parma over the last sketched attempt to snatch Mary. Even so, Owen's pension in 1584 was still only a lowly 25 escudos a month, for all his energy and diligence.[*7]

He was forced to give consideration to the future claimants, some near and some remote, to the English throne early in 1587 when the wrenching news of Mary's execution arrived. After enquiries about James VI he discarded him as a candidate and chose instead to throw all his weight behind the claim of the Spanish royal family. At first his clique was absorbed by the possibility of a Stuart-Farnese union and Gilbert Gifford, in his prison confession, declared that Allen 'was looking into the title of the son of the Duke of Parma'. Later this option was shunted aside in favour of the Spanish claim, underlined by a clutch of publications, and with Owen and Persons visiting Rome to try to induce Pope Sixtus V (d. 1590) to excommunicate James. Owen's activities received a boost in 1587 when the Earl of

---

[*] One escudo = 5 s. 6 d.

Leicester's choice of a commander to hold the town of Deventer in the Low Countries, Sir William Stanley, deserted to the enemy with his regiment. He and Owen soon struck up a partnership that would last for twenty years, while some of Stanley's Welsh subordinates – men like Captains Owen Salisbury and Peter Wynne – proved highly tuned to the plotting and intrigue that filled Owen's life.

In 1588 a group of these buoyant young Welshmen made a dramatic swipe at Ostend, receiving their instructions and password from Owen in Welsh. (A linguistic camouflage that did not throw Walsingham when he came across it, since he employed Welsh speakers such as Griffin Maddox.) Owen's activities were by no means limited to northern France and the Low Countries, for he made frequent trips to Spain and several to Rome. Sterrell and Phelippes began spying on him in about 1587 and, from *c*. 1592–6, both men had fairly frequent contacts with him.[8] This was risky and a decade later Phelippes fetched up in prison when government confidence in him was slack. In 1594 a letter from John Owen, a brother who had followed Robert to Douai, sent to Sterrell under the alias Robert Robinson, was delivered in London to the wrong Robinson and was then forwarded by the lord mayor to Burghley.

Despite the contacts between agents it is impossible on the evidence of his lengthy career to believe Owen was a double agent. It must be that what went on was devious sparring, the setting of false trails, teasing probes and pulses of lies. Parma maintained complete trust in his agent and, until the duke's death in 1592, Owen's ascendancy over English affairs at the court in Brussels was unchallengeable, even on the matter of pensions to exiles. His enemies hoped that this would end when the Archduke Ernst, 'an orthodox Catholic zealot', began what turned out to be his short period of rule, 1592–5. But Owen's well-placed friends took up his cause and he was soon operating as before. His task was an exceptionally difficult one and he deserved, it is opined, his salary of 60 escudos a month. The archduke wrote on one occasion, 'Hugh Owen is a man of great intelligence . . . diligent, very discreet and suitable for any business.' In fact, his notoriety attracted a good deal of attention on both sides, with the Spanish valuing his reports on the sailings of English ships bound for the West Indies. In presenting the material, his accuracy and detail helped him to overcome the lingering problem of being a subject of Elizabeth while serving her enemy. A pamphlet of 1595 singled out Owen when inveighing against Philip's ingratitude towards the English refugees who served him, although the record of duplicity made Spanish hesitations understandable.

Between 1596 and 1601 the extended quarrel between the 'Spanish' and 'Scottish' factions among the exiles reached a lengthy climax, with highly charged

Watson's plot, or Bye plot, was initiated by a strongly anti-Jesuit priest. Its failure led to the Gunpowder plot (1605)

denunciations to the Pope, Philip and the archdukes. It became fused in the deeper strife between Jesuits and seculars, which found expression in 1598 in the 'Archpriest' controversy. Both Hugh and Robert were powerfully pro-Jesuit – Hugh defending them in Brussels, his brother, a canon of Le Mans, doing the same in Paris. The Pope achieved a makeshift solution in 1601, but by then many of Owen's old opponents were retreating back to England, making their peace with the English government, hopeful that when Elizabeth died she might be succeeded by someone who would tolerate, if not profess, their faith. For the moment Stanley, the Owens and the Jesuits were the irreconcilables, left upholding the Spanish cause at a time when the Archduke Albrecht regarded his wife's claim with sincere scepticism. In Spain, after the death of Philip II in 1598 of a portmanteau of diseases, Owen was still well regarded and his pension was renewed in 1601 at the archduke's request.

At this point it was the attitude of the papacy, and that of the majority of the Catholic laity and secular priests in England, that made flexibility necessary. Certainly, towards the end of 1602, Robert Owen was sent by the French government on an unofficial mission to his brother in Flanders to put together a concerted effort in the matter of the English succession. Persons at this time had shifted to declaring he would surrender his life for James VI if only he would become a Catholic, and presumably the fraternal exchanges inclined that way. After three months and no firm conclusion reached James was made exultant by the passionately desired entrance into England – the earthly paradise coveted for so long. He was immeasurably helped by the calm efforts of Robert Cecil after Elizabeth's death; no foreign armies intervened and the new monarch had no need for active help from Catholics. They held optimistically to the notion that James's vague pronouncements before his accession would allow for liberty of conscience.

Their shock was therefore great when James reimposed recusancy fines in May 1603. This was quickly followed by Watson's plot, led by a strongly anti-Jesuit priest. In essence it was a repetition of the Essex revolt under new conditions and, ironically, many of those involved had most earnestly striven for James to take the throne. In what was also known as the Bye plot, the intention was not murder, but following the Hibernian mode, kidnapping. It was believed that this leverage would free James from the supposedly malignant influence of Robert Cecil, who was held to be the main cause of the king's bad faith.[9] When it failed the initiative fell to the pro-Jesuit emigrés and in July Hugh Owen, while still trying to form a pro-Spanish party among the English nobility, had a hand in sending Guy Fawkes, a soldier henchman of Stanley's from Flanders to Spain on a mission to inform Philip III. Yet even Stanley was now less ardent in the cause, because mindful at last of his estates he seemed disposed to make terms with Cecil who had achieved an unassailable position. Moreover, Philip wanted peace, so by September Robert Owen was perturbed at the way things had developed, even before James's refusal to educate his heir Prince Henry as a Catholic was communicated to the papal nuncio in Paris in December. Had the Owens and Persons got wind of this months before? A final question about the Owens concerns the family. In March 1605 the Catholic stationer Henry Owen, of the parish of St Bartholomew the Great, was indicated for being a recusant. Since he came from a prominent Welsh family and his brother was Nicholas Owen, the extraordinary contriver of so many priest-holes, including the one at Hindlip Hall in Worcestershire, the thought that they were brothers of Robert and Hugh looms up. That relationship would explain the extreme exasperation of Robert Cecil, then Earl of Salisbury, with the Owens in the aftermath of the Gunpowder plot (1605).[10]

Chapter Sixteen

Routine and Rebellion

In 1596 the Earl of Essex's secret service was about to lose momentum. Until now no one has ever adduced any reasons, but it is possible to point to a cluster of things that led to it. Simple neglect by a preoccupied earl was one reason, as well as competition from Cecil's rejuvenated network, which now received government funds. Anthony Bacon's diminishing energy due to ill health, his persistent and damaging money problems, and also the presence of du Plessis in England during September, are three additional components. After four years of success the Essex network was now coasting. Another element was the parallel personal crisis of the head of the earl's secretariat, Edward Reynolds, who, after Oxford, had assisted Paulet in guarding Mary. Now he felt wretched at the prospect of Essex taking on another unfamiliar secretary, determinedly viewing it as a rebuke for the quality of his work during the Cádiz campaign. He complained bitterly to Bacon who tried to mollify him, but with his confidence savaged he declined to write any Latin letters, because he felt his Oxonian command of the language had ebbed lamentably. Reynolds prepared to resign and only after many exchanges with Bacon did he hold back while still seeking preferment for his old age. It was a trick he managed to pull off and he died a rich man.

With Standen absent with Essex on the Cádiz expedition, and Cecil made secretary in his absence, at least one spy was anxiously rehearsing his future. Burghley, of course, had long treated the absentee with suspicion, both because he was an avowed Catholic and because it was Standen who had recommended Rolston. Years before, in September 1592, a despatch from Standen recorded that he had agreed that the younger man should seek employment by Philip II in Flanders rather than Spain, and that to enable him to report by word of mouth on matters of moment, especially those involving James VI, a trustworthy person should be sent from England to Calais to rendezvous with Rolston, revealing his identity with the phrase 'it is good to be merry and wise'. However, Rolston had another manoeuvre in mind, intending it seems to quit Spanish employ by renouncing his pension. And this is what he did, despite some hissed advice from England that he should allow things to go on as they were. But then his personal plans faltered because he was very nervous, as Standen reported, about the reception being prepared for in England: 'he meaneth to defer until he hear from you and then to meet with your confident at Calais or else at home, upon assurance from her Majesty and the council, as in this point he hath by mouth dealt largely with Lawson: which meeting being so necessary, so must it be completely kept secret.'

When Standen had arrived in Calais years before, only to have a letter already referred to stolen, he was particularly tender for Rolston's safety in Spain. He wanted his recruit alerted to events by either Alderman Brooke or Richard Craddock, making it known to the merchant resident in St Jean de Luz, one Joseph Jackson, whom Sir Robert Cecil would later employ in Amsterdam. Neither Jackson nor Rolston was well regarded by the sour and changeable Edmund Palmer, aggrieved that strangers and traitors were made so much of, and Rolston was lucky that Standen would willingly cover lapses. He continued the role in Spain that Standen had relinquished, sending information to his friend, as well as Bacon. The quality of Rolston's material is hard to judge, and there were those who declared it stale and lacking specificity. By 1596 he held himself to be in some danger, but prudently resolved to stay away from England until he knew the queen's pleasure. With Standen absent on active service this was particularly hard to unravel, and when Rolston took the risk, ostensibly coming home on a secret peace mission, he ended up in the Tower.

Standen continued to think cordially of him, but the government did not. The frowns deepened when Rolston confessed eventually that he had been sent to collect military information for Philip and also to try to buy Essex over to the Spanish interest. Clearly something of the earl's mounting financial problems had been communicated to the king. Bacon must have been alerted to what was going on with Rolston, and it allowed for the further decay of the lengthy friendship between Standen and himself. After 1596 there are no extant letters between the two men which suggests not an archival accident, but a true breach. The hiatus was probably confirmed as Standen at last came to realize that Bacon had only a mutilated court career. Early in 1598, when Standen was toiling to secure his old age by a convenient marriage to a rich widow who rejected him, it was Bacon's credit that was exhausted. It is not hard to envisage his mildly sardonic view of the proposed union with its mercenary intent. Unlike his own brother, Francis, he does not seem ever to have contemplated that route to solvency.

Anthony Bacon was at heart a kind man with a generous nature – his mother would have said withering that he was far too generous. Robert Cecil was a much more astringent and clear-eyed watcher of the world's follies. We may examine his ruthlessness by looking first at the activities of Richard Burley of Melcombe Regis, the port where Thomas Bellott lived from 1597 sending Cecil intelligence items on naval and troop movements in the Channel. Based since 1580 in San Sebastián as the factor of an English merchant, it was Burley's revelation of the espionage efforts of John Donne, already referred to, which won him Spanish approval.[1] This was enhanced when, with the outbreak of war between England and Spain, Burley and his brother joined the Armada fleet. After its defeat he sent a memorandum to Philip suggesting the recruitment of English pilots and sailors, many of whom, in the aftermath of an historic victory, suffered greatly as a result of Elizabeth's surge of parsimony. Yet while these unfortunate men might be starving to death, Philip was right to be sceptical about recruiting them when their loyalty would always be under scrutiny. Burley only received moderate encouragement from Mendoza when invited to Paris to develop his original ideas.

A year after the Armada rout, with its dreadful losses of men and materials, Mendoza reported to Martin de Idiaquez his confidence in Burley and the camouflage routine of engaging English mariners by using Breton sea captains and their ships. These vessels made clandestine trips to land priests and Mendoza thought they could purposefully return with seamen. Given the extent of scrutiny in England of ports, it is very unlikely that such a scheme could ever have worked, but Burley cherished it still and once suggested that the ship of Pedro de Zubiaur,* a trader with England for two decades with a valuable web of contacts, should be used to ferry fourteen pilots he declared were ready to change their allegiance. He may also have hoped to net the pirate Elliot, whose exploits had won him more than local notoriety.

Not long after this Burley himself came under scrutiny. In December 1592 a John Whitfield declared that the exile was still highly esteemed in Spain and was paid 40 crowns a month. But in 1593 Father Walpole wrote to Anthony Bacon that Burley was 'discovered to be a spy employed from hence'. Yet he continued his seafaring activities off the Brittany coast until the summer of 1595, when he was one of four captains of ships that swooped from Blavet, near La Baule in southern Brittany, to land men in Mount's Bay and proceeded to burn Mousehole, Newlyn and Penzance. Such small raids were impossible to predict but they stimulated intelligence efforts at home and abroad.

Sir Thomas Baskerville's report on the defence of Cornwall suggested it had been denuded of arms and munition because so much had been commanded to the fleet of Drake and Hawkins for their ill-fated West Indian voyage in which Baskerville had himself served. As for the Spanish, this thrust involving Burley did not smother the current suspicions about him, and soon he was arrested and imprisoned. He remained in gaol until the truce of 1603, following the accession of James I. In December of that year his position was reviewed by the Council of War which then thoughtfully overturned the judgement, and advised the Council of State of the skimpy nature of the evidence. In this they were surely correct for Burley was probably trapped by a ruse set up by Cecil. He was determined to have some revenge on a traitor and, according to the sailor Sir William Monson, he wrote a letter to Burley in Lisbon pretending that he was a spy for England. He thanked him suavely for a special service and Burley went to prison. Now, on his release, he received compensation through all his back pay, and there was a recommendation that he should again be allowed to serve in the Spanish navy.

If Burley had been in a position to reflect on the matter, he might have thought himself fortunate that his service had not kept him in England. George Stocker, who arrived secretly back in the country before the Armada, was captured and repeatedly tortured. Although partially crippled, he managed yet to escape with two other men from prison to live as a Spanish pensioner in Brussels. Kidnapping

---

* In 1582 Walsingham's spies had arrested a Patrick Mason, who claimed that Zubiaur had urged him to recruit John Doughty to kill or kidnap Drake.

someone abroad to bring them back to England for trial was an exercise that came to have an increasing fascination for Robert Cecil, even though it was difficult to plan in secret and even more difficult to execute successfully. When he was Earl of Salisbury, Cecil considered an attempt to snatch Hugh Owen, clearly inspired nearly forty years after the event by the pursuit and seizure of Dr Story. After the Gunpowder plot there was considerable unease in the exiled English community. From Antwerp Sir Robert Basset (who for a time maintained a fanciful claim to the English throne), wrote to his brother: 'I am advertised for certain of some plots against me either to carry me for England, as Dr Story was, or to have me made away by some desperate person.' Even so, the risks of spying and getting caught did not deter someone like Thomas Harrison who, in 1599, sketched his employment qualifications: 'I have sundry times very dangerously adventured to have my throat cut as may appear. In the house of the Lord Seaton I lay in policy to discover Holt the Jesuit fourteen days and caused him together with myself to be apprehended at Leith with all his packets for France and Spain. In Colchester, by Mr Secretary's devise I was consorted with one Deane and Shelley a seminary and lodged fourteen days in the outward prison to intercept all their letters, which was also done to the discovery of a number of traitors.'

It is curious that someone like Stephen Parrot did not end up stabbed in a ditch. An evangelical spy, he had been to Rome, Douai, Valladolid and the Benedictine monastery of San Martin at Compostella. While there he had been caught tampering with the mail and expelled. He was a witness during the trial of two former students at Valladolid who were arrested in London early in August 1600. Indeed, Roger Filcock and Mark Barkworth could hardly shrug off the three informants who had been there and dogged them – Ingleby, Singleton and Parrot. Barkworth fetched up in Bridewell with Stephen Parrot as his gaoler. When the priest sought to buy a certain freedom of movement, presumably to minister to other Catholics, Parrot's attempted extortions were so inordinate that the prisoner protested to Robert Cecil. This effort to cramp the exactions of Parrot may have brought the victim (and others) comfort in the period before his execution.

The simple ruse of an Englishman claiming to be a Catholic exile while working as a spy was always available. It incensed the genuine emigrés and constantly perturbed their hosts. Early in the 1590s Juan de Velasquez gave it some attention, but as confessional espionage increased he had to do more, especially on receiving a royal memorandum in 1596. The following year he received help from the shifty Edmund Palmer, the double agent who would reveal English state secrets and name the spies in Spain for 500 escudos. It was a bargain well struck, for Velasquez was alerted to Thomas Marchant, then living in San Sebastián while in contact with another agent living in Seville. The pursuit of Marchant, who was from the Channel Islands, took a month. When captured he admitted he was an agent for Essex and that his cousin Nicholas Le Blanc was also involved. Their cover was trade, and Marchant, who left London with cargo of merchandise in 1595, had been operating for two years.[2]

In his 1598 memorandum Cecil referred to a ship prepared ostensibly to smuggle goods to Spain. The voyage was to El Ferrol and Cecil, with Thomas Honyman, both put up 500 ducats for the ship's cargo of wheat and naval stores from the Baltic, for which there was a ready market. The intention was that the ship should spend twenty days in Spanish ports and then return home with all speed to deliver fresh intelligence. On board was at least one spy noted for 'good wit and discretion', a linguist who had lately served in 'these late actions at sea' – which must mean the marine ventures of Essex in 1596–7. It may be that Cecil had then employed him to spy on his rival. Now he passed himself off as a sailor and was paid 60 ducats before he went. Perhaps he was Thomas Wilson, who before serving in Italy travelled in Europe, and like Cecil is known to have spoken Spanish as well as Italian. Whoever it was, this intimate linking of trade with spying became an interesting component in Cecil's forward thinking. The aggressive seeking of markets for English goods within the global empire of Spain was not something Cecil would willingly fetter when the time came for peace talks in the new reign. By 1604 Cecil had a very good overview of how an end of hostilities was crucial to Spain, and he was determined to exact as many concessions for trade as possible. This sturdy approach was in part made available to him by his attention to his pan-European spy network.

Not every spy, some self-proclaimed and self-employed, was an asset. Cecil was the realist in politics who had to negotiate, buy and sometime smother the vaulting political and diplomatic fantasies of someone like Sir Anthony Sherley.[3] Allegiance was an extraordinarily elastic notion for the man introduced to James VI by Anthony Bacon, before Sherley's journey to Persia in 1598. Then, his intention was to weld a grand alliance between Persia and Western Europe against the Ottoman

Robert Devereux, Earl of Essex, 1566–1601. Assisted by the Bacon brothers, the earl used his secret service to underpin his court career, but still failed to convince Elizabeth that he should hold an important office of state

Empire. Among Sherley's suite was Abel Pinçon, a Frenchman who had studied in England and 'had run some wild courses in his youth'. He wrote an account of his journey and was later employed as a somewhat lacklustre secret agent for Cecil on the recommendation of Sir Ralph Winwood. Employed as an agent by both Spaniard and Scotland, Sherley, in the mean time, certainly corresponded with the Scottish court in the spring of 1601 when he was in Rome. Cecil had at least two men watching Sherley since his much-touted activities made Levant merchants' nerve-ends jangle. One of the watchers was Simeon Foxe, resident in Venice and studying medicine at the Univerisity of Padua, one of the foremost institutions of the day. The son of John Foxe, he was previously educated at Eton and Cambridge, and had served as a soldier in the Low Countries and Ireland. The other was Thomas Wilson who was paid £30 and who, late in the summer of 1601, was also in Venice.

Sherley and Wilson were much in each other's company, each keenly interested in the other man's behaviour. At one point Wilson wrote to Cecil that 'I am forced at this present, to change my lodging, and live very retired, and make it be given out that I am gone out of town, only to shun his impudent company, which intrudes himself every day by force, only to spy by me, whether I know of his practices.' In 1604 Wilson hankered briefly after the post of consul to the English traders in San Lucar de Barrameda. The fact that the Spanish knew him as a spy was no deterrent, but he did not get it, though 'English, Scottish and Irish have solicited me to sue for the said place'. In 1605 his reward came when Cecil installed him in London to be his secretary responsible for overseeing espionage, and his remarkable organizing abilities stood him in good stead too when Salisbury began a huge programme of building in London and at Hatfield.[4]

After 1598, given the increasingly vehement rivalry of Cecil and Essex, it is not surprisingly that the secretary's secret service in a dominant position turned inward to scatter its sometime rival's presumptions.[5] The timing is revealing, since it achieved the aim when the coincidence of two important elements gave Cecil a powerful advantage. The first was the ebbing of Anthony Bacon's efforts and the second was the death that year of Philip II. His absence from the political scene allowed for an easing of pressure as England edged both towards the end of the war with Spain and the end of the Elizabethan era. All eyes were now on the compelling figure of Essex, because his annexation of war as the key to power began to look severely lop-sided. He had some inkling of this himself, since he tried a simultaneous effort to consolidate limited contacts with James VI. This had inevitable drawbacks even so, including the fretful, meddling disposition of the king, and of course there was Elizabeth's minatory silence on the accession problem. Still, by 1598 the French ambassador was reporting that James was disposed to use the earl as his mediator in every action in England. Snatching like a child at the future and ready to exercise 'all the power of . . . mind and body in advancing his designs', Essex, who was surrounded by misogynists, allowed his relationship with the testy old sovereign to be swamped by deep fears and boyish outrage. As a child he had once shrunk from being kissed by her. Now when he should be calm, conciliatory and benign, he was instead sulky, fretting and unbalanced in a way that suggests manic depression even to the non-clinician. This was not just the fashionable affliction of melancholy worn with panache; it was a gloomy distress that perpetually undermined his confidence when dealing with the omnipresent Cecil. The latter's introspection was not self-mutilating, but a prop of policy.

The forced decision of promoting Essex to Earl Marshal had been an effort to spoon him honey after the galling failure of the Islands Voyage (1597). But as a palliative it soon lost its efficiency, and the wretched fact of Elizabeth's last years was that she and the earl were unable to communicate, except occasionally in shrill expostulations. She ignored his peremptory demands for offices for his followers like Sir Robert Sidney and still she kept silent on the succession. If Essex had been capable of rational analysis he might have recognized that there were very few real obstacles to the Stuart claim – other councillors acted accordingly. But he cut himself off from them too, exasperated by Cecil's advancement, which was underlined in 1599 when, like Burghley before him, he became Master of the Court of Wards. This gave him access to a vein of funds he could tap at a time when Essex was on the brink of financial ruin. The earl felt frantically exposed to the calumnies and sinister intentions of his court enemies, notably Ralegh, who maintained deep grievances over the outcome of the Cádiz expedition; Lord Cobham and his brother-in-law Cecil. He complained they had paid spies to trap him; had they tried it first with Nicholas Skeres, in Essex's service until his arrest in March 1595? And who was the unnamed young man of good family whom Cecil had wormed into Essex's household? The youth had been educated therein 'and was so much trusted . . . that his Lordship made no scruple to discourse in his hearing with friends concerning their most secret designs.'[6]

By the turn of the century the court struggle swirled round the defiantly ageing queen who could still kick up her skirts in a festive dance. As for Essex, his activities became so odd that Cecil thought he had reasons to justify spying, especially when the earl's faction began decrying evil councillors about the queen. Essex's agitation may have been increased by the piercing realization that by a means he could not fathom the queen's trust had settled on the crooked shoulders of a dwarfish administrator with whom he could not even duel. Essex had used his sword as a prop for his career as a courtier and politician; now without the ability to use it legitimately his vulnerability was exposed to the world's scrutiny. What brought him to the block in 1601 was terminal embarrassment.

Afterword

The theatrical potential of spying, with its excitements, betrayals and hard won consolations, naturally commended itself to dramatists. It was uniquely valuable in plot construction and in England three imbricated situations – the spying husband, the spying father and the spying duke – soon became stock material. Playwrights who used it did not hesitate to borrow freely from each other. Shakespeare, for example, in *Measure for Measure*, owed something in general to all cases where royalty took on a disguise for the purpose of political spying and more specifically he was indebted to Marston's *The Malcontent*, although the theatrical possibilities were more fully realized by the former. In *Measure for Measure* the duke is more than a mere spy; he is the impresario of the whole plot, unique in the disguise he adopts. He sets aside one mantle of authority for another which allows him the ultimate triumph of the spy – reaching the inner recesses of souls. The duke initiates, directs and resolves the action in such a way that one wonders if Shakespeare was partly inspired by Philip Henslowe, as he was by Essex for Hamlet.

The *Zeitgeist* was strongly reflected in contemporary drama and the two key texts of the end of the Elizabethan era are *Hamlet* (1601) and Jonson's *Sejanus* (1603). The first was very likely written immediately after the Essex rebellion, while Shakespeare's company were in disgrace and travelling in the provinces to avoid further scrutiny. The court of England, as Shakespeare knew by report, and the grandly imagined court of Shakespeare's Denmark were both seething with secrets. Hamlet and Claudius both plot 'to find out one another's secrets; as a result of the play-within-a-play, they identify one another as mortal enemies'. Domestic prying and state spying fuse in *Hamlet*, as they had in England by the time of Essex's trial. Both elements are essential in the dramatic gearing of the play and, as in life, the spying is often done baldly and badly, with startling and irretrievable consequences. When the king sets Rosenkrantz and Guildenstern to spy on Hamlet he effectively condemns them because his nephew stepson neatly sidesteps their efforts. A telling mistrust even seeps into his relationships with Horatio and Marcellus as he repeatedly requires them to swear oaths of secrecy; and deception is enfolded into the action when Hamlet decides to 'put an antic disposition on', a testing and febrile form of disguise. Far more potent then a mere change of clothes and overlaying the spying, it becomes a mechanism that unleashes a sequence of fatal encounters and actions, on and off stage. Shakespeare so gives his audience an

Ben Jonson, 1572–1637, used by Salisbury as
a government agent during the penetration
and destruction of the Gunpowder plot
(1605)

extended and mordant commentary on espionage, as well as acting. A pity then
that Anthony Bacon died quietly, shortly after the execution of Essex; any
comments by him on the play would have been intriguing.

In Jonson's fearsome black satire, *Sejanus*, based primarily on Tacitus (much
favoured by the circle of Essex), spies are regarded with venomous loathing:

Nero: 'Twere best rip forth their tongues, scar out their eyes,
　　　　When next they come.
Sosia: A fit reward for spies.

(Act II)

Given Jonson's personal position at the time of writing, this hatred has both a
dramatic and private context. He was then a Catholic 'writing from within a
Catholic milieu', and this was a nerve-shredding situation when, as Sabinus says:
'Every ministering spy / That will accuse and swear, is lord of you / Of me, of all,
our fortunes and our lives.' What was truly hurtful was the hateful recognition that
though most domestic Catholics were loyal and patriotic (a view not even
overturned during the debâcle of the Gunpowder plot), they could still be swamped
by the mercenary, mendacious efforts of spies and *agents provocateurs*. Further, as
has been frequently indicated herein, many spies were of apostate backgrounds,
and as a realist and moralist Jonson knew that many of them would have agreed
with the exultant, odious Macro, commissioned by Tiberius in the play to work
against Sejanus: 'I will not ask, why Caesar bids do this: / But joy that he bids me. It
is the bliss / Of courts to be employed, no matter how' (Act III). For many

contemporaries of Jonson this was undoubtedly true, and he was acutely aware that an unguarded word, spoken before the wrong listener (someone like Anthony Munday), might be recalled in anguished retrospect in a prison cell. In epigram CI, 'Inviting a Friend to Supper', he refers to wine taken at the Mermaid Tavern:

> Of this we will sup free, but moderately,
> and we will have no Pooly, or Parrot by;
> Nor shall our cups make any guilty men:
> But, at our parting, we will be, as when
> We innocently met. No simple word
> That shall be utter'd at our mirthful board,
> Shall make us sad next morning: or affright
> The liberty, that we'll enjoy tonight.

'Pooly' is obviously Robert Poley, and Parrot may be Stephen or Henry.[1] Jonson is surely alluding to Poley in the subtle three-line epigram 'On Spies' (LIX), with its rueful, personal tone, coupled with some relief that Robert Cecil, whom Jonson sought to cultivate as a patron, had discarded Poley from his secret service. The poet's claim made to William Drummond that Salisbury 'never cared for any man longer nor he could make use of him' does not seem too far adrift. 'Spies you are lights in state, but of base stuff, / Who, when you have burnt yourselves down to the snuff, / Stink, and are thrown away. End fair enough.' Poley never worked for Cecil as far as is known after July 1602, so the epigram must date from some later time. On 18 July 1602, Poley wrote to Cecil: 'How half offended, you said to me I never made you good intelligence, nor did you Service worth reckoning, is the cause I have not since presented myself with offer of my duty, although I much desire my endeavours might please you, my necessities needing your favour.' It is possible to be more precise in the dating of the Jonson epigram praising Lord Monteagle. The Catholic peer was one of the instruments for uncovering the Gunpowder plot, an event that, even in its planning, threatened Jonson by association if he was not yet in Salisbury's service; he had dined some months previously with the charismatic Robert Catesby and Thomas Winter. In the briefer epigram Jonson makes obeisance to necessity of state, but still feels revulsion at the act of spying; the domestic, yet haunting metaphor of the candle is used to make a moral point. Is there a whiff here too of self-disgust – especially in the charged word 'stink'? If Jonson was spying for Salisbury before 7 November when he was summoned by the Privy Council and asked to track a Catholic priest who was wanted for interrogation about the plot, it would not be surprising if his attitude to spying had by then become ambivalent. He complied with the council requirement and sought out the priest, who naturally distrusted him in those days of acute tension. Meanwhile, Father Thomas Wright, a friend of Jonson's prior to the plot, was interrogating Guy Fawkes for the government. Salisbury was bent on finding out all that was going on; Jonson was desperate to consolidate his modest links to the country's most powerful and secretive statesman. Unsavoury work, however, left him in an unhappy frame of mind.

Although wide-ranging investigations did not find clear evidence of foreign involvement in the plot, James and Salisbury were well aware that notable English Catholic controversialists like Persons, still in exile, were not reconciled to a Protestant regime. A spy reported the table talk of Hugh Owen and Father William Baldwin in Flanders referring to the suspect Henry Percy, Earl of Northumberland and, given the antipathy between Salisbury and the earl, the pursuit of Owen was stepped up. The capture and subsequent death under torture of Nicholas Owen, the lay brother and master joiner, seems also to have been related, for as Juan de Tassis, the Spanish ambassador in London reported to Philip III, 'the name of Hugh is more hateful here than that of the devil'. As has been pointed out, the discovery of the plot 'presented James with an awesome opportunity' to demolish finally the propaganda edifice Persons had laboured over for years. As Salisbury intended, James in his speeches after the crisis repeatedly 'emphasized the mysterious powers of a king who could thus act as God's spy, successfully discriminating between loyalty and sedition, truth and lie.'

In undemocratic or despotic regimes, drama and poetry become freighted with a suspected political significance. The government fears writers and the writers fear the government. Hence, the powerful intellectual allure of allegory in Elizabethan England, for it employs a set of agents and images to convey in disguise a moral meaning. We know allegory had a heady savour for alert minds in Ceauşescu's drab, terrorized Romania, where the foul-handed censors twitched over *Hamlet*, but could not meddle with the text without risking derision. They contrived, therefore, that it should be played in sub-arctic temperatures to half-starved audiences whose very applause had a subversive beat. In this respect the rumbustious Elizabethans who flocked to the Globe fared better. Their appetite for news (novelty) and information was deep and wide, spreading far beyond those in service to the great men. Indeed, the demand for foreign news was so insatiable that in the late 1580s it was met by a continuous flow of translated newsletters. John Wolfe specialized in the publication of French news with Edward Aggas, Anthony Chute, Francesco Marquino, John Eliot and Anthony Munday all employed by him as translators. The last named brings us back (in his role of snoop) to the court and spying, and a required acknowledgement that Elizabethan England was, by a small margin, not a truly secret state like Ceauşescu's Romania, with its abundant and awful apparatus of repression. The queen and her chosen ministers only came to the brink of creating something more ugly than a sour authoritarianism, and that under pressure.

The triumvirate of Burghley, Walsingham and Leicester purposed two essential things (as did their immediate successors): the defeat of foreign threats to Elizabeth; and the consolidation of the grip of Protestantism. Since very little political flexibility was possible in a country without broad and authentic democratic mechanisms, it is not surprising that Robert Cecil resolved the accession problems of King James in a clandestine manner. To the astonishment of many this introduction of an outside monarch was achieved without bloodshed. Variously earnest, nefarious, brutal and corrupt, all the spy masters assisted in the protection of the last Tudor. The queen had survived many real dangers early in her life and naturally buoyed herself up with subterfuge, so that disguise became the essence of her rule. To have survived for over forty years without the spy masters might have been more difficult than it proved and she was pleased to employ their skills. After all, conspiracy itself was like food and drink to the stupid *and* cunning Mary, Queen of Scots. Her eerie emotional detachment that remained yoked to soaring self-interest, was abetted by bigots like de Spes and callow innocents like Babington. Her ambitions cost many lives; the two queens were sisters in blood, 'although there were more executions for treason in the 1530s than in the whole of Elizabeth's reign'.

In favour of conspicuous consumption, but recoiling from generous funding of her spy masters, Elizabeth regarded spying as the cheapest, handiest substitute for resident diplomats. Spies were like loaves of bread – usefully sustaining but liable to go mouldy. Indeed, what she got fresh from them was always tainted 'for her own advisers (and others) . . . fed her information which suited them' – and it was often half-baked. In the end she exploited fear and the willingness of her rattled gentlemen to subsidize spying. In this way she hoped to arrive at an unbiased truth cheaply, and if we switch from loaves to fishes, it was done by trawling in the waters muddied by her own councillors. Walsingham was the greatest (just ahead of the Cecils) of the Elizabethan spy masters. His flair was to make a tiny, multi-national, shifting cluster of informers and intelligencers seem to be everywhere. Yet they were only spasmodically anywhere, unlike the Spanish Inquisition which flourished in secret as another early modern bureaucracy. The principal secretary's network was as substantial as a spider's web – barely visible and defining large gaps; so that although he developed a flinty belief in the necessity of spying, he knew too that 'an intelligence advantage does not confer infallibility'. Today his efforts seem puny and almost laughably primitive, especially in the light of interconnecting 'intelligence networks conceived and designed . . . to spy on other armies and other leaders'. These efforts, like codes now, are of breathtaking complexity. How Walsingham would have relished, for example, the US Navy's daily list of all shipping at sea obtained through a global ocean surveillance information system called Classic Wizard.[2] But even such a thing then would not have allowed him to peer further into the minds and plans of Mary, Alva, Philip II and his generals. Failures were certain as raw data could prove elusive, yet through Walsingham and his motley agents the English government in a time of crisis achieved an advantage that bemused its enemies, leading some perilously close to agonizing blasphemous thoughts about betrayals by their god.

From the first vicious success in snatching, abusing and dispatching Story, through to the discovery of the Gunpowder plot (1605) – in essentials like personnel, an Elizabethan tumult – Catholic west European powers could never feel wholly comfortable dealing with England. These islanders with their weird tongue were vigorous, unsubmissive and unpredictable; the nation and their queen imbued with a strong sense of God's providence. The Machiavellian mode had been exported to England, and so flourished hot and cold, that foreign rulers could not escape the shivery conclusion that they knew and understood far less about foggy English policy than the English divined about them. It is a notable paradox that espionage (invisible power) was a component of a visibly increasing bureaucracy all over Europe, from Edinburgh to Constantinople. When at length it reached its twentieth-century political zenith, so spying took on its most rancidly brutal form in Nazi Germany and socialist Eastern Europe. Can the declared admiration of an ex-head of the Soviet KGB (Semichastny) for today's Elizabethan secret services be a cause for even the mildest self-congratulation? A more severe judgement might be that they are expensive warped artefacts from a less democratic age, and their survival still indicates an unseemly obsession with secrets.

Abbreviations

AHR	*American Historical Review*
BL	British Library
CR	*Contemporary Review*
CS	Chetham Society
CST	*Cymmrodorion Society Transactions*
CSPD	*Calendar of State Papers Domestic*
CSPF	*Calendar of State Papers Foreign*
CSPS	*Calendar of State Papers Scottish*
EHR	*English Historical Review*
HJ	*Historical Journal*
HT	*History Today*
N&Q	*Notes and Queries*
PMLA	*Publications of the Modern Language Association*
P&P	*Past and Present*
PRO	Public Record Office
RB	*Revue Bénédictine*
RES	*Review of English Studies*
RH	*Recusant History*
SCJ	*Sixteenth-Century Journal*
SP	*Studies in Philology*
SQ	*Shakespeare Quarterly*
TCHS	*Transactions of the Caernarvonshire Historical Society*
TJHSE	*Transactions of the Jewish Historical Society of England*
TWAS	*Transactions of the Worcestershire Archaeological Society*

Bibliography

I   Manuscripts

BL Additional Mss
BL Harleian Mss
PRO SP 106/1–3 Ciphers

II   Printed Primary

Acts of the Privy Council
Bales, P. *The Writing Schoolemaster*, 1590
Calendar of State Papers
HMC Salisbury (Cecil) Hatfield Papers
The Journal of Sir Francis Walsingham, 1570–83, Camden Society Miscellany, vol. 6
The State Papers and Letters of Sir Ralph Sadler, 2 vols (ed. A. Clifford), 1809

III   Printed Secondary

Agrell, W. and Huldt, B., *Clio goes Spying* (Lund), 1983
Bald, R.C., *Donne and the Drurys*, 1959
—— (ed.), *An Humble Supplication . . . by Robert Southwell*, 1953
Basset, B., *The English Jesuits*, 1968
Beckingsale, B.W., *Burghley, Tudor Statesman*, 1967
Boas, F.S. (ed.), *The Works of Thomas Kyd*, 1955
——, *Marlowe and his Circle*, 1929
Bossy, J., *Giordano Bruno and the Embassy Affair*, 1991
Bradbrook, M.C., *John Webster, Citizen and Dramatist*, 1980
Brooks, E. St. John, *Sir Christopher Hatton*, 1946
Caraman, P., *The Other Face; Catholic Life under Elizabeth I*, 1960
Champion, P., *Charles IX: la France et le Contrôle de l'Espagne*, 2 vols (Paris), 1939
Charteris, R., *Alfonso Ferrabosco the Elder* (New York), 1984
Clark, E.G., *Ralegh and Marlowe* (New York), 1941
Code, J.B., *Queen Elizabeth and the English Catholic Historians* (Louvain), 1935
Cooper, W.R., *Notices of Anthony Babington*, 1862
Devlin, C., *Hamlet's Divinity*, 1963
——, *The Life of Robert Southwell: Poet and Martyr*, 1956
Dietz, F., *English Public Finance, 1558–1641*, 1932
Du Maurier, D., *Golden Lads, Anthony Bacon, Francis and their Friends*, 1975
Edwards, F., *The Marvellous Chance*, 1968
Evans, F.M.G., *The Principal Secretary of State* (Manchester), 1923
Foucault, M., *Discipline and Punish*, 1977
Guiney, L., *Recusant Poets*, 1938

Hicks, L., *An Elizabethan Problem*, 1964
Hume, M., *Treason and Plot*, 1908
Ingram, J.H., *Christopher Marlowe and his Associates*, 1904
Izon, J., *Sir Thomas Stucley*, 1956
Jensen, De L., *Diplomacy and Dogmatism: Bernardino de Mendoza and the French Catholic League* (Cambridge, Mass.), 1964
Kahn, D., *The Codebreakers*, 1963
Kennedy, W.P.M., *Studies in Tudor History*, 1916
Kocher, P.H., *Christopher Marlowe* (Chapel Hill, N.C.), 1946
Langbein, J.H., *Torture and the Law of Proof* (Chicago), 1977
Law, T.G., *Collected Essays*, 1904
——, *The Archpriest Controversy*, 1896
Lechat, R., *Les Réfugiés Anglais dans les Pays-Bas Espagnols* (Louvain), 1914
Loomie, A.J., *The Spanish Elizabethans*, 1963
Maclean, J., *Memoir of the Family of Poyntz*, 1886
Mathew, D., *The Celtic Peoples and Renaissance Europe*, 1933
Meadows, D., *Elizabethan Quintet*, 1956
Morris, J., *The Letter-books of Sir Amias Paulet*, 1874
Parry, L.A., *The History of Torture in England*, 1933
Raab, F., *The English Face of Machiavelli*, 1964
Ramsay, G.D., *The Queen's Merchants and the Revolt of the Netherlands*, Part II (Manchester), 1986
Read, C., *Mr Secretary Walsingham and the Policy of Queen Elizabeth*, 3 vols, 1925
Retamal, J.F., *Diplomacia Anglo-Española*, 1981
Richards, S.R., *Secret Writing in Public Records*, 1974
Richings, M.G., *Espionage*, 1934
Rowan, R.W., *Spy and Counter-spy*, 1929
Simpson, R., *Under the Penal Laws*, 1930
Smith, A.G., *The Babington Plot*, 1936
——, *William Cecil*, 1934
Smith, L.B., *Treason in Tudor England: Politics and Paranoia*, 1986
Stone, L., *An Elizabethan: Sir Horatio Palavicino*, 1956
Strachan, M., *Sir Thomas Roe: A Life*, 1989
Tennenhouse, L., *Power on Display*, 1986
Ungerer, G., *A Spaniard in Elizabethan England*, 2 vols, 1974–6
Urry, W., *Christopher Marlowe and Canterbury*, 1988
Way, P., *Codes and Ciphers*, 1977
Williams, N., *Thomas Howard, 4th Earl of Norfolk*, 1964
Winstanley, L., *Hamlet and the Essex Conspiracy*, 1924
Woodfield, D.B., *Surreptitious Printing in England, 1550–1640* (New York), 1973
Yates, F., *John Florio: the Life of an Italian in Shakespeare's England*, 1934

IV Articles in Periodicals

Adams, R.P., 'Despotism, Censorship and Mirrors of Power Politics in Late Elizabethan Times', *SCJ*, x, 3, 1979
Behrendt, R., 'Abbot John Trithemius', *RB*, lxxxii, 1, 1974
Bossy, J., 'The Character of English Catholicism', *P&P*, 21, 1962
Breight, C.C., 'The Tempest and the Discourse of Treason', *SQ*, 41, 1, 1990
Butler, E.C. and Pollen, J.H., 'Dr William Gifford in 1586', *The Month*, ciii, 1904

Croft, P., 'Trading with the Enemy, 1585–1604', *HJ*, 32, 2, 1989

Dodd, A.H., 'Correspondence of the Owens of Plas Du, 1573–1604', *TCHS*, 1, 1939

Eccles, M., 'Jonson and the Spies', *RES*, xiii, 52, 1937

——, 'Brief Lives; Tudor and Stuart Authors', *SP*, 79, 1982

Gray, A., 'Some Observations on Christopher Marlowe, Government Agent', *PMLA*, xliii, 1928

Gwyer, J., 'The Case of Dr Lopez', *TJHSE*, 16, 1952

Hicks, L., 'The Strange Case of Dr William Parry', *Studies* (Dublin), 37, 1948

Hodgetts, M., 'Elizabethan Recusancy in Worcestershire', *TWAS*, 3rd series, 1 & 3, 1965–7; 1970–2

Kalb, E. de, 'Robert Poley's Movements as a Messenger of the Court', *RES*, 9, 1933

Kuriyama, C., 'Marlowe, Shakespeare and the Nature of Biographical Evidence', *Studies in Literature*, University of Hartford, 20, 1, 1988

McBride, G.K., 'Elizabethan Foreign Policy', *Albion*, 5, 3, 1973

Neale, J. (Sir), 'The Fame of Sir Edward Stafford', *EHR*, 44, 1929

Perrett, A.J., 'The Blounts of Kidderminster', *TWAS*, xix, 1942

Pollitt, R., 'The Abduction of Dr John Story and the Evolution of Elizabethan Intelligence Operations', *SCJ*, xiv, 2, 1983

Read, C., 'The Fame of Sir Edward Stafford', *AHR*, 20, 1915

Schooling, J., 'Secrets in Cipher', *Pall Mall Magazine*, viii, 1896

Seaton, E., 'Robert Poley's Ciphers', *RES*, 7, 1931

Thorp, M.R., 'Catholic Conspiracy in Early Elizabethan Foreign Policy', *SCJ*, xv, 4, 1984

Thurston, G., 'Christopher Marlowe's Death (Parts 1 & 2)', *CR*, 205, 1964

Williams, W., 'Welsh Catholics on the Continent', *CST*, 1901–2, Appendix H

Wright, C.T., 'Young Anthony Mundy Again', *SP*, 56, 1959

V Unpublished Theses

Bleiweis, S., 'The Elizabethan Intelligence Service, 1572–85', PhD, Rutgers University, 1976

Freedman, J., 'Anthony Bacon and his World', PhD, Temple University, 1979

Morris, L., 'Some Aspects of the Work of the Elizabethan Intelligence Service', MA University of Wales, Aberystwyth, 1967

Notes

Preface

1. M. Foucault, *Discipline and Punish* (1977), pp. 50–3

Introduction

1. B. Coward, 'The Stanleys', *CS*, 3rd series, xxx (1983), pp. 144–5
2. C. Breight, 'The Tempest and the Discourse of Treason', *SQ*, 41, 1 (1990), p. 18
3. Ibid., p. 4
4. A. Haynes, 'The Elizabethan Earthquake, 1580', *HT*, xxix, 8 (1979), pp. 542–4
5. Breight, op.cit., pp. 17–18
6. A.L. Rowse, *Court and Country: Studies in Tudor Social History* (1987), p. 217
7. L.B. Smith, *Treason in Tudor England: Politics and Paranoia* (1986), pp. 249–55
8. J. Bossy, *Giordano Bruno and the Embassy Affair* (1991), p. 19
9. G.D. Ramsay, *The Queen's Merchants and the Revolt of the Netherlands (Pt II)* (1986), p. 157
10. Ibid., p. 156
11. A.G. Smith, *William Cecil* (1934), p. 142
12. Ibid., p. 144
13. Ibid., p. 146

Chapter One

1. R. Pollitt, 'The Abduction of Dr John Story and the Evolution of the Elizabethan Intelligence Operations', *SCJ*, xiv, 2 (1983), p. 131
2. Ramsay, op.cit., p. 160
3. D. Mathew, *The Celtic Peoples and Renaissance Europe* (1933), p. 316
4. Pollitt, op.cit., p. 144
5. Ibid., p. 147
6. Ibid., p. 150
7. Bossy, op.cit., p. 26
8. Smith, op.cit., p. 158
9. Ibid., p. 160

Chapter Two

1. Ramsay, op.cit., p. 161
2. M.R. Thorp, 'Catholic Conspiracy in Early Elizabethan Foreign Policy', *SCJ*, xv, 4 (1984), p. 431. Also E. Hildebrandt, 'Christopher Mont', *SCJ*, xv, 3 (1984)
3. P. Williams, *The Tudor Regime* (1979), p. 278

4. J. Morris (ed.), *The Letter-books of Sir Amias Paulet* (1874), xxi
5. J.A. Housden, 'The Merchant Stranger's Post in the Sixteenth Century', *EHR*, xxi (1906), pp. 739–42
6. P. Way, *Codes and Ciphers* (1977), p. 14

Chapter Three

1. M.G. Richings, *Espionage* (1934), p. 134
2. Ibid., p. 137
3. M. Burns, *The Debatable Land* (1970), p. 203
4. Bossy, op.cit., pp. 20–1
5. Ibid. p. 20
6. K.T. Butler, 'Some Further Information about Rocco Bonetti', *N&Q*, 195, 5 (1950), pp. 96–7
7. D. Cressy, 'Binding the Nation: the Bonds of Association 1584 and 1696', p. 217: in D.J. Guth and J.W. McKenna (eds), *Tudor Rule and Revolution* (Essays for G.R. Elton) (1982)
8. Breight, op.cit., pp. 4–5

Chapter Four

1. T.G. Law, *The Archpriest Controversy* (1896), vii
2. Ibid., viii
3. M. Hodgetts, 'Elizabethan Recusancy in Worcestershire', *TWAS*, 3rd series, I (1965–7), p. 71
4. C.T. Wright, 'Young Anthony Mundy Again', *SP*, 56, p. 153
5. Law, op.cit., ix
6. Bossy, op.cit., p. 92. Also L. Hicks, 'An Elizabethan Propagandist: the Career of Solomon Aldred', *The Month*, clxxxi (1945), pp. 181–90
7. L.L. Peck, *Northampton: Patronage and Policy at the Court of James* I (1982), pp. 6–13
8. C. Read, *Mr Secretary Walsingham and the Policy of Queen Elizabeth*, 3 vols, II (1925), p. 331
9. Ibid., p. 334
10. L. Stone, *An Elizabethan: Sir Horatio Palavicino* (1956), p. 240

Chapter Five

1. E. St John Brooks, *Sir Christopher Hatton* (1946), pp. 260–3
2. W.R. Scott, *Joint Stock Companies to 1720*, vol. III, pp. 503–4
3. Read, op.cit., pp. 370–1
4. *CSPF*, vol. II (1590–1), 647, p. 373
5. J. H. Langbein, *Torture and the Law of Proof* (1977), p. 90. Also L. Parry, *The History of Torture in England* (1933), p. 36
6. Langbein, op.cit., pp. 82–3
7. Ibid., p. 84
8. R.C. Bald (ed.), *An Humble Supplication . . . by Robert Southwell*, (1953), xii
9. W. Ingram, *A London Life in the Brazen Age, Francis Langley 1548–1602* (1978), pp. 178–84

Chapter Six

1. De L. Jensen, *Diplomacy and Dogmatism; Bernardino de Mendoza and the French Catholic League* (1964), p. 83
2. A.J. Perrett, 'The Blounts of Kidderminster', *TWAS*, xix (1942)
3. C. Devlin, *The Life of Robert Southwell: Poet and Martyr* (1956), pp. 94–5
4. A.G. Smith, *The Babington Plot* (1936), p. 95
5. Ibid., p. 107
6. Ibid., p. 110
7. Brooks, op.cit., p. 276
8. C.B. Kuriyama, 'Marlowe's Nemesis: The Identity of Richard Baines', p. 347: in K. Friedenreich, R. Gill and C.B. Kuriyama (eds), *A Poet and a Filthy Playmaker* (1988) (New York)
9. E. Seaton, 'Marlowe, Robert Poley, and the Tippings', *RES*, 5 (1929), p. 277
10. Jensen, op.cit., p. 84

Chapter Seven

1. Smith, *Babington*, op.cit., pp. 8–9
2. Brooks, op.cit., p. 274
3. Devlin, op.cit., p. 96
4. Smith, op.cit., p. 27
5. Richings, op.cit., p. 146
6. Devlin, op.cit., p. 111
7. Ibid., p. 113

Chapter Eight

1. Seaton, op.cit., p. 280
2. *CSPS*, viii, p. 690
3. Smith, op.cit., p. 176
4. *CSPS*, viii, pp. 584; 599; 602–3
5. Smith, op.cit., pp. 181–3
6. T. Maclean, 'The Recusant Legend: Chideock Tichborne', *HT*, 32, 5, p. 13
7. Brooks, op.cit., pp. 286–7. Also J.H. Pollen, *Mary, Queen of Scots and the Babington Plot* (1922), Scottish History Society, 3rd series, III, 1922
8. Seaton, op.cit., p. 281
9. Devlin, op.cit., p. 121
10. Smith, op.cit., p. 87. Also an article in *The Rambler*, new series, vii (1897), p. 106
11. Bald (ed.), op.cit., xx
12. Brooks, op.cit., pp. 277–8
13. Smith, op.cit., p. 236
14. HMC Salisbury (Cecil), III, 715, pp. 346–9
15. BL Add. Mss 6697, fol. 444
16. B.H. Newdigate, 'Mourners at Philip Sidney's Funeral', *N&Q*, 180 (1941), pp. 398–401

Chapter Nine

1. P. Way, *Codes and Ciphers* (1977), p. 24
2. R. Charteris, *Alfonso Ferrabosco the Elder (1545–88)* (1984), p. 10

3. P. Croft, 'Trading with the Enemy, 1585–1604', *HJ*, 32, 2 (1989), p. 284
4. P. Croft, *The Spanish Company*, xxi, n. 2
5. Croft, 'Trading', op.cit., p. 286
6. J. Maclean, *Memoir of the Family of Poyntz* (1886), p. 76–7
7. BL Harl. Mss 286, fols. 56–7
8. K.M. Lea, 'Sir Anthony Standen and some Anglo-Italian Letters', *EHR*, xlvii (1932)
9. L. Hicks, 'The Embassy of Sir Anthony Standen in 1603', Part 1, *RH*, 5, pp. 96–8
10. D.B. Woodfield, *Surreptitious Printing in England, 1550–1640* (New York, 1973), pp. 26–7
11. Stone, op.cit., pp. 245–7
12. Jensen, op.cit., p. 105

Chapter Ten

1. Jensen, op.cit., p. 87
2. Privy Council Registers, iv, p. 430
3. Jensen, op.cit., p. 107
4. R.C. Bald, *Donne and the Drurys* (1959), pp. 76–7
5. J. Briggs, 'Marlowe's Massacre at Paris: A Reconsideration', *RES*, new series, xxxiv (1983), p. 263
6. W. Urry, *Christopher Marlowe and Canterbury* (1988), pp. 62–3
7. M.V. Hay, *The Life of Robert Sidney, Earl of Leicester* (1984), p. 122
8. R.B. Wernham, 'Christopher Marlowe at Flushing in 1592', *EHR*, 91 (1976), pp. 344–5
9. Hicks, op.cit., p. 101
10. S. Dedijer, 'The Rainbow Scheme', p.22: in W. Agrell and B. Huldt (eds), *Clio goes Spying: Eight Essays in the History of Intelligence*, Lund Studies in International History, 17 (1983)
11. E. Seaton, 'Robert Poley's Ciphers', *RES*, 7 (1931), pp. 137–8
12. E.de Kalb, 'Robert Poley's Movements as a Messenger of the Court, 1588–1601', *RES*, 9 (1933), p. 16
13. Hicks, op.cit., p. 108
14. F.S. Boas (ed.), *The Works of Thomas Kyd*, lxix (1955)
15. Urry, op.cit., p. 177
16. Ibid., pp. 84–6
17. G. Thurston, 'Christopher Marlowe's Death', *CR*, 205 (1964) pp. 156–9; 193–200
18. de Kalb, op.cit., p. 17
19. Quoted Bossy, op.cit., p. 167

Chapter Eleven

1. D. du Maurier, *Golden Lads, Anthony Bacon, Francis and their Friends* (1975), p. 25
2. Ibid., p. 50
3. Ibid., p. 65
4. *CSPD*, ccxlii, 192, p. 21
5. Hicks, op.cit., p. 100
6. HMC Salisbury (Cecil), iv, p. 176; p. 349

Chapter Twelve

1. G.K. McBride, 'Elizabethan Foreign Policy in Microcosm; The Portuguese Pretender, 1580–9', *Albion*, v, 3 (1973), p. 194

2. Read, op.cit., II, p. 51
3. McBride, op.cit., pp. 203–4
4. Ibid., p. 205
5. J. Gwyer, 'The Case of Dr Lopez', *TJHSE* (1945–51), xvi (1952), p. 166
6. Ibid., p. 171
7. Ibid., p. 175
8. M.C. Bradbrook, *John Webster, Citizen and Dramatist* (1980), p. 76
9. Gwyer, op.cit., p. 184

Chapter Thirteen

1. Du Maurier, op.cit., p. 158
2. HMC Salisbury (Cecil), iv, p. 349
3. Bradbrook, op.cit., p. 69
4. G. Rees, *A Chapter of Accidents* (1971), p. 114

Chapter Fourteen

1. Bradbrook, op.cit., p. 56
2. Stone, op.cit., pp. 235–7
3. HMC Salisbury (Cecil), xii, p. 231
4. Mathew, op.cit., p. 315
5. A.J. Loomie, *The Spanish Elizabethans* (1963), p. 57
6. Rowse, op.cit., p. 205
7. M. Edmond, *Hilliard and Oliver* (1983), pp. 115–8
8. Hay, op.cit., p. 123
9. Ibid., p. 126
10. Devlin, op.cit., p. 227
11. Ibid., pp. 227–8
12. Woodfield, op.cit., p. 26

Chapter Fifteen

1. Mathew, op.cit., p. 313
2. Stone, op.cit., pp. 249–50, n. 4
3. Ibid., p. 255
4. Ibid., Appendix III, pp. 325–30
5. BL Harl. Mss, 1974, fol. 21g. Also W.L. Williams, 'Welsh Catholics in the Continent', *CST* Appendix H, (1901–2), p. 128
6. A.H. Dodd, 'Correspondence of the Owens of Plas Du, 1573–1604', *TCHS*, 1 (1939), p. 47
7. Loomie, op.cit., p. 56
8. Dodd, op.cit., p. 50
9. A.H. Dodd, 'Wales and the Scottish Succession', *CST* (1937–8), p. 214
10. F. Edwards, 'The Attempt in 1608 on Hugh Owen', *RH*, 17 (1984), pp. 140–1

Chapter Sixteen

1. Loomie, op.cit., pp. 66–8
2. Ibid., p. 65

3. D.W. Davies, *Elizabethans Errant, The Strange Fortunes of Sir Thomas Sherley and his Three Sons* (New York, 1967), pp. 141–3
4. A. Haynes, *Robert Cecil, First Earl of Salisbury: Servant of Two Sovereigns* (1989), p. 178
5. R. Adams, 'Despotism, Censorship and Mirrors of Power Politics in Late Elizabethan Times', *SCJ*, x, 3 (1979), p. 11
6. L. Smith, op.cit., p. 315, n. 60

Afterword

1. M. Eccles, 'Jonson and the Spies', *RES*, xiii (1937), pp. 385–6
2. D. Campbell, article in the *Independent on Sunday*, 30/9/1990

Index